THE
STATE OF
INDUSTRY

THE STATE OF INDUSTRY

CAN BRITAIN MAKE IT

ROBERT HELLER

BBC BOOKS

Published by BBC Books
A division of BBC Enterprises Ltd
80 Wood Lane, London W12 0TT

First published 1987

© Robert Heller 1987

ISBN 0 563 20588 1

Typeset by Phoenix Photosetting, Chatham
Printed and bound in Great Britain by
Mackays of Chatham Ltd, Kent

CONTENTS

THE INTERVIEWS

TO THE BRITISH MANAGER

CAN BRITAIN MAKE IT?

This book is a unique record of where British manufacturing industry stands, as seen through the eyes and expressed in the words of its own leading figures, at a crucial point in the 1980s. These top executives are all successful men engaged in sterling efforts to beat the competition in world markets, to build on the recovery of recent years so as to enter the 1990s and the next century on far more equal competitive terms than those of 1979.

The thrust of the interviews is into that future. There's little point in dwelling on the disasters of the past, except to learn from them, and that is something which these men have plainly done. The current generation of chief executives, in its realism, international outlook, capacity for detail and sense of direction, is unquestionably superior to its post-war predecessors, and is not repeating their mistakes.

But if there's no point in looking backwards, there is likewise no sense in dwelling on present improvements on that past performance. The argument is put tellingly by one of the interviewees: the comparisons that count are with the present performance of the competition – and 'competitive analysis' is one of the several phrases that recur in these interviews of like-minded men who use similar tools in positioning their companies in world markets for maximum advantage.

The interviews had the same purpose – not to seize on this statistic or that piece of business news as ammunition in the adversarial political debate between the Ins and the Outs, but to determine how much actually has been achieved against world competition and, far more important, what remains to be done, both at company and national level. You can't have (and Britain hasn't) many relatively successful companies in a relatively declining economy.

Britain's relative economic decline has many explanations, but only one mystery. Why have the British tolerated such steady erosion, in fair economic weather and foul, of their international stature? Each lost percentage point of world trade in manufactured goods; each slip down the ladder of national income *per capita*; every cent, pfennig or yen dropped on the foreign exchanges; the fact that manufacturing output in early 1986 was

4 per cent lower than in 1979 – these dry statistics represent real losses in private and public living standards and, worse still, a threat to those standards stretching far into the future.

But people believe what they want to believe. Hope has sprung eternal: and the politicians' understandable certainty that their policies will bring economic renaissance has been gladly echoed in the media and in mass opinion. On the face of it, there's no reason why British manufacturing industries should lag behind others in a Europe to which Britain is now bound by membership of the Community. That being so, isn't there always the possibility that Britain can emulate the great economic miracles of West Germany and Japan, and rise from the ashes of defeat?

The broadcast series which is recorded in these pages sought to answer that question. Is there a chance? Are the chances being taken? The idea of the series came from my producer, Gordon Hutchings, who timed it to coincide with Industry Year's closing weeks. As one of the interviewees observed, Industry Year was in itself a symptom of the national problem: other countries don't feel the need to run year-long campaigns to persuade the populace that industry matters. Against the background of heavy unemployment, industry's crucial importance should surely have been apparent enough.

Relative economic decline and an apparently everlasting jobless mountain are critical issues, but they are not crises. Slow but inexorable failures rarely stimulate radical reform until they explode into life-or-death emergencies. That truth emerges very clearly from the interviews. The companies involved were not chosen with that in mind; but the majority had been brought to the brink, had stared over into the abyss, and had then brought all available resources to bear to save their businesses from otherwise inevitable extinction.

These managements, in fact, reacted as the British macro-economy has not. Mostly led by new men, they have refused to tolerate that erosion of international stature, brought about in many cases by long years of mis-direction and mismanagement. Impending financial disaster directed attention to its roots. From making the wrong products for the wrong markets in the wrong way, these companies have moved dramatically towards the side of economic virtue, and with dramatic financial results.

Is that the answer? The seventeen companies whose executives were interviewed cover a wide cross-section of key industries: chemicals, cars, engineering, aerospace, electronics, textiles, computers. It wouldn't be difficult to find another seventeen where much the same story can be told: of 'headcounts' slashed, product lines and factories rationalised, comparative performance sharply improved, marketing thrusts reoriented towards the far larger sales available outside Britain, managements redeployed and retrained to suit the new strategy and reinforce the new energy.

Add together all these revitalised and thriving micro-economies and you should in theory have an equally vigorous macro-economy to match. Yet the seventeen top executives, while extremely confident about their own prospects in world competition, were markedly less certain about the nation's chances. This only shows the same realism which they have brought to their own companies, either in building on success (like Glaxo) or capitalising on under-exploited strengths (like ICI) or emerging from the pit (like ICL). Realistically, Britain faces some enormous disadvantages in world competition; not only is productivity still far too low in many areas, but whole sectors have been lost to foreign competition, beyond any hope of recovery.

Where industries like motorcycles, shipbuilding and much of consumer electronics have sunk below the horizon, others (notably cars) have slid half-way down. In many cases, too, the recent, badly needed improvement in productivity must be qualified by the decline in scale: double output with the same labour force, and you achieve a 100 per cent rise in productivity: maintain output with half the labour force, and the sum again works out at 100 per cent – but which company has made more progress?

This fact emerged as one strong theme of the interviews – that Britain's advances had to be measured against the continuing strong performance of international rivals who are not standing still. Sir Peter Parker has remarked, speaking of the British economy, that, 'You think you're moving, but it's the train on the next platform that's pulling out.' Against larger rivals, usually several of them, operating from the base of stronger economies, even the best British companies face continuous challenge in a world of general, acute and increasing competition.

Those rivals, moreover, gain incalculable advantage from certain aspects of the societies in which they operate. An important series in *The Times* investigated the shortfall in Britain's spending on industrial research and development. So far as the figures show (and Britain's, amazingly and uniquely, stop at 1983), total R & D spending in the age of the silicon chip has risen by far more as a proportion of gross domestic product in every other major industrial country than in Britain.

If Britain's disproportionately high military R & D is excluded, the 1983 figures show civil spending of 1.6 per cent of GDP in this country, 1.7 per cent in France, 1.9 per cent in the US, 2.5 per cent in West Germany, and 2.5 per cent in Japan – and remember that the others have far larger GDPs. The lag in civil R & D is extremely serious in itself, but is by no means an isolated phenomenon. Similar gaps exist on every measure of the foundations of economic prosperity.

Britain lags hopelessly in the proportion of income which companies devote to training; in the output of graduates of all kinds, but especially in the scientific and technical disciplines; in the rate of application of advanced techniques on the factory floor; and so on. These yawning gaps are no more acceptable for the fact that, as Corelli Barnett has pointed out in a recent book, similar deficiencies have disfigured British society for decades – even in the years, glorious in other respects, of the Second World War.

That comes back to the central mystery of relative economic decline: its toleration. How is it that civil R & D is not being vigorously promoted? Why was the government programme for forcing industry to spend more on training abandoned? Why do many companies fail to see that their own training effort, especially given the lack of adequate national provision, is vital to their own futures? Why is public spending on education, notably higher education, under acute pressure, instead of expanding vigorously to meet the standards of the international competition?

It's a curious situation – at a time when progressive managers, like those interviewed for the broadcasts, are emphatic about the need for more management education – for a government actually to cut the funds of the two best-known business schools. Industry, as the interviews show, can do a great deal to help itself, and should do more. But there are obvious limits to the ability of any one chief executive, or even many, to shape the environment in which a company operates.

There isn't necessarily any limit to the businessman's ability to see how that environment should be shaped. The identity of view and viewpoint shown by the seventeen is striking, and markedly apolitical. They do note that many governing conditions have improved since 1979, and that the reduced influence and obstructive powers of the trade unions are part of the improvement. It's very difficult to argue otherwise. And, at the same time, these men are deeply concerned about the structural defects and the underfunding – above all, in education – which make a British economic miracle much less probable.

Again, who could reasonably argue against that case? The war between the Ins and Outs, unfortunately, has not been waged on rational grounds. Britain's combination of great political stability with inherent instability of policies has been fatal to achieving the kind of consistent radical reform at the national level which would match that forced through in these seventeen companies. Britain has been governed effectively – in the sense that the Ins have exercised authority – but it has not been governed efficiently, and the decline of manufacturing industry is one of the fateful results.

They are shown by internal figures as well as international comparisons. Manufacturing accounted for only 22 per cent of the British GDP in 1984, compared with over 30 per cent in 1960. Both Germany and Japan were still around the 30 per cent mark in 1984, after a much shallower dive. So, while it's true that Britain's figures conform to a general world shift towards services, the impact has been more severe on this relatively weak economy than on others. That is a general truth. Whatever economic wind has blown, it generally blew more chillingly on Britain.

The all-in-the-same-boat argument is thus no excuse. The chill factor partly explains the emphasis placed by the seventeen on international expansion, including international takeovers and other investment. The British economy is not only too small, but too slow-growing. The consequence for many companies is that their interests outside Britain must become (in several cases, have become) much larger than those inside. This isn't saying that the British plants will be smaller than they would otherwise have been; on the contrary, their viability in world markets often depends on the world interests of the group. Internationalism does, however, mean that much of 'British' manufacturing industry will be beyond the reach of any British government.

As local industry has declined, international industry has occupied some of the empty territory. Britain has become more attractive to foreign manufacturers, especially from Japan. Once again, these plants, while important in themselves, are minor in the context of their international owners. Once again, the power of any British government to dictate the destiny of manufacturing in Britain is diminished. Perhaps that power never was so great as the politicians supposed: but its dwindling does stress still more the necessity of making Britain as attractive a country for manufacturers as any other, on all counts.

Otherwise, industry will no doubt vote with its feet. The industrialists in these interviews have voted with their careers. Professional managers all, the seventeen chief executives include six men qualified in the professions (three accountants, three lawyers); five more have degrees in engineering disciplines; three come from abroad (and three are Scots); two have MBAs (a far higher proportion than in industry at large); the average age in the early fifties is raised by the presence of three men appointed to chairmanships after distinguished careers in other fields.

All have acted in the conviction that strong international businesses can still be built on a British base, and that the grave defects exposed by recession have been eradicated for ever in recovery. The extent of their success can be judged from the words which follow, as well as from their deeds. But the interviews also reveal the truth that many micro-miracles do not, after all, add up to a macro-miracle. For that to happen, fundamental change in the national economy and its political management is essential. Otherwise, the whole will not be as good as its parts. Whether they are good enough themselves is the subject of the six chapters.

I am very grateful to the seventeen leaders of industry who gave their time so generously for these interviews and spoke so frankly. The contribution of Gordon Hutchings to the genesis and execution of the series was paramount. He is certainly the co-author of this book; the responsibility for its virtues is largely his, its vices are all mine.

CHAPTER 1

FROM RECESSION TO RECOVERY

Leaner and fitter and poised to reconquer world markets? Or shrunken and uncompetitive, condemned to further decline? You could hardly have more diametrically opposed views of Britain's manufacturing industry than these two extremes. The first, optimistic diagnosis is naturally believed by the Conservatives. Their political opponents take the gloomier view. However, if that sombre prognosis is true, the news is as bad for Labour and the Alliance as for the government. Without a thriving manufacturing sector, grand plans for the revitalisation of the British economy cannot be realised. So even the sternest political critics of Mrs Thatcher's industrial and economic policies must believe that a manufacturing renaissance is feasible.

History, it must be said, is not on their side. The decline of Britain's share in world trade in manufactured goods has continued inexorably, irrespective of political promises, programmes and hopes. Furthermore, the country's once-favourable balance of trade in manufactures has moved into large deficit. Projections of the trends from an earlier and relatively better period, 1960 to 1973, imply that before the 21st century is very old, Britain will be the poorest country, measured by gross domestic product *per capita*, in the whole of Western and Eastern Europe, with the possible exception of Albania. If that sounds unthinkable and utterly impossible, so once did many of the events that have already come to pass – like the halving of British car output over a period in which every other European country has increased production.

Britain is bang on schedule for that appointment with Albania. But what is actually happening beneath the surface of the grim statistics? Looking at the key industries, and their leading firms, can we detect signs of the kind of resurgence that lifted West Germany from the post-war rubble to economic leadership in Europe? The evidence of improvement is clear and plentiful. But is the recovery too little, too late? Or enough, and in time?

This book sets out the diagnosis of British manufacturing's health, as offered by leading industrialists, people running companies in crucial markets such as chemicals, aerospace, cars, computers and textiles. Of their dozen firms, nine have been through the full force of either storm-threatened or actual bankruptcy, massive job losses, wholesale redundancy, diminution of past market positions. Even the other companies, while less ravaged by that storm, have seen sweeping changes that make them very different from a decade ago. It shouldn't be forgotten how fearful that storm was, or how traumatic were the effects of what Sir David Plastow, chairman of Vickers, delicately calls 'paring down'.

PLASTOW To give you some idea of the scale of that paring down – we don't normally talk about headcount reduction, it's a very painful and unpleasant business – but whereas in the Seventies the payroll of Vickers was in the forty thousands, after the merger in 1980 with Rolls-Royce Motors it was in excess of 30,000. We now have a headcount of around 15,000.

It wasn't just a question of employing too many people. How they were employed made a great and often fateful difference, as John Bagshaw, chairman of Vauxhall Motors, recalls.

BAGSHAW We were having some horrendous industrial relations problems right through the industry. I arrived at Vauxhall to do some research work back in 1979. We had an unfilled customer order-book that you couldn't jump over, and yet we couldn't get the cars out of the plants, and people were just walking away from our products and going and buying wherever they could, because we just couldn't satisfy the demand. There was a lack of realisation – maybe at the shop floor level, certainly at the supervisory level – of the simple need to meet a customer's demands, and nobody was paying much attention to it. And the frustration and the rage when you went round and talked to fleet customers was unbelievable.

Company after company had the wrong approach to managing people, and to obtaining the right productivity from the right number of employees. Not only that; the whole corporate structure militated against good performance. Ronald Miller, chairman of the up-market textile group Dawson International, looks back to 1974.

MILLER We were in a terrible mess. We were almost bankrupt and we decided that something would have to change. We were at that time centralising our whole management structure and building up a team of people behind the chief executive. We had various production directors, marketing directors, who had assistants, who in turn had staff behind them. The result was that when any of our companies wanted to do something, they had to refer upwards through this whole chain of command and, of course, the reply took some time to come down. As a result opportunities were often lost.

As economic circumstances worsened after 1979, managements that in one way or another shared problems like Dawson's ran out of options. It was a case of change or die. The death wouldn't have been slow, but quick: financial extinction. At the far larger textile group, Courtaulds, the crisis escalated alarmingly at a time when it was also suffering from a self-inflicted disease – 'managerial indigestion' – after an enormous bout of diversification. The phrase is that of chairman Sir Christopher Hogg.

HOGG In the course of the Seventies after the first oil crisis, economic times got tougher, imports into this country increased, and at the end of the Seventies, early Eighties, the pound rose appreciably. The combination of all these factors hit Courtaulds' profits hard. We've always remained profitable, but profits dwindled almost to nothing in the first year of the Eighties. One way or another, we had a very large managerial challenge ahead of us in the shape of 300 or 400 separate businesses, the majority of which at one stage were making losses; we were having a poor return on capital, and were rapidly running out of cash at the rate at which we were going.

Textiles, as one of the original industries of the Industrial Revolution, could be expected to suffer setbacks in the age of the silicon chip. But Peter Bonfield, chairman of high-tech ICL, recalls what happened to the largest British-owned computer manufacturer – and his situation was little different, in its agonising financial effects, from Courtaulds'.

BONFIELD Our crunch point was about five years ago. The company had . . . grown at more than 25 per cent a year, but then the growth rate dropped off dramatically, and the cash flow situation was very poor. Basically we ran out of cash and therefore needed to be totally reconstructed on a different basis to get moving again.

'Totally reconstructed on a different basis.' That's been the recent story for most of Britain's leading companies – and many smaller ones as well. British industry was forced to get fitter and, as at Vickers, that inevitably meant leaner, much leaner. At one of the country's fastest growing sunrise companies, Apricot Computers, chief executive Roger Foster reflects on the results.

FOSTER I live and work here in the Midlands, where there's been a decimation of industry over the past five or seven years. But I have to admit that the industry now left in the Midlands is a lot more efficient, a lot sharper than it was a few years ago. So the medicine worked; but at what cost? At the cost of wiping out maybe as much as 25 per cent of businesses here, and the cost, of course, of millions of jobs. But though industry is now more efficient than it was, I think it's going to take generations before we really get back into the mainstream, competing against the Far East and America.

The reductions in manpower have come about both by cutting numbers in continuing operations and by discontinuing activities altogether – on a huge and widespread scale. Courtaulds is one example of enormous shrinkage in terms of operations. What effect has that had in terms of sales? Christopher Hogg.

HOGG It's shrunk amazingly little considering the holocaust that we've been through. We reckon that something like 30 per cent of the businesses we ran at the end of the Seventies have now completely disappeared, and yet our turnover has not gone down much in real terms; it's actually increased in nominal terms.

Even in a company such as ICL which, unlike Courtaulds, was largely concentrated on a single product range, the holocaust story is much the same. Peter Bonfield.

BONFIELD What we had to do was basically re-size the company; the overhead was too big for the size of company that we had. So we spent probably a year re-sizing it, which meant reduction of workforce, reduction of plant, reconstructing the way that we did business, reorganising, retraining, specialising in specific areas. Also, we set up a whole series of collaborative arrangements so we could get access to other people's ideas and technology, to force the company to look outwards. I think it had become relatively introspective, looking primarily at the UK market instead of the world marketplace. And computers is definitely a world marketplace.

The traumas of restructuring were not confined to the hourly-paid workforce. Many management heads fell, some of them, so to speak, crowned heads. Thorn-EMI, the TV rental, lighting, entertainment and appliance group, was one firm which lost its chief executive when the City lost confidence in its performance. Sir Graham Wilkins then moved from retirement as Beecham Group chairman to spearhead the reshaping at Thorn.

WILKINS We've certainly changed our organisational structure, and discarded quite a few things that didn't fit. We were heavily involved in traditional engineering, and we no longer are. We have reorganised the company into four major profit centres for management purposes, so that we have good management teams operating in each of those sectors; and we've pushed the profit responsibility down to the individuals running those sectors, so they are not only responsible for their profits, but judged on their performance.

This formula of disposal, regrouping, concentration and delegation has been the general response to the crisis of British manufacturing. Very effective it is, too. But the formula is hardly original or difficult to grasp. Why was it that so many companies stuck for so long with ineffective strategies and structures? Sir Francis Tombs, who heads both the Rolls-Royce aero-engine giant and the engineering group Turner & Newall, attributes the lag to basic attitudes.

TOMBS Ten years ago, perhaps a little more, we were very self-satisfied, very committed to the cushy home market. And we tended to design things for the home market at all levels of industry which the rest of the world didn't want – sometimes too expensive, sometimes just different. I think that has changed. We've become, as a manufacturing industry, very much more international, very much more ready to manufacture elsewhere as well as at home. This is sometimes represented as 'exporting jobs'. It's not, it's providing an opportunity for exporting on an acceptable basis to other countries.

Graham Wilkins singles out one aspect of this insularity, which has certainly been a prime ingredient in Britain's loss of competitive power.

WILKINS I'm convinced that the worst of our problems stemmed from the lack of understanding of the term 'marketing'. It's no good making a product in industry unless you can sell it, and sell it at a profit, and I'm not satisfied that enough attention was then being paid to the ultimate consumer in terms of finding out what that consumer wanted and was prepared to buy.

Even where firms were exporting successfully, like Dawson International's Pringle knitwear business, the group had internal faults that made the internationalism ineffective. Ronald Miller.

MILLER When we had bought a number of companies in the Sixties and Seventies, we found that they had lost touch with their markets. They had forgotten, for example, that deliveries had to be made on time. There were occasions when, once we had corrected that situation, customers used to phone up and say, we're very upset that the goods have arrived early. And we said, the goods haven't arrived early. And they said, but they have always arrived six weeks later (for example), and we'd built that into our system, and now they've arrived on time! This was a fundamental problem which we had to correct.

To emerge from the crisis, British manufacturing has had to turn its attitudes to its markets upside down. The orientation has had to change completely. For instance, how does Courtaulds now position itself? Christopher Hogg.

HOGG We have to regard ourselves as a worldwide supplier. The textile industry is a worldwide industry. It is determined by international competition. Across the whole span of Courtaulds' enormous business there is practically nothing which is not exposed to international competition, either imports in this market or, of course, competition overseas against our exports and our overseas production. And we have to determine everything we do by the best worldwide standards and not just by what seems to be adequate in this country. And therein lies the problem.

Therein lies the problem indeed. British industry, despite entry into the Common Market, had failed to see the necessity of becoming world-class, failed to seize its opportunities, failed to tackle its difficulties with enough determination. Who was to blame for the difficulties and the débâcle? The question is crucial, because if the patient is truly being cured, it can only mean that the causes of the disease are no longer so deadly in their effect – indeed, that they are gone or going. So who or what brought British manufacturing so low? David Plastow.

PLASTOW The single most important thing that has come through this very difficult period of enormous recession is the need to be an international player, or opt out. And I have to say that government in Britain over a long period of time has not really been supportive in the proper sense towards manufacturing industry. If you look at the games that have been played over nationalisation (the loss of shipbuilding and aircraft to Vickers – and it lost steel twice!) no other major economy has had that sort of disruptive influence. And if we look at the motor industry, for many years it was an economic tool of both shades of government in the way that it played games with the finance supporting the purchase of cars, to regulate the economy.

So the fault lies at the very top – in government – which is generally where the blame lies for management failure in any organisation. Francis Tombs agrees – but he spreads the blame more widely.

TOMBS Successive governments of all colours post-war have tried to pretend that we can live in isolation from the world and have been slow to realise that's not the case. Successive trade-union leaders have shared that belief, they think they can take a larger slice of the cake from somewhere, and somebody else will pay for it; and managements have not been sufficiently aware of the need to compete in the world at large. They've been protected by our home market, protected by a belief that somehow things will come right – and in a typical British way we've had to wait for things to get pretty bad before starting to adjust.

Sir Austin Pearce, the chairman of British Aerospace, also criticises the politicians, and adds another explanation of industry's difficulties – an antipathetic educational culture.

PEARCE One of the main obstacles to progress is the fact that industry is not seen as being particularly important in this country. I know some political people do feel it's important, but there have been too many political comments that industry is not important, particularly manufacturing industry. That is bad for the country, and as a result, the feeling in our educational system is that you don't train people to go into industry. The result is a very limited intake, with most of the better brains going elsewhere.

Industry itself hasn't contributed enough, however, towards finding its way out of the educational morass, as John Bagshaw discovered in the car industry.

BAGSHAW As we're digging more and more into the problems within our own company and talking to some of our suppliers and associated companies, it is evident that what is causing most problems is a serious lack of training in the past ten years, or even further back. We're finding that, as we move towards more complicated equipment, more use of computers, people have never really been trained up to it.

At ICI, Denys Henderson sees no great problem in finding the managerial, scientific and technical skills his company needs – but he does see an area of serious difficulty in the City of London.

HENDERSON I do have a real worry about the City, the way in which it forces managers to concentrate on essentially the very short-term performance. There is a tremendous pressure on fund managers to improve their portfolios. They are clearly looking at earnings per share, they're looking at profits. Now, the chemical industry is a long-haul industry, a drug takes twelve years to develop. I say to myself, it can't be right for Britain if it wants to retain good, science-based innovative industry, that the managers of those industries are forced to take decisions which are essential in the short term in order to survive financially, but which undoubtedly will be jeopardising some of the long-term prospects.

Every aware management will, however, admit that in the last analysis the responsibility for bad industrial performance rests in one place and one place only: management itself. John Bagshaw.

BAGSHAW If you went down and talked to some of our employees on the line, you'd find half the problem we face is terrible frustration. A person has a certain amount of time to complete an operation, and if the material is not there, or the part won't fit where it is supposed to fit, or the bolt won't go through the hole for some reason, you can't blame the worker for it, you've got to blame management – the management which allowed that part to come on to the line knowing, or not knowing, that it wouldn't fit. So the poor employee is standing there being blamed for it all, but we haven't put the mechanism in place to let him do it right first time. And that is why I would blame management at all levels for any problems before going out on a union-bashing exercise and saying, 'Hey! You won't co-operate with us.'

Bad government, bad management, bad marketing, bad industrial relations, bad education and training – there wasn't much else that could go wrong. So what has changed in the mid-Eighties? What, now, is going right? Paul Girolami, chairman of Glaxo, talks about government's contribution.

GIROLAMI I'm not being politically biased, but it is unquestionably easier for us to run a multi-national business from London now than it was ten years ago. That's a fact – how important a fact I don't know, but I think it's important from where I sit. Secondly, I'm very hopeful because I sense a whole feeling of direction in industry, more energetic and more realistic and less complacent. And thirdly, I have to say I think the young people coming through are better than the old ones. The old classical industrial establishments were brought up in the time when the markets were there and were theirs for the taking. The older generation doesn't have the element of competitiveness which is essential today.

Francis Tombs feels that improvement in the political environment has been matched by substantial progress at the level of the firms. What changes does he detect?

TOMBS A very much more professional approach to management, a recognition that working capital is important, and that international productivity comparisons and wage rates are also important. We've had a post-war tradition in this country, unhappily, of paying relatively low wages and employing too many man-hours to make a product, and have also been careless with the resources used within the company, principally working capital. All those things have changed, but also the labour and government climates have changed and there's now a much greater recognition on the part of trade unions and government that we have to compete in the outside world. We don't live in a protected cocoon, which was the belief for some decades.

Ronald Miller of Dawson International is sure that international, global thinking has sunk in right across the board – or perhaps it should be across the boardrooms.

MILLER I can see that markets are changing, have changed substantially over the last ten years. Just as we're talking now about the 'Big Bang' in the City of London, I think that really is a reflection of things we have seen in our markets over a number of years. People in business today are much more internationally minded. One has to be aware of competition, not just in the UK. One has got to measure competition in worldwide terms.

According to Austin Pearce, imbibing the gospel of globalism has been accompanied by acceptance of the imperatives of efficiency.

PEARCE In my view, the vast majority of British industry is far and away more efficient, more productive than it was five or six years ago. One cannot say that for all industry – there's always the bad actor – but in going round talking to other people in their industries, where an awful lot of work has gone in, people are undoubtedly more efficient.

These are, of course, generalities, and there are plenty of exceptions to prove the rule. But if you move down to specifics, you do indeed find some dramatic examples of change. At Vickers, David Plastow's management sold off no less than twenty unwanted operations.

PLASTOW And we finished with six prime operations, all of which are truly internationally competitive. Probably the biggest single message to come through those difficult times was that it was no good sitting here having a large share of the UK market (whatever it was) and thinking you could continue to develop that business, invest in it and become increasingly competitive. You really had to be international in your operations, not merely to spread the geographic risk in terms of the varying conditions of major economies, but also to be out there and to be seen to be successful in the domestic markets of your competition in product terms and in pricing and commercial terms.

'Internationally competitive' means nothing unless the market finds that the actual products made are equal to, or better than, the international competition. Graham Wilkins believes that British manufacturing can now pass this ultimate and essential test.

WILKINS We have to get across to the public that there are many products now manufactured and produced in this country which are at least as good, if not better, than many of those imported. There is still a sense that foreign manufactured products are better than those produced in the UK, but I do believe that many sectors of the market have now improved their position to the extent that the products produced in the UK are at least as good as those produced overseas.

That is supported by John Bagshaw's experience at Vauxhall. In today's car industry, as in manufacturing generally, the key word, the touchstone of effective performance, is what it always should have been – quality.

BAGSHAW We are now within one or two rating points of the best General Motors products built in Europe with the products that are coming off the line at both Ellesmere Port and Luton. This has been done by an awareness that we've got to get quality right – we've been identifying where we did have quality problems, we've in some cases sacrificed the attainment of schedules in order to build quality, we've put a lot of investment into better equipment, and we've also considerably upgraded our paint plants.

These are all highly encouraging developments – and there is, from all these chairmen and managing directors, a repeated note of confidence and resurgence. If what Christopher Hogg says of his own company, Courtaulds, were true across the whole manufacturing economy, the state of industry would be excellent indeed.

HOGG I believe that all over the group we now have much better managed businesses, much more confident and competent managers, and that slowly but surely we're not only taking business from our competitors and all the rest of it, but we are developing new products, going into adjacent areas, and that nothing is going to stop the forward momentum.

It would be wrong to suggest that any of those interviewed, including Christopher Hogg, is in any way complacent. Apricot's Roger Foster points to just one formidable question mark.

FOSTER I think we have got better because the malaise was so deep that it wasn't too difficult to improve. With the big cut-backs people would become much more efficient, and that is what has happened. But from now on, if we want to gain efficiency, it will require huge long-term investment, and I'm not convinced that the whole industrial structure here lends itself to huge long-term investment. And that is what it needs.

For all that, there are no exceptions among the industrialists interviewed in presenting a picture of British industry reformed, revamped and rejuvenated, ready at last to enter the international arena on reasonably competitive terms. The cynic can raise two easy objections. First, no chief executive is going to confess, certainly not out loud, that his company is in an unfit state, uncompetitive and badly led. Second, would the view from the top have been any different twenty years ago, before Britain plunged into industrial decline?

The objections have some force, and it remains true, of course, that the nation's macro-economic performance has provided little evidence to support an optimistic view of British industrial effectiveness. But two strong counter-arguments can be laid against the objectors. The calibre of the top executives we have heard, and will be hearing, is unquestionably high. They compare well, not only with many of their predecessors, but with their international rivals. Second, the strategies they have followed, almost to a man, are firmly rooted in the realities of the world economy in the 1980s. They know that, if you cannot concentrate on areas of strength, you cannot compete. They know that, if the company is not properly controlled internally, you cannot concentrate. And in that realism, there does lie some real hope.

CHAPTER 2

FROM CHEMICALS TO TEXTILES

In one industry at least, Britain has retained its place in the world competition, with world-class companies that are not dwarfed by their overseas rivals. That is chemicals. The key to this strong survival has been Imperial Chemical Industries. Where the car and electrical industries, for example, were hopelessly fragmented at the end of the war, ICI bestrode chemicals like the colossus it was.

ICI doesn't bestride the world scene, however. Each of the Big Three German firms matches ICI in sheer size. But the group has survived into the 1980s with impressive technology, greatly improved marketing and the strong will to compete and succeed without which today's world markets cannot be cracked. In many product areas, Britain, thanks largely to ICI, remains a major player, sometimes with an expanding presence. And in one sector, pharmaceuticals, ICI is by no means alone. Several important discoveries, from synthetic penicillins to anti-ulcer therapy, have kept big British companies in the forefront of what has been the world's most profitable industry. These scientific successes have insulated the drug companies from the disadvantages of being based in a slowly growing economy.

That has not, however, been true for ICI's other products. Every trauma suffered by the rest of Britain's manufacturers has had some repercussions on ICI and the smaller chemical firms, including, very notably, the decimation of the traditional textile industry of Lancashire. Great plans to resist competition from the Far East by massive reinvestment in bulk textiles have long since collapsed. Is the rump of British textiles a strong force with a genuine prospect of sustained growth? And can a greatly changed British chemical industry exploit its retained strengths to do more than hold its own in world competition? I asked Denys Henderson, who has just taken over as ICI's chairman, how much he feared the competition.

HENDERSON Actually, with a certain degree of arrogance, I don't really fear the chemical companies at all in terms of competition. I believe that ICI *are* every bit as good as the majors in terms of our product spread and in terms of our territorial coverage. Indeed, we are undoubtedly the most inter-national of all the big chemical companies. The areas that cause us concern are where the oil companies move into the chemical industry, because they see it as a way to add value to their basic oil and gas businesses. They're very powerful, they're financially strong but, dare I say it, they're not actually terribly expert in the way in which they break into the traditional markets. And similarly, I'm not too happy about competing with national govern-ments that choose to get into the chemical industry, because their criteria for success are quite different to ours. They're not as concerned with return on capital or profitability as we are.

That's fighting talk coming from a company that in 1980 suddenly moved from what seemed to be a perfectly sound position into perhaps its worst moments since the end of the war.

HENDERSON Yes, 1979 was a very good year for us, by almost any indicator you care to use, and it really was a tremendous shock when the world fell off the cliff edge in the middle of 1980. I remember it well because I'd just joined the ICI board as commercial director. I had the privilege of reporting a record first quarter sales, whereupon by quarters three and four we were in an unheard-of position of being in loss. There were those of my colleagues who uncharitably suggested there was a connection between my arrival and falling off the cliff.

That connection was obviously far-fetched. But surely there must have been some connection between ICI's management and its products and that falling off the cliff?

HENDERSON No, it was the markets largely. With hindsight, there had been two step-changes in demand that I don't think any of us properly read. The first was the oil shock in 1973 when the OPEC cartel put prices up dramati-cally. But they did the same thing again in 1979 with what is called the second oil shock. Now, this reduced demand through the early Eighties quite markedly. We had a particular problem in this country because, firstly (and not too many people remember this), in June 1980 UK inflation was running at 21 per cent per annum, while that of our competitors, the Ger-mans, the Americans, the Swiss and the Japanese, was, of course, very much lower than that. And secondly if, as ICI, you were a major exporter or a major earner of overseas income, you had to face up to a considerably over-valued pound. So the combination of lower growth, high domestic inflation and an over-valued currency – at least for exporting purposes – really was absolutely disastrous.

Plainly, these explanations are true and good. But there has plainly also been more to ICI's remarkable recovery than meets the eye from that account. Henderson talks eloquently of the importance of the *re*'s – as he explains.

HENDERSON The first *re*'s were fairly clearly to *re*structure and *re*duce costs. What that meant was that we had to improve productivity, we had to shed labour. And it wasn't just on the shop floor – it was right through the whole structure. For example, when I joined the board in 1980 there were fourteen executive directors. Today, including the chairman, there are eight directors in all, and that's been paralleled all the way down.

The second thing we had to do was to *re*shape our businesses and to say, if the UK, as far as one can see, is not going to represent a big enough percentage of the free world chemical market, then we have got to drive even harder to be extensive in our overseas sales. So we set out very consciously to do that. And as part of that process, because we had seen the bulk chemicals so vulnerable to the domestic inflation and to the overvalued pound, we had to move into more 'effect' chemicals than we had before, and this was achieved by a number of things, including acquisitions.

That was the second part, *re*shaping, *re*structuring. And the third part was *re*generating our businesses.

Why hadn't the *re*'s been applied before? Why did it take ICI so long to do what seems in hindsight to be so obvious?

HENDERSON I think you have to have some traumatic event which jerks you out of your lethargy. There's a huge inertia factor in industry, in all organisations really, and I don't think we did too badly through the Seventies. We made a bit less – but the thing that really shattered us was actually going into loss in those last two quarters of 1980. That's the point at which we said, stop, we have to take a good hard look. And that's when we embarked on the kind of philosophy and practical implementation which I've referred to.

A great many *re*'s have also been applied at Courtaulds, which but for the failure of a famous takeover bid would now be part of ICI. Now there's a thought. What did chairman Sir Christopher Hogg do when faced, like ICI, with that traumatic stimulus?

HOGG The strategy has been very obvious. We had to cut the red ink out of the company's financial accounts, and there were clearly two principal ways to do that. One was simply to close businesses which were loss-making, because there was too much capacity in the industry, too much supply chasing too little demand. The other and more important strategy was simply to manage better what we had. It sounds very simple when I say it like that, but the task of managing something better, if it's become run down, is really very complex and very long-term. It involves changing habits, attitudes, standards right across the business, from production and research on the one hand to the selling and marketing on the other, and you make many false turnings; it's a case of (you hope) five steps forward and not four steps back, but you inevitably make all sorts of mistakes, and it's really just a voyage of exploration.

The ICI bid for Courtaulds came in the days when big was thought to be best – although, as Christopher Hogg recalls, the customers may not have agreed.

HOGG I think our customers in the Seventies would have seen us as being large, dedicated to our businesses, rather slow-moving, not particularly inspired, the sort of supplier who, when times got tough, tended to be dropped off the purchasing line, because other people did things slightly better.

How far has Courtaulds moved from those days?

HOGG The most important single change which not only ourselves but the whole textile industry has undergone is one of what I might call customer-consciousness. It wasn't that we didn't care about our customers in the old days; it is just that we have all put a very great emphasis on paying attention to our customers and our customers' needs and have let that be the driving force in our businesses and in what we are doing. We have done things such as increase the focus on design, which was very important to our High Street customers. We started to invest in design facilities and in the status of design within our businesses, and slowly but surely the role of design has assumed an importance today which was unthinkable and unvisualisable five or six years ago – I think to the satisfaction of our customers and the benefit of our merchandise and our bottom line.

What the mammoths have been forced into by economic pressure is, of course, the strategy that has long been followed by the specialists such as Dawson International. Chairman Ronald Miller explains the story.

MILLER We've made it our policy to try and sell the best knitwear in the world, we don't try and compete with the mass market for knitwear. Our area in the marketplace is really very, very small. If one thinks of the overall market in the shape of a pyramid, we're at the very top part; there's a huge area of business for knitwear which we don't get involved with at all, it comes from the Far East and from other parts of the UK, and from the Continent as well. Our main competitors are basically companies in the UK who are trying to meet high standards like ourselves, and companies in Europe (particularly Italy) which are recognised for their flexibility, for their innovation and also for their fashion.

Even a company as enormous as ICI, with the sales of some product lines counted in billions, not millions, has been forced to concentrate far more than in the past. In the process, it even abandoned two mass markets – in polythene and polyester – where the products were its own invention. Not testimony, perhaps, to past good management, but certainly evidence of present willingness to change. Denys Henderson.

HENDERSON   There was a degree of arrogance in the chemical industry that said, if it's anything faintly chemical we can do it, anywhere in the world. This period we went through really told us, in a very simple fashion, we must be selective because our resources are not infinite. Therefore we must put those resources in the particular areas where we believe we have some strengths, and that's a process that has been happening all over the world; all the international chemical companies are doing that. I coined a phrase, that we're all busy playing musical chairs. What I mean is that we're moving out of some areas where we don't see ourselves as long-term players, and equally we are enhancing our position in other areas where we think there are some considerable strengths.

That willingness to change, to uproot established custom, has been equally evident among ICI's customers in the textile industry, as Christopher Hogg of Courtaulds explains.

HOGG   The whole morale of the industry has changed, its performance has certainly changed, and, although the industry is smaller, its prospects for the rest of this century and the next one are miles better than they were at the end of the Seventies. If you had said to me in, say, 1978 that the outlook could change as much as I think it now has changed, I would not have thought it was possible. And if you'd asked me to undertake the task I would have said, 'Hand that to some other man.' But when you have actually travelled down the road you can see how one thing leads to another, leads to another – and that the thing to be most wary of is simply despair or frustration, or whatever it is that causes you to give up. If you keep going you can in fact accomplish a perfectly extraordinary amount.

As chemicals and textiles have changed, so the horizons of managements in the industries have widened, have become much more international. ICI, for instance, has raised its North American business from 15 per cent in 1980 to a quarter, thanks to a recent paints acquisition: that quarter is now the same as its UK business, which in 1980 was 37 per cent of sales – and continental Europe today is running close behind the UK. Ronald Miller of Dawson International explains the new and prevailing international philosophy.

MILLER   We are international. From our knowledge of, and our feel for, export markets over the years, we feel very much at home in the world at large, and also feel very comfortable in owning companies overseas. We're both an exporter and an overseas manufacturer; it's the global village, after all, today. One has got to be prepared to look for any opportunities in that global village, in what we define as our area of the marketplace – that is, areas of specialised textiles throughout the world – and we have to be outward-looking, either through exports or through investment in these countries, to seize these opportunities.

Like ICI, Dawson has used acquisition as a strategic weapon. It was pipped at the post in its attempt to merge with Coats Patons at home: but purchases abroad have, Miller feels, also strengthened Dawson in Britain.

MILLER Having encouraged our individual companies to be innovative, I felt that I must be innovative myself. I wanted to get closer to some of the markets in which we're involved, particularly in the States and Germany, where there is a high spending power, and I'm interested to understand these markets, because I do believe they offer even greater opportunities for exporters from the UK. At the same time, I felt that we should broaden our product base and accordingly decided that, not only should we put extra effort into exporting to these countries, but that we should acquire companies in America and in Germany to get a better understanding of these countries and make more contacts. Ultimately, I believe this will be a benefit to our exporting from the UK – as well as these companies being extremely profitable in their own right.

Because of the action taken before recession, Dawson was able to move through the Seventies and into the Eighties without suffering like its bigger brethren. It reduced its head office – and now only seventeen people there look after its twenty-seven businesses. And the latter are firmly in the charge of their managements.

MILLER We have twenty-seven companies, all of which are independent of each other. Each is under a managing director who has a great deal of autonomy, and they all have different ways of tackling the marketplace. Some have their own sales people, some have distributors, some have agents, and we've encouraged the individual managing directors and the companies to work with whatever means they think best to tackle the market.

A company operating in 150 different markets like Glaxo has no option but to follow the same route of decentralisation: what chairman Paul Girolami calls 'a flexible organisation which somehow combines local initiative, local control, good local management with central leadership and direction'. Developing that was part of Glaxo's great change over the past six years; it has been transformed from something of a sleeping beauty into a pharmaceutical superstar. What happened to wake the lady up?

GIROLAMI Certain factors have been added to pre-existing factors which created a dynamic growth. The underlying strengths of Glaxo – and they've been the underlying strengths for fifteen years, if not more – have been a fundamental commitment to research and development, and also a vague yearning for international expansion. But this latter aspect was very much within blinkers, and when I first joined the group it was in blinkers towards the Commonwealth. The rest were 'foreigners' whom you had to treat rather carefully before you ventured – and there was a positive hostility shown towards the States and Japan. However, the germs of international- ism were there, and so was this commitment to technology.

Once again, the theme is internationalism. Yet there is an extra element in Girolami's transformation: Zantac. This one anti-ulcer drug is what's taken Glaxo into the superstar league, accounting for no less than 40 per cent of its sales – and dwarfing the other seven important drugs in its portfolio. Girolami denies, rightly, that Glaxo is a one-product company. But was that one product just a present from fate?

GIROLAMI The new product which has transformed our fortunes was a result of our continuing commitment to research and development. But that product wouldn't have had the effect it did without being associated with a simultaneous act of faith in international expansion. If we hadn't, before Zantac was taken in, decided to go hell-for-leather into the Ameri- can market and to tackle the Japanese market and to put all the strength behind the European market, that product would have been a flop. It would have been given to the American companies as licensees – we would have got 4 per cent or whatever. So Zantac must not be looked at in isolation, or as coming directly from only one aspect of our strategy, which is the improvement and emphasis on research and development. Certainly it was an outcome of that, but its commercial success was also an outcome of the fact that we had at last developed our markets. You don't make products like Zantac a commercial product, a commercial success heading for a thousand million dollars by just producing a good product in a laboratory. That's the starting point. But you know, many starting points finish where they start!

Yet another group that transformed itself before recession struck was BOC, formerly known as the British Oxygen Company. The imaginative acquisition of Airco in 1978, an American company, brought BOC a bonus: its present chairman, Dick Giordano. He explains what else BOC acquired.

GIORDANO BOC was able, through the acquisition of Airco, to enter the largest industrial gases market in the world. It is a business very much driven by scale. Moreover, the US market is the most competitive market in the world, so if BOC had any aspirations to being a world-class player in the industrial gas business, it had to be in the United States. When it bought Airco, Airco was number three in that market with about 18–20 per cent of the market, so it was a sizeable share, and gave BOC the critical mass it needed in the US. I suppose a bit of serendipity was that it also acquired a very strong health care business, a good deal larger and broader in product line than BOC's own health care business. That business has flourished over the last seven years and, of course, has now grown to a very sizeable portion of the total group.

The critical mass attained by the Airco deal is important because of something that must dominate any discussion of Britain's chances in the world that lies ahead – and that something is scale.

GIORDANO Scale is a critical factor in the gas business. It's a factor in the production of the product, in the distribution of the product, it is certainly a factor in the technology. The technical bill is so big that it can only be spread over a business of significant size. It's a little less important in the health care business, which tends to be more fragmented; on the other hand, we've done very well by dominating relatively small markets.

Any business that has scale as a factor will eventually produce lower costs to the largest and most competitive firm. As that firm grows and its market share produces larger and larger scale, its low cost base will eventually enter all the markets, including your own home market, and eventually put you out of business. In other words, you cannot hide behind the Channel or the Atlantic Ocean any more and believe that there is a UK market which will not be subjected to international competition. So, if you wish to succeed, you *must* be one of those international competitors, if not the best.

The internationalisation of BOC, though, has reached such an extent – it is even well dug-in and successful in Japan – as to question whether it is a British company at all. Would Dick Giordano still call it that?

GIORDANO Obviously since the Airco acquisition BOC has changed. It was for decades a venerable British institution. On the other hand, the merger of the two companies has not resulted in an Americanised British company. I think that the company has a centre of gravity probably somewhere in the middle of the Atlantic. It has absorbed bits and pieces of both business cultures, its methods and styles are the methods and styles of neither of the predecessor companies. What has emerged is a method and style appropriate to the new company.

But the experience of this mid-Atlantic company serves as a reminder that international competition means what it says: competing internationally, and in a very much larger and tougher league. What's it like, for example, for the Briton competing in America?

GIORDANO It means that instead of worrying about one or two competitors, the British manager would have to worry about six. It also means that, when one or two or three competitors might be willing to see prices go up or down, two or three others would go in the other direction; there's much more anarchy in the competitive environment. The other thing a British manager would have to adjust to is sheer scale – the fact that one can make goods in Massachusetts and ship them to Texas or California. That scale difference is very important and it needs to be adjusted to.

The more you play against the best competition the better, in theory, your abilities become, provided that you don't, in practice, get wiped out. It's clear that in this group of industries, Britain does have at least half-a-dozen companies of world-class calibre or potential, big enough to compete in either large-scale or segmented markets. What mustn't be forgotten, though, is that the competition is formidable, and growing all the time. Christopher Hogg points out that basic labour costs in some parts of the world are a tenth or less of those in the UK – and that's not all.

HOGG Labour cost is something that we still worry about and will do as far ahead as I can see. I think in some ways a more serious problem which we now must address ourselves to is the level of efficiency, efficiency in the broadest sense, which has been achieved by the so-called newly industrialised countries in the Far East – Korea, Taiwan, Hong Kong, Singapore – all of whom in their different ways have reached quite formidable levels of efficiency very quickly in traditional industries. They set the standards of productivity, by and large, for the rest of the world, and those are the standards that we must meet. Of course there are outstanding examples in the United States as well, of companies which are extremely efficient, often in very sophisticated parts of the industry, and we look at them too. But dominating everything, I think, is the thought of that Far Eastern efficiency which determines the standards we need to get into the business.

CHAPTER 3

ENGINEERING FIGHTS BACK

No industry suffered more from the impact of Britain's various economic traumas than engineering. Even today, the engineering companies, as a group, haven't recovered their previous peak level of output – and they will never recover the previous level of employment. You could easily paint a depressing picture of their situation. Part of the trouble has been the decline, which is surely permanent, of car production in Britain. That in itself guaranteed that engineering in this country wouldn't grow at the speed of its competitors in countries like West Germany.

Nor has there been any comfort from sectors like shipbuilding, now a mere shadow of its former self. As for aerospace, defence spending has been rising sharply, but it's been a long time since Britain launched a major civil aircraft alone, and it will be for ever before it does so again. The heads of British Aerospace and its key supplier, Rolls-Royce, of aero-engine fame, are contemplating a future which is very different from the past, in one respect at least – the fact that they cannot go it alone.

Other British engineering firms, however, are much less involved in international collaboration; what about them? Can they proceed strongly into world markets under their own steam? Has British engineering mastered enough of the harsh lessons of a difficult past to forge ahead into a much more comfortable and profitable future? One important point to bear in mind is that engineering is not truly one industry, but many, and that one company may well operate in several of these myriad markets. In some companies, though, the spread became so wide that it even baffled their own managers. Mike Hoffman explains what confronted him when he took command at Babcock International in 1983.

HOFFMAN The most difficult thing was actually to understand, what is Babcock? I think, by and large, we are much more evenly organised now. We see ourselves as four types of business: there's Babcock Energy and that is fairly self-evident, it's the power-related businesses; there's Babcock Engineering which is really the contracting operations – process-plant contracting such as Woodall-Duckham, which is a well-known name; the third business is Babcock Automation, the sort of work we do for car plants and engine-testing; and the fourth area is Babcock Industries, a group of companies which basically make things and sell them directly into the market.

Babcock was typical of engineering generally not only in its sprawl, but in its weaknesses – though it also had strengths.

HOFFMAN We had a very loyal workforce worldwide and we had put a lot of capital investment into a number of our major businesses. The areas where I felt we were weak were twofold: one, we still saw ourselves as an international boiler company with a number of other appendages, and secondly, we were more sales-orientated rather than marketing-led, and I felt both these things needed changing.

But there was another critical problem that had to be solved before Babcock could hope to benefit from better marketing and better products.

HOFFMAN One of the key priorities was to bring the direct labour cost down and I think that a good job has been done here over the years. I saw two areas which we had not yet attacked aggressively enough. One was the overhead cost; maybe we had too many sites, and we've now closed a number of sites in various places. The other area is much more difficult to attack, the cost of quality and the cost of holding inventory. That's much more difficult to get at, because you can't go in and make changes happen nearly as quickly as taking direct labour out. But it's absolutely vital to us that cost of production keeps going down.

That all adds up to a formidable programme for generating change, for reshaping a traditional company in the light of modern needs and modern markets. At Vickers, most famous for its defence industries and Rolls-Royce cars, but involved in four other important areas, output per head has doubled in five years. How was that achieved? Sir David Plastow.

PLASTOW A hard drive in terms of investment in more productive equipment, improvement in our knowledge of the business, so that we really understand where the costs are, better training of management in our manufacturing areas, coupled with the fact that our employees across the company have a better understanding of the need to be productive, the need to be competitive and profitable. All this has helped us in some of the more difficult areas where we've had to reduce headcount, which we've achieved by negotiation, by collaboration, by understanding. We've had virtually no difficulty at all in carrying out changes, by being sensitive and by explaining to people this need to be competitive. I think all of those things together have made us a more productive company. We've got further to go and we will be making further progress. By that I'm not forecasting massive reductions in headcount; I'm forecasting hopefully more sales volume with the same payroll and more sophisticated equipment. Also, we mustn't forget the need to design to manufacture. We must design from the beginning to get cost out of our product, and this is what we are doing more and more.

At Babcock, Mike Hoffman gives a classic case of what getting cost out of a product means in practice, and of the remarkable results that modern methods can achieve.

HOFFMAN In the Seventies we put up a 500-megawatt boiler that used about 10,000 tonnes of steel. By product design and improvement we've brought the weight of steel down to something like 6500 or 7000 tonnes per boiler, which has brought us much more in line with our competition, which tended to be lighter designers, anyway. And the changes we've made in our working practices have meant that we can process that steel at a lower cost. This is a typical example of what we've also done in our UK mining and in our process control businesses.

We've put a lot of work into taking a big boiler and dealing with it in modules – so that, for example, the way we construct a very large boiler is to make it up with a large number of elements from a sort of basic planning package. We're using that type of approach in our mining equipment businesses, in our electrical distribution businesses; we're trying to work from a basic minimum core number of design parts. I guess there's nowhere I feel that we've lost design edge over any of our competitors. The problem basically has always been the ability to make that design at an appropriate cost.

At Vickers, David Plastow is likewise convinced that the group is highly competitive in important product lines, and that he has the facts to prove it.

PLASTOW In some of the very highly competitive areas such as Howson-Algraphy, lithographic printing plates, we are number three in the world and pressing hard to be number two. We have invested very heavily in what we believe to be now the most productive plant in the world, and we're just beginning to gain share. Against a world market growth of around 5 per cent, in 1985 we took our growth in real terms up to something like 11 per cent. That was encouraging, because it is a very competitive business, very price-conscious. Similarly, our marine engineering area is very difficult at the moment, but we are still proving we are competitive in price terms. There are a lot of good examples where this is happening. But the point we must keep remembering is that it isn't just a matter of cost, though the cost basis is crucial. It's a matter also of having a product which will be uniquely special and good and therefore demand premium prices.

There's a new phrase about, though. Since the only market, under the new international philosophy, is the world, the successful competitors must by definition be world-class. How does Vickers shape up against this criterion?

PLASTOW If we take the various businesses we are in, just to mention one or two, in terms of the office equipment business we are the largest player in the UK, we are second in France, and now we've got this international seating company. We're fairly significant in the lithographic printing plate business; in sectors of medical research we are number one in the world and so on. In marine engineering we are the world's leading player in ship motion control, and I can go on quoting other examples. These are 'niche' businesses, and we think we are a world player. I think also we make the best car in the world.

The answer to the problem of scale – the fact that Vickers, even with some £690 million of sales, is small by world standards – is therefore to concentrate on segmented markets, and to achieve a position of market power within those segments. The strategic thinking at Babcock bears a close similarity.

HOFFMAN The way I like to look at it is, with the global presence of Babcock being seen as an international competitor in quite a large range of fields, it does mean we can make penetration gains in new businesses much more easily than small companies would do. A classic case: we bought a company in the US last year, and one of the things we've been able to do in this case is in fact enhance its performance in Europe very rapidly because of our knowledge of the marketing scene. I guess the strength we can bring is that we are global in our view of marketplaces and it doesn't really matter what you make if you've got that global sense of structure.

For the two great aerospace companies, Rolls-Royce and British Aerospace, the international path has been one, not of takeovers, but of collaboration. This isn't through choice. It's simply that the rules of the game have been changed, and for keeps, by the iron fist of economics. BAe chairman, Sir Austin Pearce.

PEARCE If you're going for an international market today, you've got to spend a lot of money. Hopefully you can get involved with people who will bring a market with them, which is one of the great advantages of being part of Airbus Industrie in the civil aircraft market. It's one of the reasons that we are actually involved in the joint programme for Tornado with the Germans and the Italians. It's the reason why, for the European fighter aircraft, we're joining with the Germans and the Italians and the Spanish. They will bring a market and that enables us to then compete in the export market against the Americans. You have to recognise the Americans have a massive home market which is virtually a highly protected, captive market. That doesn't mean to say you should not have partnerships with Americans. It depends; it must be market driven. And if you take the co-operative arrangements we have with McDonnell-Douglas for the Harrier, the big market for the Harrier is the United States Marine Corps. Now, to get into that we had to have a partnership with an American company – McDonnell-Douglas – and it is very successful. Similarly, with the Hawk for the US Navy, we had to have an American partner to get into the American market, so we went with an American company.

Rolls-Royce, as the country's only aero-engine supplier, is obviously affected by what happens at the country's only airframe manufacturer. But it is deeply involved in collaboration for reasons of its own. Rolls-Royce chairman Sir Francis Tombs explains.

TOMBS Rolls-Royce is now a strong outfit in its own right, in profitability and in technical terms. We've had for many years quite a wide network of collaborations throughout the world. We collaborate with manufacturers in America, Germany, France, Spain, Italy, Japan and other countries and we do that for a variety of reasons. One is to share technical risk, another very important one is to gain access to markets. It's becoming obvious to all of the three main engine-makers (the three companies with total engine capability are Pratt & Whitney of America, General Electric of America and Rolls-Royce) that a brand-new engine from the drawing board is unlikely to be launched by any single maker, because of the sheer cost. Therefore I think that the importance of collaboration in relation to new engines will grow.

So this industry is entering into a new kind of competition – that between collaborators. We'll be hearing about the implications of this in a moment. But nobody will ever forget that Rolls-Royce went bankrupt in 1971. In hindsight, that was the first powerful demonstration that even the most vaunted firms in British engineering had become horribly vulnerable. What has the company done since to repair the damage?

TOMBS It has been moving quite positively towards profitability, principally by rationalisation in the workforce and by capital investment in both manufacturing machine tools and in computer-aided design – the control of those tools. It has also put a lot of effort into what we call modular development, taking existing engines and adding together bits – building-blocks if you like – rather than developing brand-new engines. It is considerably smaller in manpower, and it shares that situation with a lot of British industry. A lot of British industry was heavily overmanned in productivity terms, and so we slimmed in the same way as much of industry has. We're a very much more powerful company than we were in the Sixties because we have a wider stable of engines, a much wider market and a much more solid technology base, and those are three very great strengths that make me quite confident about the future of Rolls.

That leaves the vital question. How does Rolls-Royce stack up against its two bigger American competitors?

TOMBS We are not that much smaller in terms of the engines we can offer and the recent successes we've had. We have sold a lot of engines, for example, to the 747s recently, far more than our size would suggest. The real difference between us and them is they are parts of much larger corporations, and we're a stand-alone engine-maker. Now, that has advantages and disadvantages. The advantage is that it focuses our mind, we have to be very good at our job, we've got nobody else to pick up our tab. The general belief is that the diversity of Pratt & Whitney inside United Technologies, and General Electric inside the large US General Electric, gives them strength against adverse cycles. I think that can be exaggerated. Both of those large conglomerates expect each part of their outfits to be profitable, and don't tolerate poor performance, so that in a real sense their engine divisions compete as separate entities with Rolls-Royce and are not all that different in size from us. We've been increasing our market share in a number of areas, and that can only be at the expense of the other two suppliers. I wouldn't wish to pretend that this has been particularly dramatic, but certainly we've not suffered from competition. I think that they have both come to live with us, they both recognise that we have areas of the world, and areas of expertise, that make us a solid and continuous competitor.

The logic of Rolls-Royce's situation appears sound. This is one world industry where there are only three players. Britain has one of the trio, and all of them need the others. That sounds fine – provided there's enough demand for all three. Is there?

TOMBS We've been through a period of pretty unprofitable airlines continuing to run aircraft, irrespective of things like fuel economy, or sometimes even convenience, and therefore we have an ageing fleet throughout the world which will require replacement. Added to that there is a modest growth in air travel, and we see the market for new aircraft as quite strong between now and the end of the century.

How does that market seem from Austin Pearce's viewpoint at BAe? The company is still selling civil aircraft which are its own developments. Will there be any more private ventures?

PEARCE I think there'll be a very limited number of them, very limited indeed. In fact the 146 is not just the Brits, because we have got into risk-sharing involvements with the Americans and also the Swedes. But we take the majority of the bill there, and there is a limitation to that. And of course the other problem we face is a recognition that we have got to move up-market, because if you're in the high-volume lower quality market, other countries like Taiwan and Korea are ready to come in and take it over.

I don't think there's any question in my mind that the market-driven requirement, and the finance requirement for big projects, will force companies into partnerships. When we come to some of the smaller aspects of our company – if you like, some of the missile areas and things like that where you are not talking anywhere near as much investment money, where the product is relatively cheap and therefore you can sell it much more easily – no, I think some of them can be done individually, but the very big ones, yes, I think it's got to be partnerships.

So that's the future: in the smaller world markets, where the cost of entry is lower, the policy is specialisation backed by strategic acquisition. In the larger markets, where the cost of entry has become prohibitive even for American firms, strategic alliance is the chosen answer. But both policies depend on the success of Britain's engineers and scientists in keeping their companies in the forefront of fast-changing technologies. Can that be done? Francis Tombs.

TOMBS We spend about £250 million a year on total development, military and civil, and we find about half of that from our own resources and the other half comes from defence agencies. For example, the European Fighter is European funded; there's the Ministry of Defence on their particular aircraft, the Department of Industry through launch-aid for new engines and investment in particular projects. We would expect that to continue. We think that the overall investment in R & D is comparable with that of our competitors, it has to be really. But we think that we are, for a variety of reasons, particularly efficient at the way in which we use it. We spend a lot of time looking at the way in which we control R & D expenditure and the way in which we can simplify; for example, by using computer modelling instead of running actual engines.

Maintaining the technological strength, though, presents peculiar problems in Britain, as Austin Pearce notes.

PEARCE The unique strength we have is the very high skill level of our workforce. The technical resource which we have in people has to be our real strength – it's the brain power – and my worry is that they will not be replaced because we're not producing enough people with the technical skills out of our schools and universities. If a major project were to be cancelled, what's going to happen to those fellows? Are they going to succumb to what happened in the Sixties, the brain drain, and go across and work for Boeing and people like that? Our real strength is our brain power, and we had better make sure we keep replacing it and also keep it in this country.

Nor is that the only problem clouding the future. The aerospace industry has a particular bone to pick with government.

PEARCE There's been a very high degree of inconsistency of policy. When you recognise that the life of a government is, say, four or five years and you recognise that it takes about eight years to develop an aircraft and actually get it flying, and then you expect it to have a twenty-five-year life, there's a total inconsistency of time here. And in this country we do have govern-ments which swing from one extreme to the other. The real problem is the Treasury, and the Treasury happens to operate on a one-year basis and our twenty-five-year programme is something that is very difficult to bridge. No, I'm afraid that you'll find this with many industrialists, that the problem area concerns the system operated by the Treasury.

The interface between government and industry in this country is still unsatisfactory. But even more crucial is the ability of engineering itself to break away from its own traditions and to demonstrate the speed of decision and reaction that fast-changing competitive markets demand. Can companies like Vickers rise to this challenge? David Plastow.

PLASTOW If one of our operations has a particular venture – an acquisition, a major capital programme – which needs approval in this building, then as long as the papers get through our appraisal area in head office, and into the bags of the executive committee by Friday night, every Monday at 3 o'clock we hold an executive committee meeting and we will make a decision. So it's very, very tight and there aren't whole layers through which things have to process.

The proof of that pudding will lie in the eating – in particular whether British engineering companies can grow new businesses that will take over the running as the old ones slow down. David Plastow has a hopeful example, from a very old business called Vickers Instruments, of what can be done.

PLASTOW Vickers Instruments began to develop their equipment for the chip industry – by that I mean the electronic chip – and the measurement and examination and quality control of that product. And they had a brilliant idea to have a totally automated wafer inspection and measurement system. And we backed that wholly, and put in several million pounds with some very good people, and with no prospect of earning profits in the short term; and now we have the only wholly automated equipment in this field in the world.

Nobody should doubt, however, that for all the distance covered since the darkest days, there's a long road ahead before the context of British engineering matches that of its rivals. It's difficult to see how companies can succeed against world-class competition if they can't compete on equal terms. Mike Hoffman.

HOFFMAN We don't put as many people in the UK through higher education as our Continental competitors, and in addition we don't put them through for as long a period. Both of these factors seem, historically, to have an impact on the quality of the people coming. Secondly, we have developed, by the nature of our stock market in the UK, a relatively short-term view, and I can understand that, because all our pensions depend upon it. But it means that in making change happen in older industries, bearing in mind that a large number of our UK industries in manufacturing are older industries, you've got to take a much more cautious view of the short-term impact of changes you'd like to make that will really benefit the long term.

And the third point is that in the heavy engineering businesses we're used to that export overseas, we're very 'pure' in our thinking on linking aid to trade.

The battle is still on, too, at the level of the firm. How that battle for competitive costs must be fought is perfectly clear. So are its consequences. To preserve its future, and to protect that of the British economy, manufacturing industry must take action that will solve the problem – but it will not solve another grave problem: that of unemployment. Mike Hoffman explains how he plans to raise his before-tax profit margins to 8 per cent.

HOFFMAN The way we are going to make that 8 per cent is first to try and enhance the 'value-added' of what we're selling, that is by developing products that the market really wants, rather than selling products that we've simply made for a long time. And secondly, to hit the market with the cost reduction programmes, which I think are also beginning to bear fruit. But I guess both of those mean that we tend to use less people all the time, as we put more capital in.

That statement puts the encouraging developments we've heard into context. Engineering is the heart of British manufacturing, and its setbacks explain why the West Midlands, once a dynamic centre, has become an area of high unemployment and reduced prospects. The best companies are getting their act together and are now without question far better prepared, mentally and materially, than they were a decade ago.

It's easy to forget, though, that it is not enough to look at what British companies are doing. Their rivals in other countries are not sitting around waiting for British engineering companies to catch up. The German engineering group Mannesman is double the size of Babcock and Vickers put together. Boeing has doubled the combined sales of Rolls-Royce and BAe. The British companies are large by absolute standards. Relatively speaking, however, they are in the position of anybody placed in the ring with a heavier opponent. They have to be better trained, more determined, and craftier than the opposition.

A high degree of training and education, resolution and managerial cunning have not been characteristics of British engineering in the years of decline, and it can't be said that all the deficiencies of the past have been eradicated. The country, and the industry, are still paying the price of a century's neglect of the nation's technical and educational infrastructure. In these circumstances, it is a kind of triumph that Britain still has strong contenders in there and fighting at all.

CHAPTER 4

THE ELECTRONIC SUNRISE

You cannot have a dawn without a sunrise. In industrial terms that means you cannot have a renaissance without success in the so-called sunrise industries. Of these, by far the most prominent and pervasive is electronics. It is a sector where Britain has a long tradition of innovation and exploitation in the whole range of technology. Indeed, Britain is the only European country whose computer business has not been utterly dominated by the Americans, led by IBM.

Ever since James Callaghan as Prime Minister was alerted by a television programme, entitled *The Chips are Down*, government has been spending heavily to persuade British industry, as supplier and user, to respond to the challenge of the chip. The country's software expertise, too, has been hailed as precisely the kind of growth industry required as the world shifts from manufacturing to services. Yet the country has continued to lag in every large-scale market.

In hardware and software alike, the world's leading companies are many times the size of the British contenders. Across-the-board competitors like the General Electric Company confess themselves to be small by world standards; and GEC is only a quarter of the size of GE in America, and a third of that of Siemens in West Germany and Hitachi in Japan. In telecommunications, Plessey is half the size of Sweden's L.M. Ericsson, let alone the giants of Japan and the USA.

The best record of any major player in a game which has, in any event, become much rougher and tougher is IBM (UK). Without question, Britain has a future in electronics, as overseas companies exploit the technological and human resources which exist here. But can the indigenous companies seize a larger share of the market – above all, the far larger market outside Britain? Is the appearance of little Silicon Valleys occupied by growth companies a symptom of a new and world-scale expansion? Or is this a bus that has already been missed, with incalculable consequences for the future of the whole economy?

The first point is that the electronics companies, or at least the leading figures who appear on this programme, are nothing if not ebullient. Sir John Clark, chairman of Plessey (who recently emerged from what must have been a bruising encounter with GEC, which was frustrated in its attempt to buy Plessey), speaks with great confidence.

CLARK We believe that, in the mainstream defence electronic industries which we are in, we've got a strong enough base to maintain a technical lead against competition. We feel that, likewise, we are in a good position in semi-conductors, that's the silicon chip, and also in private switching. We freely admit that we would wish to be larger in public switching, that's what we call telephone main exchanges. And, of course, this is one of the main reasons why we bought the company in America which is involved in this field.

Nor will you hear any less confident a note struck by Sir Graham Wilkins, the chairman of Thorn-EMI, who cites big improvements at his Ferguson operation.

WILKINS The television sets we are now manufacturing in the United Kingdom are as good, as reliable, as stylish, as any produced anywhere. In fact, we are currently producing television sets for Japanese companies who put their own labels on and sell them into Europe.

Roger Foster, the chief executive of Apricot Computers, believes that in the personal computer business, little Apricot can hold its own against mighty IBM.

FOSTER We can do very well against them because our overheads are much smaller than theirs, which enables us to offer much more attractive prices; and secondly, because we are smaller, we are quicker into market with new technology. Generally speaking in the computer business, IBM is the market leader and then you have a strong local manufacturer in every country. In America, for instance, that would be Apple, who are clearly the number two in the personal computer market to IBM. In Italy it is Olivetti, in the UK it is Apricot.

Peter Bonfield, the chairman of ICL, the much larger computer company, which also makes much larger computers, compares its performance, not just with IBM, but with everybody else.

BONFIELD Just because ICL last year had a 20 per cent improvement in productivity, which is good, I rely on everybody to say, don't measure against that – what did the competition do, did they do 20, did they do 25, did they do 15, are we closing the gap? Within ICL we think we have closed the gap dramatically, and on most of our measures we are now up with the best in the world. I would see that in a lot of other UK companies. But there is no cause for complacency, and just measuring against yourself is no measure. Always measure against the best of the competition, whether it's in Japan, Korea, the US or Europe.

So far, so very good. But what about the specific markets and market strengths of the British electronics companies? What changes were forced upon ICL as it pulled itself out of its severe financial difficulties? What is its new philosophy?

BONFIELD We basically said, it's no use looking at just the UK market-place, we are in an international business, so set sights higher to look internationally. We are obviously a relatively large company in UK terms, but not big in international terms and therefore we had to come to terms with that. So we said, if we're not big in international terms then we'll specialise. We decided that we'd specialise into specific industries – retail was one, and manufacturing industries. Rather than try to compete with the big US multi-nationals across the board, we would only compete with them in very specific areas.

That was one major change. The other major change was to try and get the company to think smaller, act as though it was a smaller company. We were organised in the traditional manner of British industry, which was a big sales organisation, a big manufacturing organisation, a big product development organisation; and all the decisions came up to the top of the company and therefore it didn't move very quickly.

We broke the company down into much smaller units – what we call business centres – where the marketing people and the development people get together, mostly under one roof, and they attack a particular part of the marketplace. They're typically of the order of 100 to 200 people, whereas previously our product development operation was of the order of 4000 people.

Thorn-EMI, of course, has a much wider spread: recorded music, appliances, lighting, consumer electronics, and TV rental. But what about high technology? Do its strengths measure up? Graham Wilkins.

WILKINS The technology business, taking it in general, is one of our most profitable areas, but we do not compete head-on with the major international companies such as Texas Instruments in the defence or various other areas; we concentrate our efforts in more limited areas where we can be internationally competitive, and our technology business is very satisfactorily profitable, although we could still improve it. In technology we are really very strong in radar, we're very strong in thermal imaging, and we're very strong in sensors and in security systems. And those are the areas in which we'll continue to concentrate.

The company's highest technological hopes used to lie with Inmos, the bold, government-backed bid to establish Britain as a big league player in the world of the silicon chip. Those ambitions have been cruelly disappointed. Where does Inmos stand now?

WILKINS Inmos is a totally different company, and its products are totally different to that which we bought less than two years ago. We obviously bought Inmos at the wrong time, but then none of the experts predicted that the bottom would fall out of the market in the way in which it did. When we bought Inmos, it was just making a profit, but it has lost money since because of the way in which prices have fallen in the commodity areas. Now that we are limiting the Inmos activity to more highly specialised products, and in particular the transputer, the computer on a chip, we have certainly eliminated or drastically reduced the losses. We've reduced the size of the business. The transputer is a major British invention, obviously ahead of its time, and we feel that we must give that team and the transputer a period of time in which we can determine whether we can make it into a viable and profitable commercial operation. But it will still take us probably another year before we know that.

Yet the lower-tech businesses are far too important at Thorn-EMI to be neglected, and here the note struck is more uncertain.

WILKINS One perhaps ought to be looking more at a European market for appliances, I think that's about the maximum size of the market that you can look at because so many of these things are quite heavy. We do have quite significant businesses in a few areas; for instance Kenwood, our small appliance business, is quite a large business in France. But we had to sit down and decide how we wanted to develop that appliance business in Europe, whether we wished to go into every market in Europe or limit it, and whether we wished to stay in all appliances – that is, in cookers, refrigerators, laundry equipment and small appliances. In the end, we decided it was more sensible to sell our major appliance business to Electrolux.

Britain's leading electronics companies have all had to engage in far-reaching strategic decisions like those with which Thorn is grappling. At ICL, Peter Bonfield's hard look at the company's market stance had to be accompanied by what amounted to a re-education of ICL executives, a reconstitution of the whole corporate culture.

BONFIELD We found that 'co-locating' – which is our great computer word for putting people down on adjacent desks, but putting the engineers opposite the marketing people and forcing them to work together – has produced magic results. They previously thought that you had to go to a different committee, or that marketing was something that people did with flashy shiny suits, and in fact I'm trying to encourage everybody in ICL to be a marketing man.

Paradoxically, the approach adds up to making this very large company, with £1 billion of sales, think not large, but small.

BONFIELD We actually want the company, in some aspects, to be perceived as acting like a small entrepreneurial start-up company, as you've seen in the UK with some of the micro-computer companies. It's easier in the micro-computer field, in the very, very small area, to be small because you don't require the service back-up which is actually one of the big barriers to entry into the commercial marketplace. We're trying to tread a very careful path of making it small enough to be entrepreneurial and big enough to self-generate enough money for R & D, and then we need to link up with other people, because even if we generate as much as £100 million in R & D we will still need more. With our web of alliances we actually feel bigger than number twenty in the world; I think our impact is bigger than that, anyway.

Being small in the computer business isn't a virtue in itself. It's always what you do with your scale, greater or lesser, that counts. Apricot had shot up in three years from £8 million in turnover to nearly £100 million, and then, after twelve years of profits, it slumped into loss. What went wrong?

FOSTER I think we had outgrown the management, or the depth of management, in the company without growing some of our own internal control systems, and probably for the twelve months leading up to the disaster we were running pretty well out of control, though we didn't realise it. So over-extended growth was a principal reason, for which we paid a heavy price. The second reason was, of course, the well-publicised disasters throughout the computer and electronics industry, which had probably shared a similar pattern, that is a huge boom between about 1980 and 1985 and, following that huge boom, a great slump.

That disaster came on top of a fiasco in the US, where an attempt to establish Apricot came woefully unstuck.

FOSTER We did have an opportunity to enter the United States market. A particular group of people in America wanted to handle our product. It was at a time of great success for the company, and we took a chance. We financed it separately from our main company because we knew the risks involved, and it clearly was considered to be a high-risk venture. We committed close on $20 million of funds to the venture, but in terms of the US market that really is a small sum. With the benefit of hindsight we would have needed a great deal more money than that to have succeeded in the strategy, and we would have needed a year of boom for the industry over there – whereas in fact 1985 was a year of slump in that industry, in America as well as in Europe. So we really didn't do well.

After all that, where does Apricot stand now? Far from throwing in the towel, Apricot, like ICL, has gone through a major rethink of its strategy.

FOSTER We've now got a range that is 100 per cent IBM-compatible, as it's called in the industry. Prior to that we had a range of machines that were special to Apricot, and though we had a lot of software on them, we were not standard with what has now emerged as the clear industry standard, IBM. We decided that we had to make a change to become fully IBM-compatible, in order to reap the benefits of that approach. We believed we could use our own technology to do two things: to be both IBM-compatible, and yet to keep the special features of our computers that had really been the hallmark of Apricot's success – their style, their extra performance and the more advanced technological features. Those are what had set us apart.

It has to be said that not everybody shares Roger Foster's confidence in the future for an independent personal computer manufacturer based in these islands, although many people would accept his view on the changed, but still brilliant, market prospects.

FOSTER New, more powerful processors are emerging in the personal computer market, as a challenge to the much more highly priced mini- and main-frame computers, which at the moment are a huge chunk of the overall computer marketplace. Just as one market was getting torn to shreds, so another market is beginning to open up – a market which, to my mind, probably holds even greater potential riches for the next five years than the personal computer market did in the past five. We're now concentrating all our development and energies on multi-user systems priced typically around £10,000 or £20,000, but offering all the advantages of the personal computer, along with the power of the much, much larger, more expensive computers. There is a fabulous market there, and that's a market in which we must compete, of course, with people like IBM and DEC and Hewlett-Packard.

So, Apricot's strategy is to go for growth at the top, multi-user end of the personal computer market while seeking revenue from less volatile areas.

FOSTER One of the most profitable parts of the Apricot Group, which indeed showed large profit growth even in our bad year of last year, was a 'focus' company which we ourselves own concentrating on the City of

London – ACT Financial Systems, we call it. We have developed, in-house, a range of some 2000 packages under the name of Quasar, and we sell these into very large City banks, merchant banks and stockbrokers. We actually sell computer hardware as well as software, but the essential sell is that we are offering a solution to a particular problem.

After the shock in its unlucky thirteenth year, Apricot has learnt the virtues of something rarely heard of in the go-go years: stability.

FOSTER We've put a big investment over the past few years into main-tenance – the maintaining of computers after you've sold them – and this is now a very sizeable business. We're probably in the top three or four main-tenance companies in the country. We employ some 160 engineers and it's very, very profitable to us, and, of course, very stable. At one time we talked only of growth; now we talk of stability, steady growth, sustainable growth – these are the watchwords for the future.

At Plessey, which matured from growth star to established high-tech status long ago, rethinking was just as necessary as everywhere else. John Clark.

CLARK We needed to concentrate on a number of core businesses. And this we did by the selection of public telephone switching, private telephone switching and associated office automation, defence electronics in the broadest sense of the word, and the supporting technologies of semi-conductors, known in everyday language as the silicon chip. Now that meant that over time we had to divest ourselves, in the main by sale of com-panies, of those things which did not fit into that essential core selection.

A big question mark has hung over one of these Plessey cores – public switching. The System X electronic exchange developed for British use is crucial, and it has had a difficult and disappointing start in the world markets. Is Plessey down-hearted about System X?

CLARK It is, in our belief, one of the most modern telephone switching systems in the world today. It is quite capable of being tailored to meet the needs of any international telephone network, and now that we've got a well-established installed base in the United Kingdom, our expectations for exports of System X appear to be more and more promising with the passage of time.

Plessey sought to strengthen its hand in public switching by acquiring a subsidiary company, Stromberg-Carlson, in the US – an arena where one previous electronics foray had led to difficulties. But the market offered by the so-called Bell Telephone companies looked irresistibly large.

CLARK   Each one of these companies is very nearly as large as British Telecom in its own right; and the fact is that, on the basis of the existing products in the relatively small Stromberg-Carlson, we are able to address something like 70 per cent of the total market requirement for all telephone companies in North America. Now one has to go through an elaborate process of testing, and I think it's fair to say that Stromberg-Carlson has got further to date in passing Phase 1 of the Bell Telephone companies' test procedures, and is a very long way down the road in passing the tests for Phase 2. That puts us effectively in pole position. So we take the view that our American company is facing a most exciting future.

Small though Plessey may be in relation to the leading overseas competitors, its chairman feels certain, like many of the British executives interviewed for these programmes, that in its chosen market segments his company is world-class and world-scale.

CLARK   Believe it or not, in our chosen field of silicon componentry, where we are in what they call the 'custom-design' business, we are probably within the first half-dozen in the world and are looking to a very, very considerable expansion over the next five years. In private switching, likewise, we are now a very considerable force. On defence, if you take individual product areas, I would think that in military radio sets, in radar, in naval warfare, we have as good a position as any of our competitors.

Another way round the scale problem is partnership – the device which the aerospace companies have been obliged to adopt. ICL has forged several alliances, one of them for developing the Series 39 main-frame computers with the Japanese company, Fujitsu. Peter Bonfield explains why.

BONFIELD   The reasons initially were to share development costs. We're not big in the overall main-frame market, in fact Fujitsu themselves are not that big compared with the largest in the business, and therefore we thought we'd pool some of our resources and, instead of each developing and manufacturing all products, we would share our expertise. Our deal with Fujitsu only covered the semi-conductor part of large main frames; it didn't cover the total product line. We design our computer products using their parts, which they then run down part of their production line so that we get the benefit of reduced development cost and a reduced repeat cost. The parts are then sent back to the UK and we make computers out of them.

  With all collaborations we feel there must be a win-win situation; you can't have somebody winning and somebody losing. So we obviously gain from that with Fujitsu. Fujitsu have gained by ICL's becoming a major customer of theirs in Europe, which we weren't previously; we used to buy most of our semi-conductors from the US. And that collaboration has been going now for just about five years and I think has been an excellent example of how to do it – give and take on both sides.

Graham Wilkins sums up the business philosophy which company after company, and not only in electronics, has adopted as its guiding star through the often turbulent seas of world competition.

WILKINS We shall only remain in any business sector where we believe we have management of high enough calibre, so they can compete with anyone in the rest of the world, and where we do feel we have an advantage either in product innovation or in marketing skills or preferably both. And the limiting factor as to which areas we decide to invest in is – do we have the correct people, do we have the adequate marketing skills, do we have a big enough presence around the world, and can we make good enough products cheaply enough?

As John Clark explains, it's not so easy to construct a successful strategy of this kind in Europe as it is in the homogenous United States. Europe may be as big, but it's nowhere near as united. That has serious implications for anybody selling to government agencies and public utilities.

CLARK You have to realise that, as far as Europe is concerned, the public sector – which includes telecommunications, electricity, gas, coal and, of course, defence – has in no way been liberalised so far to any appreciable degree. The member states of the Community have continued to protect these basic industries, and it's only now that we're beginning to see some of these barriers being broken down. And they will have to be broken down because, in the long term, Europe must compete; and if Europe maintains a separation of national interest then it will never be in a position to capitalise on its buying power or purchasing power.

And again, there's the point to make that the rival firms overseas are not standing still waiting for Britain to catch up.

WILKINS Undoubtedly, we shall continue to have good relationships with many of the major Japanese companies, because that is quite clearly where so many of the new inventions in electronic technology are coming from at the present time. And they are sufficiently large and sufficiently profitable to afford the vast sums of money which are required for the research and development for the new products. So to that extent they do have scale and size on their side. I think that our own British scientists are just as good, just as inventive as other scientists around the world at the moment, but you do need to spend a lot of money on research and development; and at the moment we are not adequately profitable to do that.

For all the occasional euphoria, for all the new, stronger strategies, for all the successful efforts to raise productivity, and technological capability, the British electronics industry, in which so many sunrise hopes were invested, has to overcome the disadvantages of many missed opportunities in the past and of many missing capabilities in the present. John Clark.

CLARK You can't really generalise about the electronics industry. You've got to look at consumer electronics and divide that from professional electronics, and then, of course, you've got computers, you've got telecommunications and so on, and each of these sectors has its own problems. But, without any doubt, the generalisation that *is* applicable to them all – and particularly today to consumer electronics – is that in international terms we have a very, very long way to go as against, say, the Japanese.

We've seen in the United Kingdom what the Boston Consulting Group called the demise of the British motorcycle industry, many years ago now. We've seen the demise of the radio industry. We've seen the demise of the audio industry. We've seen a massive penetration by the Japanese of the television industry. At one time we had up to a dozen, if not more, manufacturers of televisions in the UK. Today we're down to a bare handful, and unless not only the electronics industry but British industry at large wakes up to the character of international competition, the nature of it and the size of it, then there's no future for British manufacturing industry.

CHAPTER 5

HALF-WAY POINT IN CARS

If the fate of its motor car industry is the best guide to the development of a large modern economy, then it is no surprise that Britain has been in relative economic decline. The companies which came together to form the old British Leyland Motor Corporation were on paper the equals of the automotive giants on the Continent. In Britain itself, the BLMC components once had more of the car market than Ford and Vauxhall combined. Today the greatly reduced rump has around half Ford's market share; while its position as a full-range manufacturer has depended heavily on models developed with the Japanese Honda.

BL's partial eclipse would have mattered less if the American-owned companies had developed along the old lines of strong independence. But Ford is now totally integrated into a European-wide organisation, and imports many of the cars it sells in Britain, while the much-revived Vauxhall, overshadowed in Europe by the German subsidiary of its parent, General Motors, has also been importing heavily. Neither any longer fits the bill as a British company developing British cars for the world market on the lines of Volkswagen in Germany, Peugeot in France or Fiat in Italy. Only Jaguar remains a world-class contender – and Jaguar's market is small and specialised, though highly profitable. Plainly, the lack of a comparable motor industry – with commercial vehicles passing through a miserable phase – puts all British industry at a considerable disadvantage.

How serious is the situation? Are there any signs of hope? Have the labour problems that contributed to the failures of the past been put behind for ever? And has the car components business done enough to compensate for the relative weakness of its British market by building strong and growing positions in markets overseas? One thing is certain: continued decline in this sector will make general industrial renaissance very difficult indeed. The common difficulty faced by all today's leaders in the car industry – all of them, by no coincidence, new or relatively new men – is that so much damage had been inflicted before they took charge, as Sir John Egan, the chairman, found at Jaguar at the end of the Seventies.

EGAN Probably everything had gone wrong. The company had been run for some years on functional lines as part of a much larger organisation, BL. People had concentrated on all kinds of corporate objectives and not on manufacturing a good product as the principal objective. So quality was one very big problem; the whole production process was very ill-organised and disjointed, and there was very bad timing, very large inventories, very low productivity. The cars weren't selling, and the dealers weren't very interested in the product, nor were they doing much of a job to satisfy the customers with the products they had. So most things had gone wrong across a pretty broad spectrum.

At Jaguar's erstwhile parent, BL, now Rover Group, the situation was hardly likely to be any better. The torch, or perhaps it should be the hot seat, has recently been passed to Graham Day, the Canadian who used to head British Shipbuilders, an industry that has seen even more disastrous decline. Why had BL gone astray?

DAY The main reasons included an inadequate attention to the market, and therefore the market was progressively being eroded as a result of the initiatives taken by competitors. Part of that lack of success in the market was a result of very erratic industrial relations in all of the company's plants. If you added those together – and there are other examples – you'd say the company wasn't really focused. Sir Michael Edwardes – to whom I, as anybody who sits in my job, has to remain grateful – certainly addressed the industrial relations situation, and the climate in which I operate today is very different. The way in which we respond to the marketplace still has a way to go.

That last point about unfinished work is one that must be stressed. The catch-up in cars has required so massive an effort that the mass-market companies are still in a race – and not just against time. John Bagshaw, the Australian who heads Vauxhall Motors, running two of General Motors' plants in Europe, talks about productivity.

BAGSHAW I guess that is an area where we have made considerable gains. We've got a two-year wage agreement which was negotiated in 1985. This has allowed a lot of stability in the negotiating process. We are now within a few minutes of building our cars to the same levels – the same number of hours to build a car – as our other plants in Europe. Now, that sounds pretty good, but unfortunately in other parts of the world our competitors are building cars in a lot less time than we are, and that's a problem we haven't got right yet; that's where we are going in the future.

One of the major components suppliers in Britain is Lucas, famous for products like its car headlamps, Girling brakes and so on. Dr John

Parnaby, its director of manufacturing technology, strikes a very similar note.

PARNABY Our analysis of British engineering manufacture suggested that on the average, whatever measure you make, the Japanese measure will be between 10 per cent and 40 per cent better. But that was three years ago, and in some cases we've closed the gap. In other measures, we've got a way to go.

A way to go, then. But a great advance has certainly been made compared to the standards of the past – and it is overly cynical to say that this comparison isn't very demanding. The trouble was that the new generation of managers faced a problem perilously akin to that of Hercules in the Augean stables – one improvement could easily be vitiated by another mess elsewhere. Where did John Egan start the clean-up at Jaguar?

EGAN In terms of our manufacturing processes the first thing we did was to concentrate on quality and getting it right first time. There is, incidentally, a productivity multiplier on quality; if you start getting things right first time, the whole production process flows through much more easily. We also put right the inventory control aspects of the job and actually got a lot better planning into our production processes. This was a good solid platform, then, to go for productivity improvements. It really meant organising work better, giving better leadership, also people working harder. To help that we brought in a production bonus; people on the shopfloor earn something like 27 per cent of their wages through the production bonus. All of these things came together to allow a management-led increase in overall productivity. I don't think we were asking people to run around like greyhounds; but we were indeed organising the job so much better that people could work at a much steadier pace throughout the day.

At Rover Group, Graham Day also stresses the gains in productivity.

DAY The second important legacy from Sir Michael Edwardes was the push towards productivity, and that is understandably linked to the change in the industrial relations climate. But with that change came the justification for significant investment in plant and technology. In terms of getting units down the line and out – expressed any way you like, say, cars per person per year – we are certainly as good as the best in Europe. So the combination of the industrial relations and the investment which led to productivity increases has given the company, not a full lease on life, but a good leg-up into the Nineties.

It hasn't been just a question of get the industrial relations right and the rest will look after itself. On the contrary, the drive to raise productivity to the best world standards would have imposed tremendous demands even if labour relations had already been perfect. John Parnaby explains how much of British manufacturing had become, in a word, obsolete.

PARNABY Much of the design of the manufacturing systems was based on 1930s principles, and aligned to the manufacture of very high volumes of low varieties of product, through a period when we dominated world markets in many areas and where our production engineering was quite excellent within that requirement.

However, as these sorts of manufacturing system are forced to compete with an aggressive new competitor who is offering high variety, there is a strong danger that people will modify them in a relatively piecemeal way, and will use panacea methods of buying pieces of equipment or computers, to try and compete. If you're not careful you finish up with a very complex system which still nevertheless has a backbone of high-volume, low-variety business. And since these sorts of changes take place gradually, there's never quite the incentive to go right back to the beginning, use a new set of principles and produce a new design of manufacturing system which is capable of high variety and low volume.

An example of a tendency towards higher variety, together with the requirement to increase the numbers of technologies used in the product manufacturing processes, would be one of our lighting factories which makes automotive headlamp systems. It used to make a relatively low variety of products, predominantly steel-formed headlamps, circular with a rim. Progressively, that very low variety has become very large, so the business now makes several hundred types of the product.

The scale of the response required can be seen from the remarkable upgrading of the engineering operations at Jaguar. John Egan.

EGAN I hardly know of a part number that we didn't have to re-engineer on the old Series 3. We did a great deal of engineering work, and, of course, all of that was bringing in good disciplines when it came to designing new products. We were able to utilise all of the lessons we'd learnt in terms of the development process on the old product, and put those into place as disciplines for the design of new products. In the six years since 1980, we've raised the staff and hourly paid employees in engineering from something like 250 to over 1000.

We're just half-way through a capital expenditure programme of over £50 million, to design a new engineering centre which will be fully open by the end of this year, at which time the total headcount in our project engineering department will rise to about 1300 people. The budget of our project engineering department will have gone from something like £5 million to £35 million. So the whole engineering effort is on a completely different scale.

But in this industry, more than most others, improvements in your own engineering and quality aren't enough. Jaguar found at one stage that something like a quarter of its engineering effort had to go into helping suppliers redesign their components.

EGAN We make about half the car, and we buy about half of it from outside suppliers. There were bad information flows through to the suppliers; they often didn't know how badly their products were faring in the field. We put those communication processes right. We manage – in most cases now – to agree with our suppliers that they should pay for the full cost of failure, so they have a tremendous incentive to achieve the quality levels that we require.

That matter of quality is a recurrent theme in the Western car industry these days: the Japanese have set new standards, and others have been compelled to follow or to pay the price in terms of lost markets. What progress has been made at Vauxhall? John Bagshaw.

BAGSHAW The cars that are being built at our Ellesmere Port plant are going through robotic gates, which allows us to build the bodies very accurately and improve the fit and finish. We've got a lesser amount of automation at Luton, but it's a different type of body construction, so that allows us still to maintain very high quality standards. We've also upgraded the quality of our dealer network. We just haven't been satisfied with letting the cars go out the gate and expecting them to be delivered to customers without an upgraded professional attitude by the dealers. We've got what we call a 'golden quality handover' system, where the dealer and the customers jointly sign off on the pre-delivery and handover of the car, and that's made a big difference.

Once again, though, making improvements in your own operations isn't nearly enough. Is Vauxhall satisfied with the quality of its suppliers?

BAGSHAW I'm not satisfied – and I'm a supplier too, because we have in-house manufacture – in fact I'm totally dissatisfied with certain aspects of what we're doing. If we do a sheet-metal stamping, for instance, and then the worker has got to take a hammer to it to get it to fit on the line, that's not good enough. It goes right back into the engineering and design, in many cases, of those pieces; they've got to be producible and they have got to be fittable. I think we've got a lot of work to do in a lot of areas. That's us at Vauxhall and General Motors, and I'm sure it's the same for other manufacturers as well.

As a supplier, Lucas simply had to face up to the harsh realities of the new situation in world markets. John Parnaby explains what this entailed for the company.

PARNABY We recognised that the skills of the emerging competition, that's to say the Japanese, resulted from the strategy they laid down for penetrating existing Western markets. This strategy led them to have three very important skills. One was to be able economically to manufacture high product varieties; another was to achieve economically high product quality; and the third was that they were able to operate very flexible manufacturing systems with very flexible people systems. All of these skills resulted from having to concentrate limited resources on manufacturing development and having to get into other people's markets by offering features which the competition couldn't – exploiting niches, and above all, providing a cost and a quality advantage.

Lucas responded by a total restructuring of the business, a revolutionary reform based on the concept of multi-skilled teams or task forces which tackled the manufacturing problems and worked hand-in-hand with a policy of decentralisation.

PARNABY The principle is one of, essentially, dividing up into cellular units – small businesses if you like – whereby a company has a set of business units which are reasonably autonomous, which in turn are divided into product units. These in turn are divided into cells or modules, with each cell looking like a small business, designed and tailor-made for the job it has to do, so that the people who operate it can understand it and feel as if they are in control.

Furthermore, each cell understands its adjacent cells as being 'customers' or 'suppliers' and can operate the right sorts of relationships. Each business unit is then very clear who its competitors are, who is world-class competition, and what their measures of performance are and what has to be done to be competitive. Our group managing director, Tony Gill, spends a lot of his time monitoring those changes. In my area of manufacturing innovation, I see at local level that we now have several manufacturing sites operating the Japanese *kanban* system – continuous flow manufacture. It's primarily a method of providing a discipline for materials-flow control through a factory.

Adopting Japanese methods, like just-in-time delivery of components, isn't without its drawbacks, however, as Graham Day found at Rover Group. The improvement in labour relations there has been remarkable, and isn't only the result of fear of unemployment: but there's a twist in the tail.

DAY I wouldn't deny that the thought of losing one's job at any level concentrates the mind, and I think that has been a positive factor, particularly on an individual basis, whereby the individual employees realise that their future and the company's future are absolutely linked. But also in the process, management – albeit belatedly – has become much more alive to the need to communicate. We all do it imperfectly, but I think we do it better. Last year we sustained the downstream consequences of strikes at one of our major suppliers, Lucas, and as we were running 'sole-sourcing' for a lot of our components we felt the downstream consequences in less than forty-eight hours.

Once again, the industry is effectively a combined operation. But at Rover Group it isn't just collaboration with suppliers that will determine how far the company can recover: it's also collaboration with a strong member of the Japanese competition: and the reasons are very compelling for this relatively small manufacturer.

DAY For us to produce a model costs the same as for someone who is selling a million off or two million off. That drives us down two paths. One is, we've got to make sure that our models and the positioning of those models in the market are absolutely right; our margin for errors is much less. Secondly, for some market sectors we go along the collaborative route. The Rover 800 is the first strategic collaborative venture for us, which was with Honda, with whom we've had a relationship since 1978. We were able to produce an executive market car which combined our individual skills in a way which, I believe, produced an optimum product for us both, and at a lower individual cost, and we're currently involved again with Honda on another product for another market sector which we code-named YY (incidentally the 800 was XX). So YY is now progressing and we hope to have that product, in its different guises, into the market in, say, 1989.

But hanging over the whole Rover Group operation, and one of the reasons, no doubt, why the government seriously considered selling it off piecemeal to General Motors and Ford, is the poor market performance to which Graham Day referred earlier. How distressed is he by the fall to around a 16 per cent share of the home car market?

DAY Market share in isolation is not the only god to worship; it is a fairly complex formula of market share, of product mix, of profitability and so on. Also, for us, it's sustaining our total production and after a very modest performance for many years, with in some cases complete withdrawal from markets, we've now moved back very strongly in export. We've been selling well, for example, within the EEC, in Europe generally; sales in 1986 were up over 14 per cent over the previous year. We've gone into the United States with the new Rover 800 series and with the Range Rover. And I can see that perhaps on the car side alone a third of our production will find itself sold in overseas markets in 1987.

The company has not been helped, however, by the ferocious price wars in the domestic market as the manufacturers have scrapped for market share. How did that battle come about, and how's it being paid for?

DAY I'm told that the whole cut and thrust that's taken place, particularly in the UK, was really started by Austin Rover about five or six years ago. If that's true, it doesn't change my view, it's still a mug's game; and you asked where the funding comes for that. Well, whether it's out of equity or out of the banks or whatever, I don't know anybody who wants to fund that kind of exercise. That is just plain stupid.

John Bagshaw wouldn't deny that Vauxhall has played a major role in the price wars. Its parent, General Motors, invested very heavily in new products, and it demanded sales to match, before profits. Now the emphasis is changing.

BAGSHAW We've got a range of products which is second to none in the industry. We've built up a good relationship with our dealers. They are responding to our drive for professionalism, they've seen our market share come up, they are highly motivated. We've doubled the number of sales we're making each year, so we've got a growing number of Vauxhall owners out there that hopefully are loyal owners that will buy again. So we're building a very, very solid base for the future, but we are not doing it on a profitable basis at the moment. So we have really got to work to get profitability into this place in order to survive.

The consequence is that Vauxhall now has as strong an incentive as Rover Group to see the discount war cool off. But profitability at Vauxhall has been under threat from another source – the strength of the German mark. The company, not without criticism from the unions and the politicians here, was relying heavily on imports from Germany. That had disadvantages when conditions changed.

BAGSHAW A year ago everything was looking pretty good at Vauxhall. The Deutschmark was around 3.90 to the pound; it made pretty good sense, all the material coming from Germany. Today the mark is down around 2.83, and for every pfennig we are in the red about £1 million. So the difference from a year ago to today is about £100 million, just on exchange. Now we are scrambling as hard as we can go to re-source back into the United Kingdom.

That will do much to weaken the argument that the American manufacturers here simply aren't manufacturing enough, so that the true scale of the British industry is even less impressive than the meagre figures for sales by the domestic makers imply.

BAGSHAW We have got our Ellesmere Port plant now moving up very fast to 35 an hour, which is plant capacity. That has just about wiped out all the imports of the Astras and Belmonts that we saw two years ago. At Luton we've got the new paint shop coming on stream, we're moving on to the plant capacity of 32 an hour, and there will be practically no Cavaliers now imported from the Continent. So, of the cars that we sell here, we will be building nearly 70 per cent in this country, which is higher than it's been in years and years. Our reliance on imports is purely in the couple of cars that are relatively low-volume that we build in one plant, namely the Nova, which comes from Spain, and the new Carlton and Senator, which will be coming from Germany.

For the American-owned companies, their success in the home market is especially crucial since their impact in world markets can only depend on the overall strategy chosen by their parent companies. A company like Jaguar, in contrast, has to design cars like the new XJ40 to have the widest possible world appeal – and that means leaving no stone unturned, and no type of road untested.

EGAN For example, our XJ40 sign-off included 75,000 miles on the roads around Timmins, Ontario, which is one of the coldest places in the world; also 75,000 miles in Phoenix, Arizona, which is very hot, and on the dust roads in the deserts of Australia, and also in the Oman. They also included 25,000 miles at full speed round a test track in southern Italy. The actual design intent says on the original drawings that that is what the car is expected to do.

What's true for the car manufacturers must apply with equal force to the components suppliers like Turner & Newall. How bad a blow has the shrinkage of British car production been for this company? Chairman Sir Francis Tombs.

TOMBS It's obviously been a short-term blow, because if you get used to depending on a home customer, adjustment is difficult. But the resulting need to go overseas, to make products that command the respect of Germans, Italians, French and Americans, is a very good discipline. We're going to have to compete increasingly, as a country, in the world marketplace, and the decline in the UK automotive industry has made companies like Turner & Newall, with its Ferodo brake-pads and Cooper's filters, go abroad and expand their markets beyond their purely UK base. That's probably the way in which British industry has to go. It has to forget the comfortable home base, sometimes with over-engineered standards, and compete on an open market with the world's industries. And we can do it.

The strategy is obvious. But realising that strategy, in a world peopled by energetic and efficient competitors, isn't going to be easy. How successful, for example, has Lucas been at reducing its dependence on the home base?

PARNABY It varies across the different companies. Our Girling company is only 25 per cent dependent on the UK, and their factories are generally in Europe. Lucas CAV has factories across the world. Lucas Electrical is probably the least widespread of our companies, in contrast to Girling, which is probably the most widespread. And Girling have an enviable record in that most braking systems on Japanese cars are Girling designs, which is quite amazing.

So far as car manufacture is concerned, the crucial issues still surround Rover Group as the only British-owned survivor in the volume markets, where the Japanese and the European leaders, along with the Americans, reign supreme. Graham Day has only occupied his hot seat for a short time, and so he is still searching for the key to the kind of future that Jaguar has already plainly won for itself.

DAY I don't know if Sir John Egan would agree, but he was working very hard in Jag to bring about the changes which have conferred such benefit on them before he left the BL group – but the privatisation exercise, I believe, operated as a catalyst to enable John to make people focus on what he was doing, which was positive, and he's built on that strength. I think we need a similar catalyst, and I'm not sure what that catalyst is likely to be.

The true measure of where the British car industry stands today, in relation to where it should be standing, must therefore be Jaguar. It is enormously profitable, an international success, and growing fast on all fronts. To the extent that Jaguar falls short, though, the rest of the British car industry must be much shorter of the vital marks of world competition. So where does Jaguar stand? John Egan.

EGAN I'd say that we're about half-way through. There are two areas where we have to concentrate. First of all, we have about £700 million to spend, at the rate of something like £125 million a year, to put in place all the modern equipment we need to do the job properly, our engineering centre, our robotics programmes, our machining centre programmes and so on – vast capital expenditures. In a way we've missed out a generation of capital expenditures. We're using, very often, equipment that's twenty years old. We've missed out on the investment programmes in the Seventies and all these big investment programmes have to be put in place.

Secondly, I think we have an enormous training and motivation effort still. The car industry was pretty well near rock bottom in terms of leading and motivating large groups of people to work in harmony together to a common purpose. I think we've done a good job, we've made good improvements. But we're still, again, only half-way there.

CHAPTER 6

THE SUMMING UP

From the preceding chapters on the present and future of British industry, a clear pattern has emerged. Many of the major companies whose leading executives were interviewed have absorbed the impact of recession and reform and face a hotly competitive future with one shared confidence: that they can hold their present much improved positions and build on them. The best companies have rationalised their product ranges, rationalised their production (at great cost in terms of jobs), recognised that their only market is the world market, realised that they can only compete with world-class standards of performance, and decided to concentrate solely on the areas of genuine strength.

In many cases, the results have been spectacular. But has the improvement extended widely enough – among the medium-sized and smaller companies, and even in the big company sector? Has British industry merely caught up with world competition, and is it about to be leap-frogged as the others once again forge ahead? Are we in the right industries? All these are vital issues. But underlying all these questions are two other issues that have cropped up in many of the interviews.

The erosion of the Seventies has left Britain simply lacking in world-class contenders of world-class size. Even more basic, everybody agrees that the previous poor showing of British industrial companies arose partly from inadequacies in the national culture, in the nexus between industry and government, in the education system. If this is true, then the future can only be brighter if these impediments have been eradicated. The evidence is that the old failings, the original sins of the British economy, still persist in some degree. How severely do these shadows darken a national industrial prospect which cannot truthfully be described as very bright? British industry still faces huge difficulties, as Sir Christopher Hogg, the chairman of Courtaulds, powerfully explains.

HOGG The history of the world is littered with examples of nations and people doing extraordinary things, but the will is an important part, and I'm really not sure whether in this country we really have the national will to get our act together sufficiently, and for long enough, to make real headway against some of the very fundamental problems which now beset us in improving our economic performance. I mean things like the way in which the education system is organised and responds to current needs, the degree of labour mobility, the poverty trap, the rigidity of institutions – I can't find a better phrase – and it seems to me to be very descriptive of the combination of inertia and conservatism which makes it so difficult to get action.

The architect of a famous revival at Jaguar, chairman Sir John Egan, also sees major problems.

EGAN There seems to be an enormous gulf between unions and management. For example, I keep asking my trade unions whether they are interested in helping a fine company to grow and become wealthy, from which they're going to get a good return. Or are they simply demanding more money for doing less work? If they're doing the former, it's quite easy to get the two sides together down a common track of wealth creation. If they're just simply grabbing more for doing less, then, of course, the company will go out of business. That's one absolute gulf.
  A second major problem is that standards throughout most of Britain are low in every way. We're willing to have poor service in hotels and restaurants and dirty streets and so on. When you're trying to pick up a whole company to run at international levels of competence, it's difficult when the whole environment around you is often willing to accept second and third-rate standards.

Roger Foster, whose Apricot Computers has been fighting the good fight against the Americans and increasingly the Japanese, sees problems in the national culture.

FOSTER Here in this country you haven't really got either the Japanese philosophy or the get-rich-quick and have-a-go philosophy of the Americans. We therefore tend to be fragmented in our approach. The banks, I believe, aren't sure whether they're backing high-tech or not backing high-tech. And you've got traditionally a political system in which you see wild swings in the attitudes toward industry, depending upon whether you have Conservative or Labour government. So really at the cultural level we don't have the support enjoyed by the Americans and Japanese. That makes it a tough environment to succeed in the UK.

Graham Day, the new chairman of Rover Group, is a Canadian – one of several top managers coming from outside Britain who are now making a major impact on British management. And he takes a more sanguine view.

DAY I don't think it's necessarily difficult to run business in Britain. I manage here by choice, and I upset some of my Canadian colleagues by saying I prefer to work in Britain, I find it more comfortable, I find it easier, I find the response time better than I used to find in Canada. And I think if you were to speak to Japanese businessmen, both those who've established plants here and those who may be seeking to establish plants here, they view the British industrial and commercial climate as the most attractive within the EEC.

That is both true and encouraging. But it's necessary to remember that something must have been going terribly wrong for a long time to produce situations like the one described by John Egan.

EGAN For many years there seemed to be a notion in British industrialists' minds that they could spend a third of what their competitors were doing on research and development and on new capital investment, and still compete. Obviously it's nonsense.

How did this and many other obvious nonsenses persist, and why was the action to correct the nonsense so often taken only after the economic roof had fallen in? Sir John Clark, chairman of Plessey, has no doubt about the answer.

CLARK There was, and probably still is, a great lack of professionalism of management in British industry. The signs have been on the wall for years. This issue of competitive analysis, based on an identification of what is called the 'strategic business unit', is something that's been taught in business schools for the better part of twenty years in one form or another. Some companies saw the need to go into strategic planning and adjust their policies and their investment accordingly. Others didn't, and are suffering very badly today. Whether they can survive the course is a matter of conjecture.

One thing is clear about today's survivors, however. They are leaner and fitter – they have had to be. Mike Hoffman of Babcock International, the heavy engineers, sees both great improvement and continuing problems.

HOFFMAN I think those that remain are obviously becoming more competitive. The game is no easier than it was, and you're seeing much more innovative people coming through. Fixed and rigid management attitudes have changed, and the sort of young man that's now coming out as a manager has got no real memories of the Thirties, when managements were hard and dominant. We're much more flexible now, and more competitive. The area that still worries me in the UK is that we don't actually make many things that the consumer wants. There's furniture and things like that, but you've only got to look at white goods, televisions, those types of things, to see we really don't make a large number of consumer goods. So we're still too dependent on somebody else using our heavier products for us to be internationally competitive.

Dr John Parnaby, the head of manufacturing technology at Lucas, also sees a significant change in mental attitudes.

PARNABY If you go back four or five years, when we were all in the bottom of the trough, and we were perceiving the size of the problem, morale was low, because it is only when you understand the structured approach for solving those problems that you start to have the confidence that you can solve them. In Britain there were all sorts of tall stories about Japanese success being a consequence of Japanese culture, when in fact it's Japanese professionalism, the use of knowledge, the excellent use of engineers. And once people get to understand that there is a structured way of solving these problems, morale starts to rise. So on the whole we are all feeling a lot happier than we were, now we know where we are going and we know how to solve the problems.

Graham Day, however, finds that the change in mental approach still, quite literally, has far to go.

DAY If I talk to some of my colleagues or some people outside the business about ten years from now, and how we have to position ourselves and products and facilities in that kind of horizon, I watch their eyes glaze over and they sort of say, 'Yes, yes, but what are the half-year figures going to be like next year?' And I know even then, saying that, they believe they're humouring me by talking about something as far away as next year's mid-term results. And I think we pay, as a nation, a penalty for the different time-scales within which we focus our efforts.

That still leaves the question of where British industry should be heading, where it should concentrate its efforts. Mike Hoffman looks towards the newer frontiers.

HOFFMAN Inevitably you're drawn towards the information technology industries, broadly electronics and software. Those are areas for which the UK capability is very suited. Other areas where we're making advances are materials technology and bio-engineering. And I guess if I was starting out and saying, for a national plan for the UK, where would I put my resources (other than weapons-related activities which is a large part of our R & D in the UK), I would tend to look at those types of industries where we stand a big advantage in worldwide competitive positions.

At BOC, which has diversified strongly from its core of industrial gases, Dick Giordano, an American, warns against placing too much hope either in the sunrise industries or in the services which some people see as the Great White Hope of the British economy.

GIORDANO First of all, I think it is wrong to segment the old industries from the newly emerging or new industries, often described as the 'sunset and sunrise' industries. They really are integrated. After all, the pattern of industry is set by final demand. If people buy automobiles, those automobiles will be made with steel, perhaps less steel than before, but they will also incorporate a considerable amount of new software on the factory floor, perhaps some of the newest and most exotic materials from so-called new or emerging industries. If we don't have an automobile industry, not only will we lose the old industry of making steel, but we will not have the newly emerging industry of software or new materials.

These industries complement each other; we cannot allow our industrial base of so-called old industries to disappear, and hope to have a robust and viable economy purely of newly emerging industries. The same argument is often made that we can get along with service industries and don't need manufacturing. That, too, is rubbish. If we're going to be successful and have a robust economy, we must have enough of the old industries as a basis on which the new industries will emerge.

That is surely right. Unless British manufacturing can find a role in world markets, Britain won't be able to recoup its losses in the world economy. True, manufacture in these islands doesn't have to be British-owned. The country has many attractions as a site for branch factories of overseas companies. Is that a viable future? John Clark of Plessey has reservations.

CLARK You can have a situation where your indigenous industry is investing a great deal of its own resource into a given product area, and yet your inward investor is simply an assembler of goods, and he's not therefore competing on equal terms in any shape or form with the British manufacturing company. The inward investor, in almost every case, is no more or less than a satellite factory of a foreign country, but the consequence of bringing more competition into the UK – where probably a lot of competition exists already – doesn't in fact make the cake any larger. It just spreads it more widely and more thinly. In the event it's almost bound to damage your indigenous British manufacturing company.

Those inward investments are already substantial and will become more important still. So the challenge to British firms comes not only in markets outside the UK, and not only from imports into the UK, but from highly efficient competitors camped, not on their doorstep, but inside the house. Graham Day of Rover Group looks at the size of the challenge.

DAY So there are clearly elements in British industry, British commerce which are world-class by any standard. But I believe that the changes which had to come about have come about more slowly in some sectors than in others – and the automobile business in the United Kingdom is one of them. The changes have taken place very rapidly. They've been changing rapidly for five years, but when the competition was up and running in a more aggressive and more sophisticated way fifteen years ago, it just makes life a little more stressful than it otherwise might be.

John Parnaby spells out the stretching demands which modern market conditions impose on those companies which want to compete.

PARNABY They have got to keep a very close monitor on their market and be sure they know what the customer wants – not what they *think* the customer wants. That's the difference between marketing and selling. Beneath that they have to accept that every part of the business strategy has to be competitive, so that the manufacturing strategy has got to be just as competitive as the product strategy. That, in turn, leads on to the idea that we have to have a much healthier regard for knowledge, and innovation through knowledge and through education, and therefore keeping up to date, scouring the world for good ideas, not being embarrassed to admit that we don't know things.

Being willing to learn from other people is a critical part of that. This innovation process we're going through is quite clearly education-led, and we have to recognise that we're now stuck with it forever. It's not a question of now moving back into line and then saying with a sigh of relief, 'that's it for another thirty years until the next crisis'. It's got to be a continuous improvement process, and if you look at the best-run Japanese businesses who've already done all this innovation, the thing that strikes you about them is the structured management of continuous improvement.

Mike Hoffman sees the need for a major thrust in innovation.

HOFFMAN We've got to be in areas where we can use a high level of expertise combined with a level of international marketing capability, which I actually believe the UK has. I don't think we've exploited it nearly enough because we became soft in the immediate post-war period, when you didn't have to go out and innovate and market. And that's where the Germans and the Japanese crept in. But I don't believe the battle is lost in any way in that respect. You've got to invest in products and recognise that product life-cycles are much shorter than they've ever been in the past. And then you've got to get out and make sure you sell them while the life of those products is current.

Hoffman thinks, however, that the chances of achieving the necessary leap forward have been improved by recent changes.

HOFFMAN There have been two changes really: one is that technology has moved forward dramatically, and in fact you could almost argue that if you were entering advanced manufacturing technology fields now, it really wouldn't matter whether you had ten-year-old technology or thirty-year-old technology, because the change has been so dramatic as to wipe out both of those at a leap. The other element is, whether one likes the politics or not, that the environment created in the last seven or eight years, politically, has been such that the dominance of trade unions, and the fact that one always had to listen to their views on everything, has declined.

But is the continuing propensity of British employers to increase wages by more than the rate of inflation as severe a danger as Mrs Thatcher and her ministers make out?

HOFFMAN I actually don't believe that it matters whether you pay people more than inflation, providing you are reducing the total cost of your business. If, for example, you're moving towards a much more technologically based business then you might have to pay your people arguably twice as much as they're paid now. But if you use 20 per cent of the people with the new technologies, then in fact the actual annual payment doesn't matter. It's where you're not getting the productivity gain with those increases that it really matters. You see, we're still a very low-wage economy in the UK.

If the unions are no longer an important obstacle to industrial progress, that removes one of the main post-war excuses for indifferent company performance. John Clark at Plessey has one or two precise points about government policy, another of the continual bugbears. But in general he has this robust statement to make.

CLARK I don't think that there are any external forces that are working to the detriment of British industry, as far as I'm concerned. The problems with my company are the problems that need to be dealt with by its management; and I would make the same point for the rest of British industry.

Is British management up to dealing with its problems? The idea that there are human deficiencies, that the inhabitants of these islands simply provide worse managerial material, is plainly rubbish, as Denys Henderson, chairman of ICI, observes.

HENDERSON I do not believe that our American or Japanese counterparts work any harder than we do. I don't believe they're any more intelligent. I think they are a little more single-minded in the way that they drive towards their targets. I think that they may be more market and customer-orientated than we have been. And particularly in the case of the United

States, they are infinitely quicker in taking new ideas, good research and translating them into hard market products.

In other words, it comes back to attitudes. And what forms attitudes? As Graham Day says, it's investment – but not in machinery.

DAY I would want to invest in people first and in hardware second. You can invest in hardware – up goes your depreciation charge and, if you borrowed money, your servicing charge. But unless you have the people right, it's not going to be fully productive. I'm concerned about investment in people to produce professional managers, not only managers by accident, and I think that starts very early in someone's career.

Sir David Plastow, the chairman of Vickers, likewise has no doubt where the root of the problem lies when it comes to competing against the Japanese, Germans and Americans.

PLASTOW They've had very well-trained people with training systems much better than ours. At the very highest level of technology I think we still have an edge, but at the mid-management and operator level clearly we've got a great deal to do to catch up. That's probably the most significant thing of all. If we take the Japanese example particularly, we must remember that they've had a solidly protected market before they moved out. Until 1970, when their motor business had reached something like three million units, it was virtually impenetrable, and from that volume base they got to work on the world. So they managed their affairs in a very forthright and ruthless manner, which we haven't done here. In the case of North America, a massive domestic market is a good start. But overall I think the biggest single thing is the depth of training and education, which we have got to get right.

Graham Day expands on the educational argument.

DAY In order to create wealth we can't simply manipulate the City. We have to generate it from, say, manufacturing. If that is to happen we have to have better and better people in manufacturing, and those people have to be trained, whether their basic education should be in engineering or in finance or whatever. But that's not what's critical. What's critical is what they do after that.

As Graham Day says, these days competition involves concepts like market segmentation and product differentiation. You can't succeed in marketing without understanding these concepts in theory and in practice.

DAY You don't get that in an engineering school, you don't get it in finance –
you get it, I think, in a formalised business education, which can be done on
block release, day release, sending people away to short courses, or perhaps sending them away for two years. But that's where I'd put my money.

It isn't a question of top education for top people. The need for
education and re-education, training and re-training extends right down
through the company. John Egan.

EGAN The problem we've got in this country is that, compared with our
competitors in Germany and Japan, from top to bottom the workforce is
probably badly educated – only a third or a half the number of degrees, 'O'
levels, 'A' levels and so on – and we, like any other company in the UK,
have to put a tremendous impetus into training, and also into creating the
motivation environment where the first line of supervision, for example,
can do a very good leadership job. Often we've seen foremen in this country
as a sort of oiler of the wheels, whereas really the most fundamental part of
his job is to be a leader. And I think often we haven't understood in this
country that business, especially big business, is an enormous leadership
challenge.

The best British managements have not only seized on these truths, they
are acting on what they realise is the great imperative of their times – as
at Jaguar.

EGAN We spend something like 1.25 per cent of net sales on training. This
compares with something like 2 per cent for a similar German company.
So we still have some way to go. But we spend something like eight times
the national average on training, so many companies in the UK really have
hardly started on this long road.

Lucas is one of the companies which have gone a long way down that
road, despite the difficulties put in its path by the defects in British
academic provision. John Parnaby.

PARNABY We spent over £40 million last year, internally developing a wide
range of training courses, a heavy proportion of which were in relation to
manufacturing development. We have open learning courses on Japanese
systems engineering, we've got courses on simulation that we've done
ourselves. We've built up a modular structure of about forty modules of
training, and it's been done by our group training functions in collaboration
with the business training units, but pulling in engineers to do the details,
so the professional choice of methodologies was there; and also pulling in
academic staff from universities and polytechnics who had particular skills
that were relevant. It has been inordinately difficult because when you

looked around the British academic world, there actually wasn't a great deal of knowledge of these sorts of skills.

The fact that progress is sometimes hard to achieve is no excuse for failing to tackle essential tasks. And essential is the word, as Peter Bonfield, chairman of the computer group, ICL, strongly emphasises.

BONFIELD We insisted on two things: one was that we would not reduce our investment level in research and development, which we didn't, and the other was that we would increase our level of training, management training, marketing training and general training. That has really started to pay off. We started initially with a very large marketing training pro-gramme, we then expanded that into management training, and we've put over 2000 people through that training programme – I would think one of the largest of its kind in the UK – and the results have paid off handsomely.

The fate of British industry thus lies in its own hands. Nobody should underestimate the size of the task – and nobody would, least of all the industrialists we've heard from in this series. Their efforts have shown that all is not lost, that the line to which British manufacturers have been forced to withdraw can be held, and that selective advance is possible from those positions. The magic word in management circles these days is 'world-class' – and John Egan finds that he can use it to describe a good many companies.

EGAN We're seeing around us many companies, especially our suppliers, beginning to achieve world-class levels of quality standard. We have a Supplier of the Year award ceremony every year, where something like thirty-eight British suppliers will be getting these awards. We really mean these are world-class standards, these are excellent companies. It does your heart good to see the enthusiasm and excellence generated within these companies.

   However, I think that it's a painful process because we're actually having to recreate the industrial fabric of the nation at a time when there's almost a world recession. It's much easier to do it when the rest of the world is grow-ing. But we see a lot of companies fighting and inching their way forward. I think there's a lot of courage and a lot of strength in a country with the heritage of the United Kingdom. If we keep on trying, and as long as we don't believe there's any magic wand that the government can throw in and suddenly make it all easy, then we might make it.

We *might* make it. That seems to me a very judicious summing-up, to which I'd only add one thing. If we *don't* make it, the consequences for the standards of living of all people in this country, and for the standards of much else that the British rightly hold dear, will not be pleasant. Indeed, those consequences hardly bear thinking about. And that is what's truly at stake in the state of British industry – all our futures.

THE INTERVIEWS

FROM CHEMICALS TO TEXTILES

DENYS HENDERSON, CHAIRMAN, ICI
SIR CHRISTOPHER HOGG, CHAIRMAN, COURTAULDS
RONALD MILLER, CHAIRMAN, DAWSON INTERNATIONAL
PAUL GIROLAMI, CHAIRMAN, GLAXO
RICHARD GIORDANO, CHAIRMAN, THE BOC GROUP

DENYS HENDERSON, CHAIRMAN, ICI

Denys Henderson took over the chair at Imperial Chemical Industries on 1 April 1987. Aged 54, he is the group's youngest ever chairman. He succeeded one of the great communicators of modern British industry, Sir John Harvey-Jones, and promises to be another. After this pair, it will be difficult for any ICI successor to revert to any more formal mode.

ICI's central management problem, with which Henderson has grown up in the company, has been to retain its place among the great chemical companies at a time when its home market – which contained most of its assets – accounted for an ever-decreasing share of world demand. The answer was to 'internationalise' the company, which sounds superfluous for a group that has actually been multi-national ever since it came into being as a result of a four-company merger in 1926.

Although he has never worked full-time overseas, Henderson emerged as a leader of this new international movement. A lawyer by training, he worked in successive divisional secretariats after joining ICI in 1957. His chance to excel in the field came in the mid-1960s. From overseeing new ventures for Nobel division (explosives), he moved to take charge of catalysts and technology licensing for agricultural division, and later sales and marketing, for fertiliser division; ending up (like one of his predecessors in the chair) as head of paints division before going on to the ICI main board in 1980.

As a director, his portfolio included most of the business areas with obvious multi-national potential – pharmaceuticals, agrochemicals and paints – together with new groupings in polyurethanes and other speciality chemicals which were managed, from the outset, on a worldwide basis. In

1984 he was instrumental in setting up the corporate acquisitions team, which was responsible for ICI's great leap forward in the US with the Beatrice Chemicals and Glidden purchases. Henderson moved into the chair at a high point in ICI's history. In 1986, profits pre-tax broke the £1 billion barrier for the second time on sales of £10.2 billion – a far cry from the £5.7 billion of sales and £284 million of profits at the low point of 1980.

The company has also greatly improved its penetration of geographically scattered markets for speciality and other 'effect' chemicals, and reduced its dependence on commodities (whose UK producers have lately been combined into a huge Chemicals and Polymers Group with new pan-European terms of reference). Reflecting its new marketing orientation, ICI now divides itself into consumer/speciality products (nearly £4 billion of sales in 1986), industrial products (£4.5 billion), agriculture (£1.8 billion) and oil and gas (£500 million) – and it is the first of these, the closest to the ultimate consumer, which has shown the greatest growth.

Over the next five years Henderson is going to have to pace himself in a job which Harvey-Jones has called a 'killer'. He nevertheless intends to retain a handful of extra-mural appointments as a non-executive director of Barclays Bank and Dalgety, and governor of Henley Management College. Whether he will stay on for a second term after 1992 need not be decided yet. Remarkably, he is the first ICI chairman for two decades who has been able to consider the possibility of more than five years at the top.

ICI always seemed to sail on through thick and thin. Were things really going that well by the end of the Seventies, and the early Eighties?

Yes, 1979 was a very good year for us, by almost any indicator you care to use, and it really was a tremendous shock when the world fell off the cliff edge in the middle of 1980. I remember it well because I'd just joined the ICI board as commercial director. I had the privilege of reporting a record first quarter sales, whereupon by quarters three and four we were in an unheard-of position of being in loss. There were those of my colleagues who uncharitably suggested there was a connection between my arrival and falling off the cliff.

What was going wrong?

It was the markets largely. With hindsight there had been two step-changes in demand that I don't think any of us properly read. The first was the oil shock in 1973, when the OPEC cartel put prices up dramatically. But they did the same thing again in 1979 with what is called the second oil shock. Now, this reduced demand through the early Eighties quite markedly. We had a particular problem in this country because, firstly (and not too many people remember this), in June 1980 UK inflation was running at 21 per cent per annum, while that of our competitors, the Germans, the Americans, the Swiss and the Japanese, was, of course, very much lower than that. And secondly, if, as ICI was, you were a major exporter or a major earner of overseas income, you had to face up to a considerably over-valued pound. So the combination of lower growth, high domestic inflation and an over-valued currency – at least for exporting purposes – really was absolutely disastrous.

Did that effectively price you out of the market?

Not in all our products. But in the basic commodity chemicals we were being priced out of the market, and I remember very clearly, at that time we were losing on average something like eighteen pence per pound on every pound sterling of exports. Now that figure, of course, is an amalgam of a lot of different products. We were still making good money on our higher added-value things like pharmaceuticals or speciality chemicals, but on the basic commodity chemicals we were losing an arm and a leg.

I'm bound to say, too, that our cost base at that time was still too high. We had been improving our productivity since the early Seventies very consciously to match that of our major competitors, the three large German companies and the Americans, and we'd been making some progress. But against the unparalleled adverse circumstances that I've outlined it was crystal-clear that that improvement was just not strong enough. So we had to move towards very drastic restructuring and cost reduction.

What were the main principles at work in that restructuring?

They are what I call a number of *re*'s. The first *re*'s were fairly clearly to *re*structure and *re*duce costs. What that meant was that we had to improve productivity, we had to shed labour. And it wasn't just on the shop floor – it was right through the whole structure. For example, when I joined the board in 1980 there were fourteen executive directors. Today, including the chairman, there are eight directors in all, and that's been paralleled all the way down through the company.

The second thing we had to do was to *re*shape our businesses and to say, if the UK, as far as one can see, is not going to represent a big enough percentage of the free world chemical market, then we have got to drive even harder to be extensive in our overseas sales. So we set out very consciously to do that. And as part of that process, because we had seen the bulk chemicals so vulnerable to the domestic inflation and to the over-valued pound, we had to move into more 'effect' chemicals than we had done. That's been done by a number of things, including acquisitions.

And the third part was that we had to *re*generate our businesses. So we looked very carefully at which new businesses we should push quite hard, and we made a conscious decision to get bigger in our advanced composite materials, to be sold into the defence and aerospace industry; to get into chemicals for the electronics industry; to step up our polyurethanes business; and latterly to enter the plant breeding business by buying seed companies, firstly in the United States and secondly a small one here in the UK. So it's been a very considerable *re*-orientation of the company.

What lines have you felt obliged to abandon? Have you narrowed the product base?

In some ways, yes, because what the recession of the early Eighties taught us was that the world was no longer our oyster. There was a degree of arrogance in the chemical industry that said, if it's anything faintly chemical we can do it, anywhere in the world. This period we went through really told us, in a very simple fashion, we must be selective because our resources are not infinite. Therefore we must put those resources in the particular areas where we believe we have some strengths. That's a process that has been happening all over the world; all the international chemical companies are doing that. I coined a phrase, that we're all busy playing musical chairs.

What I mean is that we're moving out of some areas where we don't see ourselves as long-term players, and equally we are enhancing our position in other areas where we think there are some considerable strengths. For example, we sold our interests in a company called FII in the United States, which was basically making fibres, because although we have now got a really quite good fibre business, it is essentially confined to Europe, in speciality polyester fibre and polyamide (nylon). Our interests in the States did not look to us like a good long-term bet – so we got out.

Germany, Japan, the United States, have very powerful chemical industries. Where are they most difficult to face, in what product areas and on what points of competiton?

Actually, with a certain degree of arrogance, I don't really fear the chemical companies at all in terms of competition. I believe that ICI *are* every bit as good as the majors in terms of our product spread and in terms of our territorial coverage. Indeed, we are undoubtedly the most international of all the big chemical companies. The areas that cause us concern are where the oil companies move into the chemical industry, because they see it as a way to add value to their basic oil and gas businesses. They're very powerful, they're financially strong but (dare I say it?) they're not actually terribly expert in the way in which they break into the traditional markets.

Where in particular has that happened?

Fertiliser is a good example. The chemical companies came into the fertiliser business in a very big way in the Sixties and Seventies, made a complete mess of the market for those of us who'd been in it for a long time, and then withdrew, leaving a fair shambles behind. Similarly, I'm not too happy about competing with national governments that choose to get into the chemical industry, because their criteria for success are quite different to ours. They're not as concerned with return on capital or profitability as we are. They may be concerned with generating employment, they may be concerned with helping particular locations that have run-down traditional industries, and people forget that there are large parts of the European chemical industry that are actually state-owned.

The Norwegian chemical industry is state-owned, a portion of the Dutch chemical industry is state-owned, the Italian chemical industry has a large state ownership, France, of course, nationalised its chemical industry under the Mitterand administration in its early years. So the British and the Germans in many ways are the last bastions of the traditional 'free' chemical industry in Europe. If you get a situation where you've got a combination of an oil company and a national government, as one finds in the Middle East, then you have the worst of all worlds. Although I wouldn't say that I feared the competition from that source, I view it with some concern, basically because they're playing a different game by different rules.

What kinds of things are you going to have to concentrate most on in the next five years?

We would actually say we weren't placed too badly now. If you take the period 1982–6 our sales have gone up nearly 50 per cent. That's not too exciting, but it's over £10 billion in sales – not too bad against the relatively modest home market of less than 4 per cent of world output. But in that period, pre-tax profits have gone up 392 per cent. We're paying a lot more taxes, but our net income has gone up by 380 per cent. So against the background where the sales have only gone up 40 per cent, I don't think that's too bad a performance. Furthermore we believe that the shape of our businesses now is infinitely better than it was in the early Eighties. Now we see ourselves as having a pretty robust shape in terms of product and territory, a very good low-cost structure and, right now, with currency the way it is, our main export markets are looking quite attractive.

In fact, the export markets across the world are essential to your survival – a point brought home by your quoting the UK market size as a mere 4 per cent of the world total.

It is a problem, because if you remember that we are competing with the giant Americans, they have as a home market about a third of the world demand. So they start with a pretty solid basis. You can argue that it is no longer appropriate to think of the UK as the home market, because the UK is part of Europe, and the European scene is about the size of the American market, if you add in the UK. The difference is this: one market in the

United States, one currency and more or less the same language; in Europe, many different languages, a lot of problems in terms of crossing frontier barriers, a lot of different currencies, an infinitely more complex, difficult market in which to make money.

So, yes, the fact that we are an international company, but operating from a relatively small home base, is a disadvantage. But British we are, and British we shall undoubtedly remain; and our intention is to go on becoming ever more international, but to use the UK as our skill base. Something like 70 per cent of our research and development is still done here because, fundamentally, we get jolly good people.

British management has taken a lot of caning in the last ten years. When you meet and compare Japanese, Americans, Europeans, how fair do you think that criticism has been?

I can't speak for the rest of British industry, but I'm not sure it's entirely justified. I do not believe that our American or Japanese counterparts work any harder than we do. I don't believe they're any more intelligent. I think they are a little more single-minded in the way that they drive towards their targets. I think that they may be more market and customer-orientated than we have been. And particularly in the case of the United States they are infinitely quicker in taking new ideas, good research and translating them into hard market products. We have been slow in doing that. We're not short of innovators, we've got plenty of good scientists, plenty of clever chaps, but they are slow in actually getting into the marketplace. It may be something to do with risk-taking, it may be that the British – traditionally over-taxed, poorly paid by comparison with the Americans, and possibly with some of the Continentals – are unwilling to take the risk. I think that's improved in the last few years.

I think the better tax regime of this decade has helped. People are stimulated. I think there is a greater entrepreneurial spirit than there might have been in the past. But there are many things we could have done better. I believe that we didn't sufficiently tackle our cost structures in the Seventies. I believe that we probably spent too much time over-managing the industrial relations scene, which we had to do. Certainly in the Seventies, we all spent an awful lot of time on the government/industry interface. That has to a large extent declined considerably in the last few years.

We are freer, if you like, to manage the business in an internationally competitive way. And I think that's another problem. Whereas we have always had to compare ourselves with our international competitors – there is no point in comparing yourself with another British chemical company, you have to look internationally – I suspect that that hasn't always been true of large sectors of British industry.

Another intriguing point is that people could see that things were sliding in the Seventies. They could see the problems, all the way from inflation through to industrial relations. Why did it take so long to respond?

I think you have to have some traumatic event which jerks you out of your lethargy. There's a huge inertia factor in industry, in all organisations really, and I don't think we did too badly through the Seventies. We made a bit less – but the thing that really shattered us was actually going into loss in those last two quarters of 1980. That's the point at which we said, stop, we have to take a good hard look. And that's when we embarked on the kind of philosophy and practical implementation which I've referred to.

So even in ICI the roof had to fall in?

That's right. That's what caused the very sharp change in direction. I have no doubt whatsoever that we would have gone on improving our performance year by year in a steady sensible fashion, but it took something like the 1980 situation for us actually to say we have to have a step-change in the way we are tackling this problem. There are those who say nothing went right in the Seventies; I don't agree with that. We were going the right way. But we were going in a somewhat leisurely fashion.

Looking at industry in general, do you see that it's going to be a particularly difficult task to try and restore some of that lost ground?

Oh yes, because you can set all sorts of strategies and tactics, but there are some chaps out there called competitors who are hell-bent on making sure you *don't* make progress. It's a rough old world, there's no doubt about that. We have some advantages: the present level of sterling makes our exports look a lot more competitive, though I'm a bit worried by the dollar now. I do believe that people are out and about and selling very hard indeed, but the world doesn't owe us a living. It's going to be a long hard slog. The point one has to remember is that when we joined the EEC, people tended to look outwards and say, look at this lovely big new market, at the same time forgetting that the Germans, and the French and the Italians were looking inwards at us and saying, here's a nice new market and we are going to have a go. We as a company have seen our UK customer base – in some areas – decline somewhat. But equally we have seen our market share in Continental Europe, over the last ten years, grow at something like two and a half to three times the general market rate of growth. So we've been making quite a lot of progress across the Channel. We can't actually be too surprised if people have made progress the other way.

What do you see as the most worrying obstacles to running a British industry?

There is the problem of relatively modest growth in the UK in the industrial scene, and the problem of stability. Most industrialists absolutely hate currency fluctuations. I've said that in 1980 one of the most painful factors we had was an over-valued currency. Now I can say that I'm much happier with life because obviously sterling looks more competitive. But what I don't like to feel is that one of the major factors influencing ICI's profit is the factor totally outside our control: currency. So we would like to see a greater degree of stability, obviously at the right level, than we have at the moment. Education? Yes, I worry about education, but so far we've managed to get the supply of good minds, well-trained minds that we want.

I do have a real worry about the City, I must say, the way in which it forces managers to concentrate on essentially the very short-term performance. There is a tremendous pressure on fund managers to improve their portfolios; they are clearly looking at earnings per share, they're looking at profits. The chemical industry is a long-haul industry – a drug, for example, takes twelve years to develop. Now, I say to myself, it can't be right for Britain, if it wants to retain good science-based innovative industry, that the managers of those industries are forced to take decisions which may be essential in the short term in order to survive financially, but which undoubtedly will be jeopardising some of the long-term prospects.

SIR CHRISTOPHER HOGG, CHAIRMAN, COURTAULDS

Among the giants of the Sixties, Courtaulds seemed one of the most certain to succeed. Under the charismatic leadership of Frank Kearton (now Lord Kearton), the company expanded rapidly, acquiring scores of companies downstream from its basic business of fibre manufacture. That, too, was vigorously developed: new fibres were added, while Kearton also embarked on a bold endeavour to restore the fortunes of Lancashire cotton with massive investment in new plants.

This wave of expansion grew from the impetus provided by the defeat of a takeover bid from ICI. But after Kearton's retirement the strategy imploded: unable to compete on cost with cotton imports, bogged down with too many bad downstream investments, and caught in a European-wide crisis in synthetic fibres, Courtaulds slipped from star to has-been. In the second half of the Seventies, earnings in real terms plummeted as profit margins collapsed.

That was an unpromising platform for Christopher Hogg, who became chairman as 1980 began. Much worse was to follow. As Hogg tackled huge debts and massive restructuring and redundancies, the profit problems deepened: in 1980–1, Courtaulds lost £17 million after tax. Hogg had worked for Courtaulds since 1968, and had the benefit of exceptionally wide experience of the group's businesses – International Paints, British

Celanese, British Cellophane (all of which he chaired), fabrics and clothing (with main board responsibility for both).

Hogg is also exceptionally well qualified among top British executives. After taking First Class Honours at Oxford, he obtained a Harvard MBA, and then taught for a year at IMEDE, the Lausanne business school. After three years with the merchant bank which became Hill Samuel, Hogg joined the Industrial Reorganisation Corporation, created by the Labour government as the means of curing or averting the type of trouble which hit British industry, including Courtaulds, in the Seventies.

The new chairman's work at Courtaulds, both in dealing with the immediate crisis and in rebuilding the group strategy, has won wide recognition – including a knighthood. From the nadir of 1980–1, profits rose tenfold before tax in the next year. Because of retrenchment and recession, sales have grown only slowly since then: but in 1985–6, the company made £143 million on £2.17 billion of turnover, a 20 per cent return on capital employed and nearly three times the level Hogg inherited.

The reshaped company's businesses fall into two main groupings. Chemical and industrial products represent just under two-thirds of operating profit, coming from synthetic fibres, chemicals and plastics, woodpulp, paint, packaging films and plastic products. These activities rest on industrial marketing and technology – including technical service. The remaining third of profit stems from the textile group. Its many businesses are in spinning, fabrics and clothing, and their common logic is that of consumer marketing. They mostly trade in the UK, in contrast to the industrial companies, which account for most of the 53 per cent of turnover generated by exports and overseas subsidiaries.

Hogg, now 50, is a man of wide interests. He became non-executive chairman of Reuters in July 1985.

By the end of the Seventies Courtaulds was in fairly deep trouble. What had happened?

Courtaulds made its first fortune in the last century out of black silk Victorian mourning crêpe. In this century, it pioneered the synthetic fibres industry with the first of the man-made fibres based on cellulose, and pursued that course very strongly, and with enormous financial success, from the early years of this century. The business developed in time into other forms of synthetic fibre, but it became clear that this by itself was not enough, and since the middle Fifties Courtaulds has been trying to diversify its business – albeit into fields it was familiar with – and has bought up other fibre producers.

But it also, from the middle Sixties, started to integrate downstream in the textile industry by buying, first of all, companies which spun yarn, and then companies which made fabric, which dyed and finished fabric, which

made garments, and indeed went through the whole gamut of textile processes – concentrating on the Lancashire rather than the Yorkshire
industry, but acquiring and investing in, over the period 1963–73, an enormous range of textile activities.

In the process of doing this it gave itself considerable managerial indigestion. It was taking on a colossal challenge, and managers who had spent
their whole lives in fibres, which is at least half a chemical processing
industry as well as a textile one, found themselves trying to do duty in fabrics, an area which was very different from that to which they had been
used. Furthermore, they had to cope with newly acquired companies, many
of which had been bought in stages of some financial disarray. In the course
of the Seventies, after the first oil crisis, economic times got tougher,
imports into this country increased and, of course, at the end of the
Seventies, in the early Eighties, the pound rose appreciably. The combination of all these factors hit Courtaulds' profits hard. We've always remained
profitable, but profits dwindled almost to nothing in the first year of the
Eighties.

One way or another, we had a very large managerial challenge ahead of
us in the shape of 300 or 400 separate businesses, the majority of which at
one stage were making losses. We were having a very poor return on capital,
and were rapidly running out of cash at the rate at which we were going.

Faced with that particular problem, what strategy has the company adopted?

The strategy has been very obvious. We had to cut the red ink out of the
company's financial accounts, and there were clearly two principal ways to
do that. One was simply to close businesses which were loss-making,
because there was too much capacity in the industry, too much supply
chasing too little demand. The other and more important strategy was
simply to manage better what we had. It sounds very simple when I say it
like that, but the task of managing something better, if it's become run
down, is really very complex and very long-term. It involves changing
habits, attitudes, standards, right across the business, from production and
research on the one hand to the selling and marketing on the other, and you
make many, many false turnings. It's a case of (you hope) five steps forward
and not four steps back, but you inevitably make all sorts of mistakes, and
it's really just a voyage of exploration as it were.

*What about looking at your markets? Has your perception of the problems
changed your approach?*

The most important single change, which not only ourselves but the whole
textile industry has undergone, is one of what I might call customer-
consciousness. It wasn't that we didn't care about our customers in the old
days, it is just that we have all put a very great emphasis on paying attention

to our customers and our customers' needs, and have let that be the driving force in our businesses and what we are doing. We have done things such as increase the focus on design, which was very important to our High Street customers, and started to invest in design facilities and in the status of design within our businesses. Slowly but surely the role of design has assumed an importance today which was unthinkable five or six years ago – to the satisfaction of our customers and the benefit of our merchandise and our bottom line. That's simply one aspect, but it's an important aspect.

Do you now regard yourself as a home, a European, or a worldwide supplier? Where do you concentrate?

We have to regard ourselves as a worldwide supplier. The textile industry is a worldwide industry. It is determined by international competition. Across the whole span of Courtaulds' enormous business, there is practically nothing that is not exposed to international competition, either imports in this market or, of course, competition overseas against our exports or our overseas production, and we have to determine everything we do by the best worldwide standards and not just by what seems to be adequate in this country. And therein lies the problem.

What are the most crucial points on which you have met the competition? What's strengthened you against your competitors?

I think we just manage our businesses better. We know what it's like to be not successful; we have had that memory, we don't want to go back there. We do so many things better, but we don't think we do them perfectly. We are always conscious that the world is a changing place, that our competition is international, that even when we think that we have the best standards in the world – as we do on some things – we can't afford to be complacent, and I don't think we are.

The essential ingredient is this one of determination to do better, which is what drives the business forwards. And one hopes that it drives the business forwards in all parts, so that we're not just getting better at production, or better at design, we're getting better across the board in an integrated way. As long as we keep doing that, I don't think I shall worry too much about the competition. If we can cope with the last five years, we can certainly cope with the next five or ten.

What are the most critical competitive factors? Price, or quality, or getting the designs precisely right?

Textiles is an infinitely varied industry; that's one of its great fascinations. Some things are sold on price alone, and some things are sold simply on exclusiveness, so that the amount paid by the final customer can bear no relation whatever to the cost of producing that article. It is an enormous mix. We find right across our business that one of the most difficult problems to cope with is the sheer range and diversity of what we now do, and what things we really ought to be taking into account, in order to add value to the product in the customers' interest.

At one time the big bogey used to be other countries' cheap labour. What worries you now about the competition?

Cheap labour still does, because there are countries in the world whose basic labour cost is a tenth or less than that in the UK. In the parts of the textile industry which are labour-intensive, as for instance the manufacturing of clothing is, that constitutes one hell of a competitive advantage. In some ways a more serious problem that we now address ourselves to is the level of efficiency which has been achieved by the so-called newly industrialised countries in the Far East – Korea, Taiwan, Hong Kong, Singapore – all of whom in their different ways have reached quite formidable levels of efficiency very quickly in traditional industries. They set the standards of productivity, by and large, for the rest of the world, and those are the standards that we must meet.

Of course, there are outstanding examples in the United States as well, of companies which are extremely efficient, often in very sophisticated parts of the industry, and we look at them too. But dominating everything is the thought of that Far Eastern efficiency which determines the standards which we need to get into business.

The Far East used to be known as a 'coolie economy' which competed simply on price, but you suggest that it is now competing on management and technology as well.

Very much so. The Japanese have set a formidable example to the rest of the Far East, which has been pretty quick to copy them.

We're miles and miles away now from the position where you could look at a label 'Made in Hong Kong' or 'Made in Japan' with scorn. You know that as a consumer of so many things, and it's certainly true in the textile industry. They set very, very high standards.

What are your most difficult markets?

Every market is difficult to sell in because the competition is so international. It is a genuinely worldwide industry in which goods move around pretty freely, and therefore they find their way into every market. And when you think you've got a soft market, or a 'niche' as we say, it's not long before you find that somebody else has also discovered it and is raiding your profitability. There's very little shelter from the wind in the textile industry.

Courtaulds has slimmed itself down considerably compared with what it was ten years ago. Do you now regard it as a stabilised company that is likely to stay at this size, or do you see it as one which can, or should, expand in the next ten years?

I think it's shrunk amazingly little considering the holocaust that we've been through. We were thinking about it last year, and we reckoned that something like 30 per cent of the businesses that we had at the end of the Seventies have now completely disappeared, and our turnover, in fact, has not gone down much in real terms – it's actually increased in nominal terms. So the whole of that business has been replaced; on the whole I'm not surprised that that's so, because when you get on to an improving trend in a business and things start to go right, there are many reasons why your business and your sales then start to increase.

Of course, what you're trying to do is to improve profits first and fore-most, because it is the profits which safeguard the cash flow and it's the cash flow which keeps the company alive. But the process of improving profits makes you do all sorts of things in the business which actually will help to push up your sales in the end.

I believe that all over the group we now have much better managed busi-nesses, much more confident managers, much more competent managers, and that slowly but surely we're not only getting business from our competitors and all the rest of it, but we are developing new products, going into adjacent areas and so on – and that nothing is going to stop the forward momentum.

One is seeing some fairly major initiatives taking place in the international markets as people like Calvin Klein and Benetton really open up a whole new concept of marketing. Are you missing out on that sort of operation?

I don't think so. There'll always be enormous opportunities to make money in textiles and, as you say, Benetton has brilliantly exploited an idea, Klein in an entirely different way has done the same thing – and so have many others. Those kinds of opportunities will always be there; it's an ever-changing industry, and when you're good enough to grasp something you go out and get it. For the time being my main and immediate yardstick is our own bottom line, and looking at where we have been and where we need to go to. That's improving all the time. It could very well be that in the years to come we will not only be capable of but we will actually implement similarly startling or successful worldwide initiatives.

What has most surprised you during the time you have been chairman?

One of the things that I have been most struck by is what can grow from small beginnings. Here we are, six or seven years on into the Eighties, and that's not a very long time by industrial standards, where time-horizons are long, and yet as a result of the efforts of Courtaulds and of other companies in the British textile industry, the whole morale of the industry has changed. Its performance has certainly changed, and, although the industry is smaller, its prospects for the rest of this century and the next one are miles better than they were at the end of the Seventies. If you had said to me in, say, 1978 that the outlook could change as much as I think it now has changed, I would not have thought it was possible. And if you'd asked me to undertake the task I would have said, hand that to some other man. But when you have actually travelled down the road, you can see how one thing leads to another, leads to another, and that the thing to be most wary of is simply despair or frustration, or whatever it is that causes you to give up. If you keep going you can in fact accomplish a perfectly extraordinary amount.

Looking more generally at British industry, has it become more competitive or less competitive in the last five years?

It depends on what you mean by British industry, because the answer varies from one industry to another, and varies above all with whether the industry is by its nature exposed to international competition, or whether it's mainly domestic. Retailing is obviously a domestic industry, it has to take place in the High Streets of this country. In a different way, making bricks is a domestic industry because it's difficult for anybody to be cost-competitive if they've got to bring their bricks across the water into this country in the first place, so the competition is limited to domestic sources.

For industries like textiles where goods can be carted around the world easily, the competition is growing all the time, and not just because there tends to be an endemic worldwide over-capacity in all levels of the textile industry, but because international competition has hotted up as the world's economic development keeps on growing, as it has done since the Second World War. Anybody who works in international industry now must see that the pace of growth in technology of all kinds, and of communications, is forcing industries to be globalised. Anybody who wants to participate in those industries had better watch out and take the standards as international ones. Those standards are getting tougher all the time.

Looking at the general environment in which businesses are being run now, what do you think the principal problems are in making progress in the future?

We do tend to be more insular and inward-looking than other countries are. All this leads us very often to prefer our own standards, and our own ways of doing things. And that's bad news for all those who operate in this country, whether in manufacturing or in services, but who have to meet international competition, because the standards that have to be met are international standards of excellence, they're not British standards of excellence, and they apply across the board. They apply in fundamental things like education or housing mobility as well as in more precise things – the actual number of cars per worker that you can turn out in a day.

If I could change one thing in this country, I would want to raise greatly the level of consciousness of what's going on in the world and the importance of matching best standards of international performance, if we want to have a higher standard of living. I do not think that is sufficiently understood, and I do not think that people who set out to improve things in this country automatically ask themselves first and foremost, where is it done best overseas and what can we learn from that? And it's those questions that the Japanese ask themselves with such devastating effects, and which we are really not very good at asking.

Do you get the sense that the Japanese have learnt a lot from other people?

The Japanese are the world's best plagiarisers, but nothing wrong with that. They took a look at themselves way back in the last century, saw how far they were behind the rest of the world, looked at the people that they wanted to copy, did so very effectively, and have done so with increasing effectiveness under the vastly different circumstances that have prevailed in Japan since the Second World War. If you don't do something well and you want to do it better, look at the people who do it well, and don't have any hang-ups about copying them. We don't seem to think that way in this country, and perhaps people in general don't think that way naturally. But that seems to me to be the obvious place to start.

A lot of British companies have picked themselves up by the boot-straps in the last few years, but the rest of the world has gone on. We have been sliding in our shares of the world market, we now have a deficit in trade in manufactured goods. Do you see that as something that's going to continue or can the situation be recovered?

It can be recovered. Whether it *will* be recovered depends on whether we have the national will to recover it. And that's a different matter. From what I've been saying about the textile industry, I feel that if you've got sufficient determination there's nothing you can't do. The history of the world is littered with examples of nations and people doing extraordinary things, but the will is an important part, and I'm really not sure whether in this country we really have the national will to get our act together sufficiently, and for long enough, to make headway against some of the very fundamental problems which now beset us in improving our economic performance. I mean things like the way in which the education system is organised and responds to current needs, the degree of labour mobility, the poverty trap, the rigidity of institutions, a combination of inertia and conservatism which makes it so difficult to get action. Those things take a long, long, long time to change, well beyond the lifetime of any one Parliament. To change them will require a national will which extends over governments of different complexions, and over a long period of time, and it's that which I'm not certain about. If we had that, of course we could change. If we don't have that then the outlook for the Nineties and for the next century is not good.

How has management changed? Has the general level of competence in British management risen?

I can only talk about what I see happening in Courtaulds and there I'm filled with admiration. The poor performance of Courtaulds in the second half of the Seventies in some sense was due to management, but above all management at the top of the company. And I myself was one of those! The people lower down who have to take the heat and burden of the day and run the company – really run the company – are the people that I have great admiration for, because I've watched them, under very, very difficult circumstances over the last few years, so often make extraordinary changes which they themselves would not have thought possible.

I'm definitely a believer in the fact that if you give people clear enough challenges, and they understand why they have to face them, then they will move mountains to meet these challenges. That's certainly what I've seen internally at Courtaulds.

RONALD MILLER, CHAIRMAN, DAWSON INTERNATIONAL

Ronald Miller took one of the classic routes to the chair of a major British company. A Scottish accountant, born in Edinburgh in 1937, he moved south to London and the Midlands for his first jobs in industry. After joining Dawson International in 1968 in the finance function, as group accountant, he became chairman and chief executive fourteen years later, at the relatively early age of forty-five.

While the rise of accountants to the top is common enough in British industry as a whole, a marketing company is less likely to choose a chief from an accountancy background. Dawson, although the possessor of some of Scotland's proudest brand names (Ballantyne, Pringle, Braemar, Barrie, Glenmac and McGeorge), started to fail in making the most of its market strengths in the years immediately after Miller joined. From 1971–4 the knitwear side made losses in two years and vestigial returns in the other two.

Promoted to finance director, Miller was one of the few executives to survive the management shake-up of that period. He was an architect of a classic exercise in decentralising what had become an over-centralised organisation. The switch had classic results. From very little profit and a dangerously high overdraft, the company in six years advanced to sales of over £113 million and profits of £17.6 million in 1980–1. The marketing impetus and the company's dynamic were provided by the chairman Alan Smith, but his mercurial and highly personal style of management had helped to create the group problems which centralisation was mistakenly intended to solve.

Under Miller's control, the marketing success has continued as the organisation has become far more effective. Since 1982–3, the financial year in which he became chairman, sales have doubled from £139 million to £285.5 million, while profits have risen in step, reaching £42 million in 1985–6. Much of the growth reflects not only the rise in sales of the high-quality brands, but a vigorous expansion overseas, with which Miller has been particularly identified. A West German company in hand-knitting yarns was acquired in 1983, followed in 1984 by an American business which is the largest maker of thermal underwear in the US.

The result is that 30 per cent of Dawson's turnover now comes from manufacture abroad. Since half of the British production is exported, the company is heavily dependent on overseas markets for its success. Its early swing away from the UK and its emphasis on the top end of the textile market, coupled with the success of decentralisation, effectively protected Dawson from the ravages of the recession which hit nearly all the rest of the textile industry. Profits and sales have slipped only once in the last decade.

Dawson's expansionist ideas, however, suffered one major setback: merger with Coats Patons, a larger and very diverse textile group, which seemed to be going through smoothly, was pre-empted by a rival bid from Viyella. All the Dawson businesses, though, are set for further organic growth: the knitting and clothing companies (with £142 million of sales in 1985–6); spinning, weaving and fur fabric companies (£115 million); and the raw material and processing interests (£28.2 million). Miller was awarded a CBE in 1985.

What sort of company was Dawson ten years ago? Was it going in the right direction?

Just over ten years ago, in 1974, we were in a terrible mess, we were almost bankrupt and we decided that something would have to change. We were at that time centralising our whole management structure and building up a team of people behind the chief executive. We had various production directors, marketing directors, who had assistants, who in turn had staff behind them. The result was that when any of our companies wanted to do something, they had to refer upwards through this whole chain of command and, of course, the reply took some time to come down to them. As a result, the opportunities were often lost. So we tore all that away in 1974 and put in a very decentralised form of management. Even today we've only got seventeen people in our head office: twenty-seven companies and seventeen people.

Looking more particularly at the Eighties, what kind of response have you been making to the markets?

Our theme for the Eighties has been one of innovation. I adopted this theme when I visited one of our customers in Italy, a tiny little boutique in a back street in Rome, and he said, we love your products, your colours, your designs are wonderful, you have *fantasia* (which I'm told is the Italian for innovation). And I adopted that as a theme, innovation in all its forms – through the products, through an outward-looking approach from every-one concerned in the business, through personnel development, manu-facturing, marketing, all sorts of aspects. This is the theme I've tried to get running through, and I think it has been rewarding.

Have you changed your approach to the way you market and sell products?

Not substantially. We have had a range of agents and distributors, and our own sales people. We have twenty-seven companies, all of which are independent of each other, and each is under a managing director who has a great deal of autonomy. They all have different ways of tackling the marketplace. Some have their own sales people, some have distributors, some have agents, and we've encouraged the individual managing directors and the companies to work with whatever means they think best to tackle the market.

We were fortunate in establishing a sales organisation in Europe back in 1963, and from the experience gained there we feel very much attuned to the European market. For example, we have been able to take advantage of our membership of the EEC by having our own sales force based in Europe with easy access to the markets and an understanding of different coun-tries, foreign languages, use of currency. We were fortunate in doing that in those early days, and we've used that advantage in other areas of the busi-ness since then.

You referred to a bad time in 1974, to something near bankruptcy. What was causing that?

We'd lost our way. We had centralised our management decision-making processes, we had bought a number of companies with very poor manage-ment; companies which themselves needed a lot of money pumped into them to make them profitable. So we were losing out, both on our new acquisitions and on the original business. We had effectively lost our will to manage.

When we bought a number of companies in the Sixties and Seventies, we found that they had lost touch with their markets. They had forgotten, for example, that deliveries had to be made on time. There were occasions when, once we had corrected that situation, customers used to phone up and say, we're very upset that the goods have arrived early. And we said, the goods haven't arrived early. And they said, but they always arrived six weeks later (for example) and we'd built that into our system. And now they've arrived on time! This was a fundamental problem which we had to correct.

So one area in which you've had to improve is in management techniques?

Yes, controls, understanding of what is going on at the individual companies. While we've given the companies a great deal of autonomy, we still like to know what is going on, and to work with them on what is going on.

Does that mean you now have regular reports, with rigid standards of financial performance, which you expect them to meet – and to explain if they don't achieve them?

That is an important corner-stone of our whole group philosophy – regular reporting. We forecast three days after the end of the month estimated sales and profits for that past month, which is followed ten days after the end of the month by a full report from each managing director.

What sort of people are you competing against, and where?

I can see that markets have changed substantially over the last ten years. Just as we're talking now about the 'Big Bang' in the City of London, I think that really is a reflection of things we have seen in our markets over a number of years. People in business today are much more internationally minded. One has to be aware of competition, not just in the UK. One has got to measure competition in worldwide terms. Europe is our major market outside the UK. America, leaving aside acquisition, comes after Europe, and although we do sell to Australia and the Far East and Japan, they are smaller in comparison.

What are the critical factors in the competition for your product?

We've made it our policy to try and sell the best knitwear in the world. We don't try and compete with the mass market for knitwear. We're best known for our knitted garments, our world-famous brand names: Pringle, Braemar, Ballantyne, Barrie. One sees them in all the best shops throughout the world, a tradition of quality and design and colour. Our area in the marketplace is really very, very small. If one thinks of the overall market in the shape of a pyramid, we're at the very top part of that. There's a huge area of business for knitwear which we don't try and get involved with at all, which comes from the Far East and other parts of the UK, and from the Continent as well. Our main competitors are basically companies in the UK who are trying to meet high standards like ourselves, and companies in

Europe, particularly Italy, who are recognised for their flexibility and innovation and also for their fashion.

Have you been able to invest enough to acquire top-edge efficiency?

Our rate of investment has increased dramatically in the last years. We've always spent a lot of money on updating our equipment, but the changes taking place in technology are increasing at a rapid rate. For example, I was recently at one of our knitwear companies where they've installed some new machinery – made in Japan – where it's possible to design a pro-gramme on a screen, and knit a sweater in very short time thereafter, the kind of thing that would have taken someone several days to produce by hand in the past. So these are radical changes and we certainly want to be in the forefront of them.

How critical is the size of the group? You have recently shown interest in large-scale acquisition. Why?

Having encouraged our individual companies to be innovative, I felt that I must be innovative myself. I wanted to get closer to some of the markets in which we're involved, particularly in the States and Germany, where there is a high spending power. At the same time I felt that we should broaden our product base and decided that, not only should we put extra effort into exporting, but also acquire companies in America and in Germany to get a better understanding of these countries, make more contacts. Ultimately I believe that will benefit our exporting from the UK, as well as these com-panies being extremely profitable in their own right.

That obviously gives you a marketing and distribution advantage. Does it also offer you a greater economy of scale for production at home?

Not directly. The acquisitions, as with all our companies, will stand on their own, and not be inter-related with the other companies. But ultimately, with greater sales in the States or in Germany arising from our deeper knowledge of these countries, we will be able to put more merchandise through our UK companies, which in term will lead to some economies of scale.

How do you see the group – as an exporter or as an international manufacturer?

We are international. From our knowledge of, and our feel for, export markets over the years, we feel very much at home in the world at large, and also feel very comfortable in owning companies overseas. We're both an exporter and an overseas manufacturer; it's the global village, after all, today. One has got to be prepared to look for any opportunities in that global village, in what we define as our area of the marketplace, that is, areas of specialised textiles throughout the world. We have to be outward-looking, either through exports or through investment in these countries, to seize these opportunities.

Certain traditional products like Scotch whisky have always been said to sell themselves, which has proved to be untrue. Is it proving to be untrue in your company as well? Can you rely very much on the cachet 'Made in Scotland'?

The 'Made in Scotland' label is really something which hasn't been developed to its real advantage. A Scottish label in itself is one of the best brand-names the world knows and our aim is to expand that Scottish association with quality – the classic look – into knitwear which has design and colour and flavour which matches the best foreign competition. For example, Italy is often looked at as having the ability to produce more fashion than any other country in the world. Well, we have that ability in Scotland, but it's not recognised, and it's up to us to ensure that we put a lot of hard work and effort into achieving the real potential which I believe is there.

What do you think were the main problems that led to that long slow national relative decline in the Seventies?

I think we lost confidence as a nation. What I'd like to see happen in Britain is more of the spirit that one comes across in some overseas countries, where there is a recognition of the need to have a very strong industrial base and the recognition of reward for effort and an understanding of why this is necessary. That's why I think Industry Year (1986) has been so important as a first step towards cementing in this understanding at the early levels, before people have left school, for example.

So you agree with the people who say there is an anti-industrial culture?

Yes I do, and I think perhaps it's been of our own making as industrialists. I'm not blaming it on people from outside. We've been so beset with dealing with our problems that we haven't raised our heads very much above the parapet. And it's up to us as industrialists to talk about ourselves, talk about our companies, get people in to look at our companies, get them to see that they are part of the community, that they are producing successfully, they are creating jobs, that it is essential for all these things to be there.

What about the education and training system – can you always get the skills and the talent that you need?

Not as easily as I'd like to. A lot of our companies are in small towns and villages, and it's sad that often, once people qualify in universities away from their home area, they don't return. It's very difficult to encourage other people into some country areas, people who have lived in towns all their lives. We are working harder at trying to create many local environments where we can create the interest to hold people and prevent them drifting away.

What about labour relations? Do you think they're more stable than they used to be?

We're very fortunate by and large in that we have a very good workforce. As I said, our companies are in small towns and villages – I was going to say throughout Scotland, but also now in America and Germany – and with our decentralised form of management we've been able to create closer identity between management and workforce, which certainly didn't exist ten years ago. We're working very hard at this, and I believe that it's this sort of partnership which is going to help both management and workforce gain in the future.

British companies have lost a lot of their share of world markets; do you see this being regained?

In terms of volume, I really don't see this being regained. I think we've got to pick out the specialised areas in the world marketplaces, and develop these. We've got to think of the quality areas, the innovative areas, look at what's in the world around us and see what we can learn in one country to apply to better advantage in another country. Trading is international today and I believe this can, with experience and knowledge of overseas markets, be used to advantage in the UK.

To what extent are you at the mercy of the fluctuating currency?

About half of our UK business is exported, and therefore currency does play a significant part. In the UK, we are very much tourist-related in large parts of our business, so obviously currency plays a large part there indirectly. I certainly would like to see greater stability of relative values of the pound to other currencies, which would give us greater confidence in planning ahead. The recent weakening of the pound against European currencies must be a significant benefit to UK exporters, and we will certainly be doing all we can to grow from this new base. Having said that, I hope we won't find that, once we've embarked on a course of action, levels move rapidly either way in the months or years ahead. What I'm looking for is stability in the currency markets to enable us to do some longer term planning, and also to give our customers and agents and distributors more confidence in that regard.

PAUL GIROLAMI, CHAIRMAN, GLAXO

Glaxo is rare among large manufacturing companies in having earned a high return on sales and capital throughout the traumas of the past decade. That reflects its position in ethical pharmaceuticals, which has been the world's most profitable industry since the war. But nothing in Glaxo's earlier record prepared outsiders for the explosion in profits and growth from the 1980–1 financial year onwards. In that year pre-tax profits, at £87 million, were barely higher than four years previously – even though sales had risen by nearly half.

In the next five years, sales doubled to £1.4 billion while profits multiplied six and a half times to £568 million: a rate of expansion and a level of profitability (55 per cent on net capital employed) probably without any parallel for a large British company. The key to this magnificent performance was a single product: the drug, ranitidine, marketed under the name Zantac – an extraordinarily effective treatment for ulcers and other gastro-intestinal disorders.

Paul Girolami, the chairman since 1985, and before that chief executive from 1980, has been deeply involved in the transformation of the company: not, however, as a pharmaceutical expert or a marketing man, but from an accountancy base. An LSE graduate, born in 1926, he qualified in 1953 and joined the well-known practice, Cooper Brothers. It was just setting up its consultancy business, of which Girolami became a founder member, and a director when the consultancy was turned into a company. Girolami worked as a consultant for many companies in many industries and companies (including heavy engineering, oil exploration and textiles).

His first role on joining Glaxo in 1965, however, was as financial controller. That involved introducing electronic data processing and initiating and developing the still current systems for finance and budgetary control, planning and management information. In 1968, appointed as Glaxo's first financial director, Girolami began to widen his sphere of operation outside finance. The defence of Glaxo against a bid from Beecham in 1972 was a crucial event in which Girolami was deeply involved. He also played a key role in developing many of the overseas interests in Europe, Latin America, Africa, the US and the Far East – including Japan, where he organised the Glaxo businesses and is now president of the three associated companies.

In the US, Girolami bought Meyer Laboratories (now Glaxo, Inc.) in the late Seventies. In what turned out to be a masterly stroke, however, Glaxo entrusted the American marketing of Zantac to a joint operation with a rival which had a far larger presence in the marketplace – the US subsidiary of the Swiss firm of Hoffmann La Roche. Zantac could thus be promoted immediately by a sales force matching the US majors in size, at a time when Glaxo, Inc. was still in the early stages of development.

In the latest financial year, all but 3 per cent of sales came from pharmaceuticals; at the start of the decade, if wholesaling is included, the figure was only half. Ten years before, half the sales were in the UK: the ratio has now fallen to 15 per cent. Research spending over the period has risen from £34 million to £123 million. The most vital statistic, though, is that for anti-ulcerants. A decade back, they contributed nothing to sales. Now they account for a stunning 43 per cent.

It seems that in the last six years Glaxo has changed direction, reorganised itself, taken a new look at markets. It used to be thought of as a worthy but rather dull company, plodding along. What's been going on?

Certain factors have been added to pre-existing factors, which created a dynamic growth. The underlying strengths of Glaxo – and they've been the underlying strengths for fifteen years, if not more – have been a fundamental commitment to research and development, and also a vague yearning for international expansion. But that aspect was very much within blinkers, and when I first joined the group it was in blinkers towards the Commonwealth. The rest were 'foreigners' whom you had to treat rather carefully before you ventured – and there was a positive hostility shown towards the States and Japan. However, the germs of internationalism were there and so was this commitment to technology. I wanted to inject two or three additional elements which would turn this basic element into a very dynamic force.

The first is that internationalism really means tackling all markets, and in particular the major markets, even though they are very different and very difficult and very risky. What I mean is going in as 'first person'; not saying we'll do it through agents or exports, but setting ourselves up there as a company taking on local colours and tackling that market as a national. Very difficult, but that's what we did.

The second element was to answer the question: what are we trying to do? What is Glaxo? Is it milk, is it babies, is it surgical instruments, is it genetics? Is it all these? We emerged from this rightly or wrongly (and I think very much rightly) saying: no, we want a specific objective, we address all our resources to a high-quality business, and we want to look at the potential of a business which is medicines, prescription medicines – that is our job.

Thirdly, the other important element here – which is talked about a great deal and tends to be approached in terms of models and textbooks – was how we organise a group around a single purpose. Geographically, the group is very large, covering the whole world – 150 markets today – but the local market is a small one. We've developed by trial and error into a flexible organisation which somehow combines local initiative, local control, good local management with a central leadership and direction. I think it was this combination of two latent forces with a new direction which has given the group its dynamic.

But the other interesting thing that has happened is that, in five to six years, you more than doubled your sales turnover. That period saw the spectacular rise of one particular drug, Zantac, which is largely responsible. How did that happen?

The new product which has transformed our fortunes was a result of our continuing commitment to research and development. But that product wouldn't have had the effect it did without being associated with a simultaneous act of faith in international expansion. If we hadn't, before Zantac was taken in, decided to go hell-for-leather into the American market and to tackle the Japanese market and to put all the strength behind the European market, that product would have been a flop. It would have been given to the American companies as licensees, we would have got 4 per cent or whatever. So Zantac must not be looked at in isolation or as coming directly from only one aspect of our strategy, which is the improvement and emphasis on research and development. Certainly it was an outcome of that, but its commercial success was also an outcome of the fact that we had at last developed our markets. You don't make products like Zantac a commercial product, a commercial success, heading for a thousand million dollars by just producing a good product in the laboratory. That's the starting point. But you know, many starting points finish where they start!

So there's no truth in the notion that in pharmaceuticals an advanced product will sell itself, that people will come and fetch it?

No, it will not sell. In fact, any good product which makes money doesn't sell itself. I find that notion superficial and a snare. It's the sort of thing which our competitors would urge upon us, 'Glaxo, my goodness you've got such wonderful products, don't bother to sell them.' That's what I would say if I were Smith Kline. I certainly don't say it to our troops. You've got to sell it and sell it hard, because if you don't it won't be sold, however good it is.

What effect has it had on your marketing techniques? For example, in this new expansion in the United States, have you changed your way of doing things in the company?

We've always been a very good marketing company. That's not to say that all our companies are equally good – some of them are not very good at the moment – but we've always produced examples of the very best marketing in this pharmaceutical area. We've known how to market products for a long, long time. The answer is teamwork and a sense of direction and a determination to make the most of what you've got. There's a national message there.

I don't think we are any different from any other industry really. Though we strive to get a better product, the fact of life is that we are not the only clever people in this world. In fact, there are a hell of a lot of clever people, and when we get a better product we tend to rely on the fact that it is only marginally better, and this is where the whole process of marketing comes in. You've got to price it right, you've got to use all the management techniques employed by Glaxo, as by any other successful company, to beat the competition.

Certainly the competition in pharmaceuticals isn't as nakedly in terms of price as in some industries, but price comes into it and so does everything else – quality and design and persuasion and teamwork and meeting deliveries.

As you go round the world, as you meet other people in business, do you feel that British industry is getting more competitive, is gaining more know-how than it had ten years ago?

I have to answer with some caution, because we tend to be a bit of an in-bred industry. In recent years, the atmosphere in which Glaxo can operate on an international scale has become much better. It comes out in all sorts of ways. I'm not being politically biased, but it is unquestionably easier, there's no question about that, for us to run a multi-national business from London now than it was ten years ago. That's a fact – how important a fact I don't know, but I think it's important from where I sit. Secondly, I'm very hopeful because I sense a whole feeling of direction in industry, more energetic and more realistic and less complacent. And thirdly, I have to say I think the young people coming through are better than the old ones. The old classical industrial establishments were brought up in the time when the markets were there, and they were theirs for the taking. The older generation lacks the element of competitiveness, which is essential today. The young people are much better, and when they come through you will see a fundamental change. They're not through at the top yet, they're not through at the boardroom, but they will come.

What do you think about the problem of getting more people to take an interest in industry, as opposed to other kinds of professions, at a young age? What do you think about our ability to educate and train them to be suitable for industry?

Even in the young people leaving universities, there's a prejudice against coming into the industry. I detect it, but I don't know the reasons for it. I think there are cultural inhibitions in our society, as in many European societies. Compared with the Americans and the Japanese, there are undoubtedly cultural obstacles in Europe and in England. The glamour isn't there, the pay isn't there. I'm not making a point about pay, but the two go together. You can't have symbols and not have money in your pocket. I think it will change, however. It will not change by propaganda; it will change automatically when the companies are staffed by the people now coming through, who have the zip and the fire and the style which other young people appreciate.

Can you detect what makes industry unattractive?

It hasn't got the sex appeal of the professions in one way. And pay is only one part of it. Take the way that many industrial people still behave when they come up against the other classes or functions of society – such as the City, such as the professions, such as government. They tend to behave as if they're the poor relations, the uneducated ones. They are not very articulate when it comes to meetings and they seem to be at a lower intellectual or social level.

The other thing I detect – and there is nothing much we can do about this – is that a career in industry, unless it starts with some functional challenge, tends to begin by doing a lot of boring jobs. You have to wait a long time for the glamour. Young people are not patient and they've got plenty of years ahead. They think, am I going to sit there for fifteen years, moving up level after level after level, when my brain is so great? And yet it's no good saying, oh well, I'll get the bright chap and put him at the top, because they're quite useless at the top. They have the brains, but it demands a hell of a lot more than brains to run a company. Brains is one element, sometimes not even a necessary element.

But do you think there's been an improvement in management know-how, in the general motivation of managements, when you compare them with, say, the Americans?

In know-how, I don't think we are very deficient, if deficient at all. I think our managers are as knowledgeable as the Americans. The motivation is a little different, and our style of running things isn't the same. We tend to be a little gentler, less forceful. But that's changing. I think that's not going to hold us back in the future.

Which competitors alarm you most?

In the pharmaceutical industry I would fear American competition more than any other, because – and this is the reason why we are setting up research there – they have a very dynamic, scientific approach to life. On average, they're making more scientific progress than in Europe or in Japan, and their management style is tough, rough, used to competition.

That's where we should fear the competition. I don't mean this in a nasty sense, but I think that's where we have to measure in the end; we have to measure ourselves against the Americans.

RICHARD GIORDANO, CHAIRMAN, THE BOC GROUP

Dick Giordano is by no means the first company chairman to reach high office by way of a takeover. But to be appointed chief executive of a group within eighteen months of leading a vigorous but unsuccessful defence against that takeover is extremely unusual.

When Airco was acquired in late 1978, Giordano had been president and chief operating officer of the US industrial gases company for a little more than six years. The two businesses were already connected, since BOC owned just over a third of Airco. That link was forged by Giordano and Sir Leslie Smith (then chairman of BOC) to help protect Airco against an American predator in 1973.

BOC's opportunism, using a second US attempt on Airco as the signal to launch a bid of its own, was highly unwelcome to the Americans. Under the circumstances, Smith's promotion of Giordano to run the combined businesses was a management decision of exceptional imagination. It recognised the abilities of an immensely capable executive. It also accepted the realities of the situation. Airco was only fractionally smaller than BOC. It was easily the group's most important possession, and the one with greatest potential for influencing their joint results; but its management team was suffering all the humiliation and uncertainties of losing a takeover battle.

An American executive of impeccable East Coast credentials (Harvard and Columbia Law School), Giordano had joined Airco as assistant secretary in 1963, and risen rapidly through the ranks of a typical divisionalised US industrial company, highly focused on its domestic markets, under strong central direction. BOC was an equally typical, fairly loosely co-ordinated, diverse and geographically dispersed UK public company. Although the initials once meant British Oxygen Company, it had accumulated a wide variety of other businesses and, even before the merger, earned half its profits overseas.

The recession which began in 1979 – coinciding with Giordano's arrival in London – devastated BOC's traditional markets in steel-making and metal-working on both sides of the Atlantic; and the familiar round of rationalisations and redundancies followed. The UK welding equipment business was sold (its US equivalent has also since been divested). The company also disposed of most of the lesser UK diversifications. Under Giordano, BOC has been reorganised into two main product-oriented divisions – gases (£1.4 billion of sales in 1985–6) and health care (£517 million), with special products and services (£192 million) and carbon and carbide (£169 million) making up the rest. All divisions operate on a world-wide basis, managed from the company's new world headquarters in Surrey, although the chairman and his senior executive team spend much of their time in the US.

For all the severity of recession, BOC came through hardly scathed. Pre-tax profits have grown in every year but one since 1978, reaching £192 million before exceptional items (on a turnover of £1.9 billion) in 1985–6. This record was helped by the group's multi-national spread. But it also partly reflected success in developing new markets in the foods and electronics industries and, above all, in health care, which includes anaesthetic pharmaceuticals and the equipment for delivering them.

Giordano became chairman of the company, retaining the role of chief executive, in January 1985.

What have been the benefits of the BOC–Airco marriage?

From BOC's standpoint, it was able, through the acquisition of Airco, to enter the largest industrial gases market in the world. It is a business very much driven by scale. Moreover, the US market is the most competitive market in the world, so if BOC had any aspirations to being a world-class player in the industrial gas business, it had to be in the United States. When it bought Airco, Airco was number three in that market with about 18–20 per cent of the market. This was a sizeable share, and it gave BOC the critical mass it needed in the US. I suppose a bit of serendipity was that it also acquired a very strong health care business, a good deal larger and broader in product line than BOC's own health care business. That business has flourished over the last seven years and, of course, has now grown to a major portion of the total group.

Where do you see your main growth markets in the future, both for gases and for health care products?

The gas business is a very diverse portfolio. There are many gases in the portfolio, some of which come out of the air, some of which come as by-products from chemical streams, some of which are extracted from natural gas; these gases are very simple molecules, and because of that they are extraordinarily versatile. As long as we continue to provide them at lower and lower cost to our customers, the demand grows.

The gases now range through almost every part of the industrial fabric. Decades ago they were associated mostly with metal bashing, but these days oxygen has actually become one of the smaller volume gases in the portfolio. For example, in the UK today we sell more nitrogen for one single application – food freezing and chilling – than all of our oxygen business. In many ways the gases business is regarded as a surrogate for industry as a whole. It tends to grow faster than industry. We estimate that its natural growth rate in volume is somewhere around two times GDP. So it is a GDP, a gross domestic product, business. By that I mean in countries where you may have a great deal of wealth, but not much population or gross domestic product, you don't have a big gas business.

GDP is normally associated with population as well as wealth, so in countries where there is only wealth, such as Saudi Arabia, there is not a very big gas business. Our interest is in being in countries where there is a large and rapidly growing gross domestic product. Obviously, if our business is growing at a multiplier of two times GDP, the Japanese GDP growth of 5 or 6 per cent could mean 10 per cent plus growth for us. As a result, over the last four or five years we've been making a determined effort to get into the business in the Far East.

Two and a half, three years ago, we were the first company to acquire a publicly quoted Japanese company in the industrial gas business, in Osaka. We have recently concluded a deal for a 50 per cent joint venture with the dominant company in Taiwan. We are in negotiations in Shanghai for a joint venture in industrial gases which would be a first on mainland China, and we are already represented in almost all of the countries in the Pacific rim – Indonesia, the Philippines, Hong Kong, Singapore, Malaysia, and obviously Australia and New Zealand as well. That is the fastest growing part of the world and we have to learn how to do business out there, and be certain that we are firmly footed.

In health care, our main businesses are in pharmaceuticals, principally pharmaceuticals used in the surgical theatre, and in the critical care support systems of the surgical theatre – in the intensive care unit, in the recovery room and sometimes in the hospital room itself. Our equipment ranges from anaesthesia equipment, respiratory care equipment, monitoring equipment; we make a wide range of equipments that monitor vital signs in the surgical theatre, and we are very large in intravenous therapy. It is quite a broad product range, and also includes a newly bought service business, Home Health Care in the United States. This is a new and growing business, centred around serving people who are chronically ill in the home rather than in the hospital, driven principally by the cost-containment measures that the US government is pursuing. This product line enjoys a considerable growth rate, and new technology is a very important aspect of its future.

What about competition? Where are your main competitors coming from?

The gas business is one characterised by a heavy investment; it is a business of scale. We estimate that it often has an investment-to-sales ratio of one and a half or two to one for new facilities. Moreover, it is also characterised by a very heavy investment in technology, both in the technology of producing the product and in the technology of application of a product – that is, its use. We spend a great deal of money on developing new ways in which these versatile gases can be used by a potential customer – for example, to make his process more effective.

Because of that, over the last two or three decades the business has become increasingly concentrated in the world. More and more of the smaller competitors are dropping by the wayside, not able to keep up with the technical parade, or with the massive investments required to be in the business. The business is now concentrated, probably to the tune of six or seven world competitors accounting for 80 per cent of the business in the whole world.

Some would have thought that might make the business less competitive but in fact it has intensified the competition. It seems as if, wherever you go in the world, whether it's Japan or Korea or Taiwan, you'll bump into all the same faces – all the formidable competitors scratching for a position in this business. We expect that kind of competition, we are used to that kind of competition, but clearly this will be a very competitive business for the foreseeable future.

In health care the competition is more fragmented. We do not meet a single company, for example, anywhere in the world that competes across the board in all of our health care products. In many cases, we have dominant market shares, and we are a very large company in that particular competitive arena. It is probably less sensitive to competition, as long as you are technically innovative and constantly marching ahead of your competitors in offering new products.

What aspects of competition cause you most concern? Are we talking about competitors who invest more, competitors who produce more efficiently, or competitors who have a stronger foothold in the market?

In our gas business, the most important changes to have affected the business over the last couple of decades have been technical. In other words, the shift-changes in the business that have altered the competitive posture, that have made one company move ahead of another company, or one company fall behind, have been major technological changes – technological changes which have reduced costs, introduced larger scale, or provided major breakthroughs in customer applications enabling one competitor to steal a march with the customers. So to that extent I worry, always worry, about whether our technology is the best available; and we keep a sharp eye on the technological changes that we can see in our competitors.

In the case of the health care business, again it is technically driven. Our pharmaceutical research has produced the two drugs that now make us a

great deal of money. We need output from that research effort that will
replace those drugs and continue producing a family of profitable drugs.
Similarly, in the case of our medical equipment, it is technically driven. We
must be certain that we get the new products out, that we get them out
rapidly, that we acknowledge or recognise their limited life and have a
constant flow of new products following.

I worry less about whether we have enough money. We are a sizeable
company with good cash flow; we don't have any problem funding our
aspirations. Obviously I worry about competitors getting toe-holds in
places where I may not be competing, or developing products I would like
to be in. But that concerns me less than whether we stay at the top of the
technical parade.

Have you become more selective in the businesses you're competing in?

In the sense that, if you looked at BOC in the Seventies, you would have
said it was a very diversified company which is now much less diversified,
the answer is yes. Commencing in 1979 we have sold off approximately
twenty-five businesses – it must be in excess of £300 million of turnover. So
we've attempted to simplify our portfolio in an effort to manage it better, in
an effort to be more selective.

However, some of our businesses are actually quite integrated. You can
sell oxygen or nitrogen in tonnes per day through a pipeline to customers –
that could be described as a bulk commodity business. Then, we also sell
high-purity nitrogen in teacupfuls for twenty times the revenue we get for a
similar unit through the pipeline. I'm not sure I can choose to be in one and
not in the other, because of the critical mass required and the technological
base. Much as we would like to be more selective and only compete in the
higher value-added parts of the business, often the business is so
integrated, both financially and technically, that one cannot make those
choices so easily.

*I suppose the danger you are suggesting is that you could easily become isolated
in a number of specialist businesses none of which remain viable?*

Well, none of which will produce defensible, durable businesses that will
be able to withstand the competitors' actions over a long period of time. It's
a bit like selling a product in the market and some of the customers are less
profitable than others. If you limit yourself to only the profitable customers,
you may find that you cannot achieve the volume and scale that enables you
to make money in the first place.

And scale is important in your business?

Scale is a critical factor in the gas business. It's a factor in the production of
the product, it's a factor in the distribution of the product, it is certainly a

factor in the technology. The technical bill is so big that it can only be spread over a business of significant size. It's a little less important in our health care business, which tends to be more fragmented. On the other hand, we've done very well by dominating relatively small markets.

How does this relate to what has been suggested as the motto for the Nineties, which is 'world-class or die'?

I believe that's true. Obviously, there are exceptions, such as in a totally domestic business like the retail business, but to the extent that one is making products that have application throughout the world, the market is no longer Britain, it's no longer Europe, it is the world. Either get out there and compete in the world, or retreat.

What makes that so crucial?

Because the business that has scale as a factor will eventually produce lower costs to the largest and most competitive firm. As that firm grows and its market share produces larger and larger scale, its low cost base will eventually enter all the markets, including your own home market, and eventually put you out of business. In other words, you cannot hide behind the Channel or the Atlantic Ocean any more and believe that there is a UK market which will not be subjected to international competition. That means that if you wish to succeed you *must* be one of those international competitors, if not the best.

After what you've described, BOC hardly seems a British company in the traditional sense, that is, a British-based company exporting overseas. Where is its centre of gravity now?

Obviously since the Airco acquisition BOC has changed. It was for decades a venerable British institution. On the other hand the merger of the two companies has not resulted in an Americanised British company. I think that the company has a centre of gravity probably somewhere in the middle of the Atlantic. It has obsorbed bits and pieces of both business cultures; its methods and styles are the methods and styles of neither of the predecessor companies. What has emerged is a method and style appropriate to the new company. One of the things we have to watch out for is that, although we do not use either British or American style as a reference point, we do not convey to all of our non-Anglo-Saxon companies in the countries in which we do business, that the Anglo-Saxon method is the only reference point. Almost all of the countries in which we do business have traditions and customs that are quite effective; and although we want to be certain that they are totally in the twentieth century, we don't want to impose our way of doing things on them.

Looking at the relationship between people in Airco and people in BOC, did you have to require them to get together and work together, or did it just happen?

It never just happens. Different cultural bases like to keep doing things the way they did them before. But we recognised that, where Airco and BOC's businesses were similar, we had to take a world view. We had to be certain that technology and managerial skills were moving freely both across the Atlantic and to other overseas companies. We made a number of organisational changes which tended to place heavier emphasis on technology and product, and placed an overview on their activities which made them think about businesses in world terms.

For example, in some cases where we actually had two or three different companies making the same product in health care, we pushed all of that business – in terms of technical development and managerial skills – into one centre of excellence. By way of example, we are the world leaders in making vaporisers, which are important in the anaesthesia product line. We were making them in France, Britain and the United States. We now only make them in a brand-new plant for this purpose in Leeds in Yorkshire. And we've taken similar sorts of steps. The result of this has been to internationalise parts of the business. Clearly, in the case of gases, we had to integrate our technical efforts on both sides of the Atlantic so that we weren't suffering a great deal of duplication, and could be certain that we were getting the best results for our money invested.

You now run this company from a British base after a lifetime's experience in the United States. What have you found to be the most noticeable contrast between the two business environments?

I think the two single most important differences are in the arenas of competition and industrial relations. Because the US market is so much bigger than Britain's, so much bigger than any other market in the world, it always attracts the most competition. So in our business, particularly in gases, the US market is far more competitive than the British market. And I suspect this is true in most other businesses as well. Intense competition tends to produce a different business environment that requires a somewhat different outlook in terms of how you meet it.

Clearly, the history and traditions of the two countries in industrial relations are quite different. When one works in Britain, one has to adjust rapidly to the fact that trade unions are very much in the political environment. Without passing judgement on that, it does require a different approach to dealing with unions. Moreover, the union traditions in Britain have produced a wide range of unions more allied to crafts than to industries, and that's a very different approach. And lastly, the industrial relations environment in Britain does not have the very comprehensive legislative framework that it enjoys in the United States, in spite of the fact that new laws have been passed here during the last six or seven years. That forces you to go about your business in a different way. We tend to have in the United States, within our plants, less of the 'us and them' which characterises some of the locations here in Britain. Therefore the process of adapting to it is one that any foreigner must go through in order to do business.

If a British manager were to do what you've done in reverse, go to the United States to run a company from that base, what would impress him most? You've mentioned competition, for instance. What impact does that make on the day-to-day behaviour of top managers?

It means that instead of worrying about one or two competitors, the British manager would have to worry about six. It also means that when one or two or three competitors might be willing to see prices go up or down, two or three others would go in the other direction; there's much more anarchy in the competitive environment. The other thing a British manager would have to adjust to is the sheer scale – the fact that one can make goods in Massachusetts and ship them to Texas or California. That scale difference is very important and it needs to be adjusted to.

The scale of the market also requires the manager to adjust to a much bigger price-tag for entry. Businesses that can be entered into in Britain at X require ten times X for entry in the United States. Obviously the cultures are different, but I don't think the cultures themselves are so different that they are a bar to an American coming to Britain, or a Briton going to America, and we have a fair number of examples of successes in both directions.

You haven't mentioned countries very much, but one presumes Japan is a country that might worry you in competitive terms. What impresses you about Japanese business methods?

First of all, it's extremely difficult to understand Japanese business methods. Much is written on the subject, but the culture is a veiled culture in terms of what actually goes on. In our own business, much to our surprise, we found the Japanese to be considerably behind the Westerners. In other words, you can look at the industrial gas business in Japan and you will find its technology and practices five years or so behind Britain and the United States.

I can't explain this, except perhaps to speculate that, because it is not an export-oriented industry, it has not been at the forefront of the Japanese drive to excel. Traditionally, or more commonly, Japanese companies that *are* in the export industries have been excellent, have been world leaders.

But behind that are a good number of domestic industries which would surprise us with their lack of technology and lack of efficiency relative to their Western analogies.

Clearly, though, the Japanese commitment to the company, to the product line, to the business is different. We don't have wild-cat strikes in our Japanese plants. If there's any protest it expresses itself by wearing a headband while working, or maybe walking out in front of the office before the actual starting time of work. The Japanese also work very hard and, in spite of the consensus that is so often described between Japanese management and labour, it is quite an authoritarian environment. If people are treated well, and consulted and communicated with, they will often do what they're told at considerable sacrifice to themselves.

Finally, what about the relationship of the old industrialised businesses as we know them and the way they're going to relate to the newly emerging industries of the world? What's that relationship going to be; how are we going to have to adapt?

First of all, I think it is wrong to segment the old industries from the newly emerging or new industries, often described as the 'sunset and sunrise' industries. They really are integrated. After all, the pattern of industry is set by final demand. If people buy automobiles, those automobiles will be made with steel, perhaps less steel than before, but they will also incorporate a considerable amount of new software on the factory floor, perhaps some of the newest and most exotic materials, from so-called new or emerging industries. If we don't have an automobile industry, not only will we lose the old industry of making steel, but we will not have the newly emerging industry of software or new materials.

These industries complement each other; we cannot allow our industrial base of so-called old industries to disappear, and hope to have a robust and viable economy purely of newly emerging industries. The same argument is often expressed that we can get along with service industries and don't need manufacturing. That, too, is rubbish. If we're going to be successful and have a robust economy we must have enough of the old industries as a basis on which the new industries will emerge.

ENGINEERING FIGHTS BACK

**MIKE HOFFMAN, MANAGING DIRECTOR, BABCOCK INTERNATIONAL
SIR DAVID PLASTOW, CHAIRMAN, VICKERS
SIR AUSTIN PEARCE, CHAIRMAN, BRITISH AEROSPACE
SIR FRANCIS TOMBS, CHAIRMAN, ROLLS-ROYCE**

MIKE HOFFMAN, MANAGING DIRECTOR, BABCOCK INTERNATIONAL

Nearly all of Mike Hoffman's career has been spent in Britain, but he gained invaluable experience both of restructuring a major manufacturing operation and of North America in his last job before joining Babcock International – president of the Farm and Industrial Machinery Group of the loss-making Massey-Ferguson in Toronto. Hoffman is a mechanical engineer (graduating from Bristol in 1961) and has worked for three of Britain's best-known engineering firms – Perkins Engines (a Massey-Ferguson subsidiary), Associated Engineering and Rolls-Royce.

Hoffman joined the latter as a graduate apprentice on leaving Bristol. He rose up the manufacturing and technical sides to become manager of the Aeroparts Facility in Crewe. In 1970 Hoffman moved up to become general manager, and also a director, of a Rolls-Royce subsidiary, Cannon & Stokes. On its takeover by Associated Engineering, Hoffman joined the board of AE subsidiary Hepworth & Grandage and then took charge as general manager of the newly formed AE Turbine Components, specialising in hot-end components for aero-engines.

The move to Perkins Engines as managing director in 1976, followed by the chairmanship of Perkins worldwide, put Hoffman in charge of a diesel engine-maker of the highest repute. Like many other British engineering companies, however, Perkins had developed problems during the years of relative success which came home to roost after the oil shocks of 1973. Hoffman had to rationalise the product range and restructure the company to a significantly smaller size: at the same time, he invested heavily in Perkins' future. Hoffman was the initiator of the first programmes for converting gasoline engines to diesel, from which sprang the Austin Rover O Series and the Iceberg Project for the Rover V8.

The Toronto post at the parent Massey-Ferguson came in 1981. He stayed there, running a company whose sales were $1.2 billion, until August 1983. At that time, Babcock International, a widely spread engineering group best known for its boilers, had already come back strongly from its trough at the turn of the decade. Pre-tax profits had all but halved to £17.3 million between 1979 and 1981, even though turnover had risen from £845 million to £956 million. By 1983, though, turnover was over a billion, and profits had recovered to £37.4 million.

The two subsequent years saw little growth in sales and profits – which were actually lower than those made in 1976 on 40 per cent lower turnover. The precipitate drop in return on capital employed, from 25.2 per cent to 11.5 per cent over the period, pointed to the necessity of the restructuring on which Hoffman, the experienced hand in these matters, embarked. He also initiated extensive modernisation of a business which covers an enormous range, including automotive and furniture hardware in the North American businesses (total 1985 sales, £382 million), a nuclear reactor pressure vessel for a Trident submarine in the Power Group (£282 million), installing a continuous ship unloader in Hong Kong in the Contracting Group (£80 million), wire-drawing machines for China (Industrial and Electrical Products Group, £115 million), a plaster plant in Alexandria (Overseas Group, £416 million), and conventional welding lines for car plants in Germany, South Korea and Czechoslovakia.

The latter are among the activities of FATA European Group, which is spearheading the company's push into automation markets with high-tech products like AGVs (automatic guided vehicles). Babcock shares its chairman, Lord King, with British Airways. In the first half of 1986, turnover and profits both improved as Hoffman's medicine continued to improve the group's health.

When you came to this job in 1983, what did you conclude was going right and going wrong with the group as a whole?

The things that were going right were that we had a very loyal workforce worldwide, and we had put a lot of capital investment into a number of our major businesses. The areas where I felt we were weak were twofold: one, we still saw ourselves as an international boiler company with a number of other appendages, and, secondly, we were more sales-orientated than marketing-led. I felt both these things needed changing.

In terms of marketing, we tended to know about our competition, but we'd not done enough competitive analysis and we had not looked where our competitors were going, rather than understanding where they'd come from, which is rather the traditional approach. Second, as a result of that, we had tended to live longer with some of our products than we would have done if we'd anticipated where markets were moving to. So, by and large, we had a number of old products that we had to move out fairly quickly, and we had to have a fast-track programme to develop some new ones.

Did your relationship with customers help you to research their needs?

We had a good relationship with our customers, particularly in the boiler company, Babcock Power. We knew our customers very well. We had long and enduring relations with them technically, because if you run a power station with a boiler made by Babcock it runs for forty or fifty years. Those were the easy people to deal with. It was much more difficult the nearer one got to the consumer – for example, in some of our decorative hardware markets, and things of that nature. But once we got the hang of what we were looking for, we found it relatively easy to get statistics.

There's a clear engineering relationship across the whole range of things you do, but the product list is very wide and goes into a huge number of markets. Did you conclude that it was an untidy collection of businesses?

The most difficult thing was actually to understand, what is Babcock? I think we are much more evenly organised now. We see ourselves as four types of business: there's Babcock Energy and that is fairly self-evident, it's the power-related businesses; there's Babcock Engineering which is really the contracting operations – process-plant contracting such as Woodall-Duckham, which is a well-known name; the third business is Babcock Automation, the sort of work we do for car plants and engine-testing; and the fourth area is Babcock Industries, a group of companies that basically make things and sell them directly into the market. Those are the four areas of our company. It's much easier to understand it on that basis than looking down a horrific list of different names.

What were the critical operational problems you had to solve?

One of the key priorities was to bring the direct labour cost down, and I think that a good job has been done here over the years. I saw two areas which we had not yet attacked aggressively enough. One was the overhead cost; maybe we had too many sites, and we've now closed a number of sites in various places. The other area is much more difficult to attack, the cost of quality and the cost of holding inventory. That's much more difficult to get at, because you can't go in and make a change happen nearly as quickly as taking direct labour out. But it's absolutely vital to us that we keep cost of production going down.

How have these improvements paid off in competition?

I'm probably best able to illustrate it in the power group. The investment programmes, and the flexibility agreements we've got with our employees, mean that we're fairly close now to putting iron on the ground – for example, putting boiler steelwork in position in a foreign country – that will compete on a base-cost basis with the Koreans or the Japanese. Where we have difficulty in those areas now is competing, sometimes, with the financial support provided for these various different nations. But I think with the investment that we've made, we can put the iron on the ground at a competitive price.

Which countries worry you most in terms of getting the orders?

If you look at our UK-based companies – but remember, we are a global group – the majority of the things we make are at the heavy end of the engineering spectrum. The most difficult places to compete with now are Korea, to some extent Taiwan, Japan – certainly in the big construction type projects. In some areas we see Italy and one or two of the continental European companies coming at us. But the toughest people undoubtedly are the Koreans and the Japanese.

How have you improved your competitive edge over them?

I'll give you a classic case. When we put up a 500-megawatt boiler in the Seventies, it used about 10,000 tonnes of steel. By product design and improvement, we've brought the weight of steel down to something like 6500 or 7000 tonnes per boiler. So we've already had a material cost advantage now, which has brought us much more in line with our competition, who tended to be lighter designers anyway. And the changes we've made in our working practices have meant that we can process that steel at a lower cost. And that's typically what we've also done in our mining and in our process control businesses, in the UK.

What about the engineering know-how?

I think that's where we have a definite edge. We've put a lot of work into taking a big boiler and dealing with it in modules – so that, for example, the way we construct a very large boiler is to make it up with a large number of elements from a basic planning package. And we're using that type of approach in our mining equipment businesses, in our electrical distribution businesses; we're trying to work from a basic minimum core number of design parts. But I guess there's nowhere I feel that we've lost design edge over any of our competitors. The problem basically has always been the ability to make that design at an appropriate cost.

Where do you see the main growth areas in the world markets?

From a UK standpoint, the USSR is one area. We see China as an opportunity in some of our power-related businesses. The other area is really the

United States, although our current activities in the US have been based more on acquisition than exporting from the UK.

Currently you've got a gross margin of around 3½ to 4 per cent. What problem areas are you going to tackle to improve that?

Our £1.2 billion turnover is split roughly into £700 million in contracting – that's the energy-type companies and the engineering companies. And we're looking at before-tax profit margins, for those types of businesses, of around 3 to 3½ per cent – because by and large we're agglomerating other people's hardware and products. The other £500 million is in product-related businesses; our target there is a minimum of 8 per cent before tax, and we're generally heading towards that area.

Automotive components, where it's very difficult to make that sort of return, are a large part of our business, and in the last two or three years a lot of our clean-up activities have depressed the apparent margins from those businesses. But the way we are going to make that 8 per cent is, firstly, to try and enhance the 'value-added' of what we're selling, that is by developing products that the market really wants, rather than selling products that we've made for a long time. And secondly, to hit it with the cost-reduction programmes, which I think are also beginning to bear fruit. But both of those mean that we tend to use less people all the time, as we put more capital in.

How important is the scale of the Babcock operation to you as an international business? Would you like to be bigger?

The way I like to look at it is that, with the global presence of Babcock being seen as an international competitor in quite a large range of fields, it does mean we can make penetration gains in new businesses much more easily than small companies would do. A classic case: we bought a company in the US last year, and one of the things we've been able to do in that case is to enhance its performance in Europe very rapidly, because of our knowledge of the marketing scene.

I guess the strength we can bring is that we are global in our view of marketplaces, and it doesn't really matter what you make if you've got that global sense of structure. It helps, for example, if you're going into China with one of our small companies, if you can talk to somebody who's been operating there for a longer period and knows the form. And that's one of the things we've tried to do within the company; to set up a series of communication groups where people in like types of either geographical environments or product areas are able to talk to each other and feed on expertise.

It's often said that much of Britain's decline in the heavy industry area was inevitable, that industries must die. But was that really so?

I actually think it was. There have been two distinct phases. In the post-industrial revolution era, really up until the Fifties, British manufacturing industry was able to sell almost all that it produced, because of the shortage mentality after the Second World War, and because of the dying Empire preferences. So we weren't forced to innovate. And that meant we ended up in the Sixties still selling Morris Minor motor cars in the Philippines and Indonesia.

The second phase began with the Sixties when we became more attuned to the lame-duck mentality. We expected government to support heavy industry even though it wasn't necessarily competitive. And also we developed the 'sponger' mentality, whereby industries and individuals became used to the State helping them. And that type of climate didn't produce innovators. So it was almost inevitable that shipyards which were designed, say, on the Tyne for producing fairly low-tonnage vessels on small slipways, were never going to be internationally competitive with Korea, and places like that, where they built the massive slips. To a large extent the very structure we lived in caused manufacturing to decline.

You've been in engineering now for twenty years. What did you feel during the Sixties and Seventies? Was it frustration, or did you not quite see what was happening?

In the Sixties, one was sensing that we were not making any real competitive advances outside the UK, except in very leading-edge technology – aero-engines and one or two products like that. But you sensed, working in a factory as I did, that there were so many old-fashioned ways of doing things that you would never actually overcome them.

There have been two changes really: one is that technology has moved forward dramatically. In fact, you could almost argue that if you were entering advanced manufacturing technology fields now, it really wouldn't matter whether you had ten-year-old technology or thirty-year-old technology, because the change was so dramatic as to wipe out both of those at a leap. That was one element: the rapid change in technology.

And the other one is, whether one likes the politics or not, the environment created in the last seven or eight years, politically, has been such that the dominance of trade unions, and the fact that one always had to listen to their views on everything, has reduced. People have become much more concerned about work-place environments for their own benefit, and therefore are more willing to concede working-practice changes.

Do you feel that British engineering companies are becoming more competitive?

Those that remain are obviously becoming more competitive. The game is no easier than it was, and you're seeing much more innovative people coming through. Fixed and rigid management attitudes have changed, and the sort of young man that's coming out as a manager now has got no real memories of the Thirties, when managements were hard and dominant. We're much more flexible now, and more competitive. The area that still worries me, in the UK, is that we don't actually make many things that the consumer wants. There's furniture and things like that, but you've only got to look at white goods, televisions, those types of things, to see that we really don't make a large number of consumer goods. So we're still too dependent on somebody else using our heavier products for us to be internationally competitive.

Are you concerned about the fact that wages are rising faster than inflation?

I actually don't believe it matters whether you pay people more than inflation, providing you are reducing the total cost of your business. If, for example, you're moving towards a much more technologically based business then you might have to pay your people, arguably, twice as much as they're paid now. But if you use 20 per cent of the people with the new technologies, then in fact the actual annual payment doesn't matter. It's where you're not getting the productivity gain with those increases that it really matters. You see, we're still a very low-wage economy in the UK.

Operating a business in the UK, what do you see as general obstacles to progress?

I'm bound to look at it from the viewpoint of the business that I run, and I see three areas. First, the educational standard of people that are coming into the business at all levels still needs enhancing. We don't put as many people in the UK through higher education as our Continental competitors, and in addition we don't put them through for as long a period. Both of these factors seem, historically, to have an impact on the quality of the people coming up. Secondly, we have developed, by the nature of our stock market in the UK, a relatively short-term view, and I can understand that, because all our pensions depend upon it. But it means that in making change happen in older industries, bearing in mind that a large number of our UK industries in manufacturing are older industries, you've got to take a much more cautious view of the short-term impact of changes you'd like to make that will really benefit the long term.

And the third point is that in the heavy engineering businesses we're used to that export overseas, we're very 'pure' in our thinking on linking aid to trade. I agree with the UK government, that this really shouldn't be the competitive element. But the French and the Japanese and the Italians are all very powerful in the sort of aid that they give. If we can't cut it out internationally then we've just got to pay the price and compete with it – if we want to stay in internationally exporting businesses.

What aspects of world markets do you think Britain should be investing in?

Inevitably you're drawn towards the information technology industries, broadly electronics and software. Those are areas for which the UK capability is very suited. Other areas where we're making advances are materials technology and bio-engineering. And I guess if I was starting out and saying, for a national plan for the UK, where would I put my resources (other than weapons-related activities which is a large part of our R & D), I would tend to look at those types of industries where we stand a big advantage in worldwide competitive positions.

Do you think there are certain types of industry where we can afford to abdicate?

Shipbuilding is one that we're sensibly out of. We've got to be in areas where we can use a high level of expertise, combined with a level of international marketing capability, which I actually believe the UK has. I don't think we've exploited it nearly enough, because we became soft in the immediate post-war period when you didn't have to go out and innovate and market, and that's where the Germans and the Japanese crept in.

I don't believe the battle is lost in any way, but you've got to invest in products and recognise that product life-cycles are much shorter than they've ever been in the past, and then you've got to get out and make sure you sell them while the life of those products is current.

SIR DAVID PLASTOW, CHAIRMAN, VICKERS

Sir David Plastow came into prominence in British industry through one of the earliest and most remarkable transformations of a famous national business – perhaps the most famous of them all. The Rolls-Royce car firm, under the umbrella of the aero-engine company to which it had given birth, was an epitome of the classic British sin of putting product before both production and profit. While the reputation of the cars remained unique, the company had lost money for a dozen years before, paradoxically, it received the kiss of life from its parent's financial death.

Plastow at the time of the 1971 collapse had worked for Rolls-Royce for thirteen years, having begun his career as an apprentice at Vauxhall Motors. (He is unusual among the seventeen interviewees in not having been to university.) By 1971 he was managing director of the car division, and was the obvious choice to head the newly independent firm which rose from the ashes of the bankrupt parent. With his broad experience (including four years as marketing director), Plastow implemented a strategy that was no less successful than Sir John Egan's later work on Jaguar Cars: the now public Rolls-Royce achieved an astounding run of rising profits – in round millions, four, five, six, nine, eleven, fourteen and a half.

The fact that this move from long loss to star profit growth had been achieved with the same cars, the same factory, the same workforce and much the same management had important lessons to teach about responsibility and direction – lessons that have since been followed in turnround after turnround in other companies. But Rolls-Royce was still too vulnerable to market conditions, especially in the United States, and the merger with Vickers in August 1980 seemingly offered an opportunity to combine different strengths and eliminate separate weaknesses.

Vickers had long epitomised another classic syndrome of British management: combining too many disparate businesses, of many shapes and size, without creating a strong strategy that could make sense of the whole. Plastow, as chief executive of the merged group, found himself with a much less tractable task than the Rolls-Royce turnround, and in the worst possible circumstances, with the engineering industry in deep recession. Profits in the early Eighties fell to almost half the level of 1976, despite a more than 50 per cent rise in turnover to £655 million in 1983. In the next two years, sales growth halted as Plastow restructured the company – losing turnover and jobs, but sharply improving profits.

Profits before tax doubled between 1983 and 1985 to £49 million. More important than the strong financial recovery has been the build-up, partly through acquisition, of a group of international businesses focused on specific markets and modelled on the same management principles that, in transforming Rolls-Royce, won Plastow the title of *Guardian* Young Businessman of the Year in 1976. Ten years later, he was knighted in the New Year's Honours. He became chairman of Vickers at the start of 1987.

The process of change has turned Vickers from a company once associated mainly with military hardware into one where defence accounts for only 11 per cent of sales, coming fifth after marine engineering, business equipment, lithographic plates and supplies and the still famous cars. The latter form the largest division, with £176 million of sales, two and a half times the 1985 defence business. The latter, however, now includes a tank business greatly strengthened by the purchased Royal Ordnance Factory in Leeds. The group has also become overwhelmingly international: two-thirds of its sales are now outside the UK.

What sort of condition was Vickers in at the turn of the decade?

It was rather a special case, because in 1977 more than half the assets and something like two-thirds of the earnings were ripped out by the nationalisation of our shipbuilding and aircraft interests. That was a very serious blow to the company, and we were left with a disparate portfolio in lots of different sectors, and totally inadequate compensation for that ravaging of our assets. Then in 1980, Rolls-Royce Motors – that's the cars, diesels and a few other bits and pieces, non-aerospace – were merged into Vickers. That complicated the variety of the portfolio even more. On top of that, of course, we had the beginning of difficulties with the world economy, and we were faced with a very interesting business situation.

What were the worst problems?

Primarily we had this broad, diversified portfolio without having decided which bits needed, and could afford, to be supported. We sat down over a period of a year and came to one particular conclusion, and that was that we could only afford to retain within Vickers those businesses which were going to be truly internationally competitive. As a result, we sold twenty operations, we liquidated a property portfolio, and the overall outcome was that we reduced the gearing, over a period of three years, from something in excess of 55 per cent to 'the teens'. We finished with six prime operations, all of which are truly internationally competitive.

That's probably the biggest single message to come through those difficult times: that it was no good sitting here having a large share of the UK market, whatever it was, and thinking you could continue to develop that business, invest in it and become increasingly competitive. You really had to be international in your operations, not merely to spread the geographic risk in terms of the varying conditions of major economies, but also to be seen to be successful in the domestic markets of your competition, in product terms and in pricing and commercial terms.

What effect has this paring down had on employment?

To give you some idea of the scale of that paring down – we don't really talk about headcount reduction, it's a very painful and unpleasant business – but whereas in the Seventies the payroll of Vickers was in the forty thousands, after the merger in 1980 with Rolls-Royce Motors it was in excess of 30,000. We now have a headcount of around 15,000. Of course, now we're growing again. Over the last twelve months or so we've bought five new companies, and we are doing that strictly in support of those key business areas, to make them more internationally competitive.

What have you been able to do about the internal running of the company, the professional skills, the way it operates?

We are by now a properly market-led company rather than resources-led. The question is not, how should we fill the factories, but what does the customer want, and at what price? We've greatly increased our emphasis on research and development to meet that objective. At the centre here we spend a great deal of time questioning operations managements on their knowledge of competition and how they're meeting it.

We have done a lot on the financial control side, we have what we call our 'flash reporting' system: at the end of every four-week period, by the noon of the following Thursday, we have a full financial picture of the corporation in terms of profits and cash, sales and orders. And that has been particularly important; we can get to work on the problems quicker and take the opportunities as well. Also, we've got a more sophisticated approach towards volatile foreign exchanges and have been able to have a more stable trading position as a result of that, particularly in North America with one or two of our major businesses.

We've been more and more concerned about training. We take a great deal of interest in the 'richness of the mixture', in terms of the professional qualifications of our senior people. More than that, we're really tackling training right through the various operations right down to the shop floor. There's a great deal of work to be done.

In addition, we've spent a great deal of time on communications. Throughout our UK operations we have detailed team briefings every four weeks, making sure that every employee knows what his or her role is and where their business stands in international terms.

Taking the first of those headings, marketing, is there any noticeably different way in which you are approaching the marketing; is there now more investment in it?

We encourage investment overseas. The acquisitions I referred to just now are really an extension of that thrust, having both manufacturing and marketing assets on the ground in North America. In the Far East, having an office in China, in Beijing, is a case in point. That is part of the drive we put into improving our knowledge of the marketplace, so that we can respond more effectively with better products.

In five years you have doubled output per head. What have been the main contributing factors?

A hard drive in terms of investment in more productive equipment, improvement in our knowledge of the business, our systems (so that we really understand where the costs are) and better training of supervision and management in our manufacturing areas. Coupled with that, our employees across the company have a better understanding of the need to be productive, the need to be competitive and profitable. That has helped us in some of the more difficult areas where we've had to reduce head-count, and we've done that by negotiation, by collaboration, by understanding. We've had virtually no difficulty at all in doing it, by being sensitive and by explaining to people this need to be competitive. We have got further to go, and we will be making further progress. By that I'm not forecasting massive reductions in headcount. I'm forecasting, hopefully, more sales volume with the same payroll and more sophisticated equipment. Also we mustn't forget the need to design to manufacture; we must design from the beginning to get cost out of our product, and this is what we are doing more and more.

Do you have any 'us and them' attitudes left in the company?

Yes – 'us' being the company and 'them' being the Japanese, the Germans, the Americans, the French and so on. I'm more and more sure that's so. All my senior colleagues and myself, when we go into a plant, make a habit of talking to our individual employees, be they machine shop operators or on the drawing board or sweeping the floor, and asking them standard questions: How are you doing? Who are your competition? And I get, increasingly, responses which encourage me to believe that the understanding is there, and that over the years we shall be getting more effective as a result.

How competitive are you now, comparing yourself with the world class of companies with whom you are competing?

In some of the very highly competitive areas such as Howson-Algraphy, lithographic printing plates, we are number three in the world and pressing hard to be number two. We have invested very heavily in what we believe to be the most productive plant in the world now, and we're just beginning to gain share. Against a world market growth of around 5 per cent in 1985 we took our growth in real terms up to something like 11 per cent. That was encouraging because it is a very competitive business, very price-conscious.

In our marine engineering area, very difficult at the moment, we are still proving we are competitive in price terms. But it isn't just a matter of cost, though the cost basis is crucial; it's a matter also of having a product which will be uniquely special and good, and therefore demand premium prices. It's too easy really to go down the cost-driven road. At the top end you try and move your prices by getting a good product; and you're working hard at the cost base, too, and therefore optimising the margin. The competition can touch us in everything we do. We're not totally unique in anything, and we have to work hard to maintain our competitive standing and our market share.

What do you think are the most crucial elements on which the competition is dangerous to you?

Clearly the product; that's where it all starts. If you haven't got a satisfactory product which is effectively priced and properly supported in the market-place, you are dead anyhow. But after that you've got to have world presence, the ability to be seen to be effective in the main markets of the world – that's clearly a big plus – and the ability to generate sufficient cash to go on investing in R & D, productive equipment and marketing development. That's why you have to be a world player. That's why you can't just be a UK operator any more in manufacturing.

Is Vickers strong enough in its range of activities – speaking in world terms?

In office equipment we are the largest player in the UK, we are second in France – and now we've acquired an international seating company in Germany. In the lithographic printing plate business, we're number three – pressing two – in the world. In some sectors of the medical equipment market, we are number one in the world. In marine engineering, we are the world's leading player in ship motion control – in controllable pitch propellers, for instance, we have well over 40 per cent of the world market. I can go on quoting examples. They are 'niche' businesses, where we think we are a world player. I think we also make the best car in the world.

Would you claim that Vickers has moved fast enough, been sufficiently dynamic?

Buying five international operations to latch on to those areas where we have a bit of a track record, where we have some competence, has been a very dynamic period. Since it all took place in about twelve months, after the investment and recasting of the previous four years, which was a difficult period, I think that we do now show a fairly busy corporate activity. We are not about to get out of those areas of competence. There's been a great deal of merger and aggressive predatory activity in the British and other markets over the last year or so. We watch that and, certainly, if a great opportunity came along we would probably make a move. But we believe that we serve our shareholders best by investing further in areas where we have got a reasonably solid international position.

What has British industry gained from the travail of the economy since 1979?

The single most important thing that has come through this very difficult period of enormous recession is the need to be an international player, or opt out. I have to say that government in Britain over a long period of time has not really been supportive in the proper sense towards manufacturing industry. If you look at the games that have been played over nationalisation – I mentioned already the loss of shipbuilding and aircraft to Vickers, and it lost steel twice – no other major economy has had that sort of disruptive influence.

If we look at the motor industry, for many years it was an economic tool of both shades of government in the way the latter played games with the finance supporting the purchase of cars, to regulate the economy. Governments of both colours may shout and scream about manufacturing industry, but what I've just referred to was actually very damaging and very destabilising. Our competitors on the Continent, and of course in the Far East and America, did not suffer those wild influences on investment programmes, and I'm very worried about this game of politics in the UK, when it impinges on industry.

Another criticism about what makes the business environment difficult concerns a lack of investment funds. Is that fair in your experience?

I don't think it is. Those who complain about the short view of the City and so on are probably a little unwise. In my experience, there's never been any shortage of investment money, given that the case in question looks sound. Sometimes we twitch a bit about the volatility of share prices and so on, but I have never found shortage of money being a problem in developing this business at all. What it does mean is that one has to work very hard with the investment community to make sure they properly understand what the management's up to, and develop confidence in it and its track record.

The Japanese and German alternatives are often quoted by industrialists, but I'm not sure that I would feel comfortable in those particular cultures, with heavy influence from those who come in alongside. I'd rather be a little bit more flexible, a little more entrepreneurial, in a way that we are allowed to be within the British capitalist system.

What edge do you think the Japanese, the Germans and the Americans have had over us?

They've had very well-trained people with training systems in depth, much better than ours. At the very highest level of technology, we still have an edge, but at the mid-management and operator level clearly we've got a great deal to do to catch up. That's probably the most significant thing of all. To take the Japanese example particularly, remember that they enjoyed a solidly protected market before they moved outside. Until 1970, when their motor business had reached something like three million units, it was virtually impenetrable. And from that volume base they got to work on the world. They managed their affairs in a very forthright and ruthless manner, which we haven't done here. In the case of North America a massive domestic market is a good start. But overall the biggest single thing is the depth of training and education – which we have got to get right.

What have you done to improve your own training?

We called in a firm which related our training needs to the competitive environment, and not just to what the local management thought they needed. We have a long way to go and we have to spend more money; we're spending nothing like enough anywhere in the company, although the performance is better in some parts than others. I'm sure that's typical of the whole of British industry. The Germans and the Japanese have the edge in the context of in-depth competence right through their payrolls; they have got better educated people and they spend more time and effort on maintaining that competence.

Are you prepared to nurse something along in a loss position for some years, if you believe in it?

Our tolerance varies, depending on the prospects. One of the virtues of our particular portfolio is that we are able to allow one, or perhaps one and a half, of our six main businesses to have a dull period. But not for very long. If we believe that there's been some misjudgement and that particular element, or total business, is not going to be a world player, then we are quite prepared to take the necessary action to root it out and convert those resources into other things. I mentioned that we sold some twenty operations. We sold them because we couldn't make them into these big international operations, and that was a painful process.

A particular example was the Rolls-Royce diesel engine business, which was pre-eminent in the UK. It has the bulk of the engine options for big heavy trucks, it was the lead engine-maker for the British Army's fighting vehicles, but it wasn't an international player. It broke my heart, having been associated with it for twenty years, but now it's part of Perkins which is a big international diesel business. It's got a much better future and is already showing the benefits of its new home. Most of the operations that we've sold have gone into places where they have played a supporting part to a bigger operation, and therefore done much better as a result.

Are you concerned by the fact that at Vickers half the turnover now comes from two businesses, the lithographic plates and Rolls-Royce?

The other four operations are growing fairly rapidly, so that we don't become over-dependent on those two. The other thing to point out is that more than two-thirds of our sales are now no longer dependent on the UK, so we seem pretty well to have fulfilled our ambition to be a proper international operation as a manufacturer.

How important is defence to the new Vickers?

Our principal activity in defence is tank making, and it's the only business of significance which has been in the Vickers portfolio for more than twenty years. We started the idea of tanks during the First World War. We have a factory up in Newcastle which we rebuilt in 1982, and that was 90 per cent export. Recently we acquired, in a deal with the British government, the Royal Ordnance Factory at Leeds and inherited a £2 million order-book as a result. We are going to rebuild that plant totally, very similar in lines to the facility we have in Newcastle. We will make sure that it can make money with a relatively small output. We do have the ability now to be a real inter-national operator in the tank business. We have the widest range of heavy fighting vehicles of any company in the world, and we have fine technology. We have a series of production contracts which are in pretty good shape. However, remember that defence is less than 15 per cent of Vickers – and I have to keep saying that, because we are regarded by some as still the armourers of the world!

SIR AUSTIN PEARCE, CHAIRMAN, BRITISH AEROSPACE

Sir Austin Pearce came to the top post in British Aerospace after an out-standing career in the oil industry. He was a brilliant student at Birming-ham University, gaining his Ph.D in chemical engineering in 1945, when he joined the American-owned Esso Petroleum as a technical assistant at its Fawley refinery. Eleven years later he transferred to London as General Manager (Refining). In 1968 he became managing director. For eight years he was Esso's chairman and chief executive, retiring in 1980 at the age of 58.

Pearce had become a member of the Organising Committee for British Aerospace while still chairman of Esso. That role involved preparing the industry for nationalisation (a measure that passed the House of Commons by a single vote). As BAe's chairman (from April 1980), Pearce's task was the opposite – preparing the company for privatisation. The first State asset to be privatised, BAe has been a success on every financial count. The shares, offered at 150p in 1981, shot up to 405p in 1984 and 490p the next year, when the government sold its remaining stake in the company.

The performance of the shares, which sold at over 660p in early 1987, has been underpinned by a solid profit record since 1982, when the com-pany made a small loss after tax. As sales rose from just over £2 billion in that year to £2.65 billion in 1985, pre-tax profits improved to £156 million, two and a half times the highest figure before privatisation. BAe's private life has had its share of excitement. Thorn-EMI made a takeover bid which was rejected by BAe, and further complicated when the General Electric Company intervened. In the event, BAe stayed independent.

Since first winning that independence, the company has changed its product mix substantially. Military aircraft, which dominated sales in 1981, have grown, but guided weapon and electronic systems work has expanded more rapidly to become almost as large. Civil aircraft business has also grown substantially. Much of BAe's workload is the fruit of collaboration with partners overseas. On the military side, the European Fighter Aircraft involves four national partners, with Britain (one-third) getting the largest share. Here BAe is building on the successful three-way collaboration on the Tornado, which has been the basis for major overseas orders.

Defence collaboration is also important to BAe's missile business, although its own programmes for the RAF and the Navy are the backbone of sales which totalled £922 million in 1985. Over a third of that output was exported. On military aircraft and support services, the export ratio was twice as high: £616 million exported out of sales worth £945 million. Both businesses were highly profitable, with trading profits of £113 million and £136 million respectively. Space projects accounted for £129 million of sales, three-quarters exported.

The most spectacular overseas sales performance, that in civil aircraft, was not matched by profits. In 1985, BAe lost nearly £5 million on its £650 million of sales, of which all but £48 million went abroad. Again, collaboration is crucial. Since Britain's belated entry into the Airbus contract, winning the work on the wings, BAe has become a key member of the consortium. The company has 25 per cent of the work on the new A320 version, which has been outstandingly successful in gaining orders; the Airbus saga has, however, depended heavily on government funding, much to American annoyance.

BAe's own aircraft, like the small 146 jetliner and the 125 executive jet, are continuing to sell. However, the future in the civil market plainly rests on European collaboration – and on continuing success in selling its results into the US market.

Do you think industry is more or less efficient now?

In my view far and away the vast majority of British industry is much more efficient, much more productive, than it was say five or six years ago. One cannot say that for all industry – there's always the bad actor – but in going round talking to people in other industries where an awful lot of work has gone in, people are undoubtedly more efficient.

What do you think has changed to bring that about?

First of all, the realisation that you cannot depend entirely upon the home market. The British market is too small. Therefore you've got to be international, you've got to be competitive. The only way to be competitive is to be more efficient. There has also been a degree of stability, as far as the government is concerned. We've not had the problems of being worried as to whether one day we're going to be nationalised, and the next day we're going to be denationalised, which has very, very serious impacts on investment. Because people have been able to see a degree of stability they have been able to invest consistently.

If one looks at our competitors like Japan, like Germany, like the United States, you do find that they have an industrial policy which is consistent over many years, and that's really what industry is all about. We are long-term investors, we cannot do anything on a short-term basis except in some of the very small companies. Consistency of government policy and the determination to do things have been the two key factors.

Is the way people analyse and tackle markets getting better?

The CBI recently did a study of the better and the not-so-good companies in this country. They found that the better companies, first of all, had a much stronger financial and cost control discipline, which is back to efficiency. Secondly, they paid much more attention to the market, the customer; and thirdly, they paid more attention to their employees. If you did those three things then you could really compete.

What do you think are the main obstacles to further progress?

One of the main obstacles is the fact that industry is not seen as being particularly important in this country. It's not seen as being particularly important at some of the political levels. I think that is bad for the country. The feeling in our educational system is such that you don't train people to go into industry. The result is that you get a very limited intake, and a lot of the better brains don't want to go into industry. As a result you find that people in relatively small jobs in the City, particularly in the merchant banks, will probably get salaries two or three times as high as very senior people in industry. Our culture is not really industry-orientated – yet we started the Industrial Revolution. And in 1986 the UK had to have an Industry Year. The Germans don't have one, the Japanese don't need one. We do! It's very much a cultural problem.

Is it a question, do you think, of not having enough potential entrants to choose from, or is it also a shortage of specialisms?

Because of the cultural situation, because of our educational system and the pressures put upon it, the number of people who are going into the technical subjects has in fact been dropping. Therefore there is a shortage. And that is where we have to start, because if we don't teach our children, if we don't train them to go into these types of subjects, then the pool of talent for recruitment for industry is bound to be much smaller.

How has your attitude to your markets changed?

One of the first things that we've had to do is pay much more attention to the market, what the market is for our products. As I've said, the British market is too small; you've got to go international. If one goes back into the Sixties, some of the aircraft built by the British companies were specifically aimed at people like BOAC and nobody else. The Trident is a classic example: it was built for a British customer, and that British customer didn't want to take very many, so it was not a good idea.

Now, if you're going for an international market, you've got to spend a lot of money. Hopefully, you can get involved with people who will bring a market with them, which is one of the great advantages of being part of Airbus Industrie in the civil aircraft market. It's one of the reasons that we are actually involved in the joint programme for Tornado with the Germans and the Italians. It's the reason why, for the European Fighter Aircraft, we're joining with the Germans and the Italians and the Spanish. They will bring a market and that enables us to then compete in the export market against the Americans. You have to recognise the Americans have a massive home market which is virtually a highly protected captive market. All their development costs are paid for by the American government, and everything else is incremental cost. We have to do something similar, basically through partnerships, which have to be European. Now that doesn't mean to say you should not have partnerships with Americans. It depends; it must be market driven. And if you take the co-operative arrangements we have with McDonnell-Douglas for the Harrier, the big market for the Harrier is the United States Marine Corps. Now to get into that we had to have a partnership with an American company, and it is very successful. Similarly, with the Hawk for the US Navy we had to have an American partner to get into the American market, so we went with an American company.

Do you think there is still too much reliance on government patronage? Is it something that can be avoided more in the future?

This depends upon how the rest of the world is going to behave. Getting into any of these projects – new fighter aircraft, the new big civil aircraft – costs an awful lot of money, and in a competitive world. Let's take the situation in Europe. You have Aérospatiale, which is a nationalised company and therefore it is part of the French policy that it should be successful. Result: a lot of help from the French government. You have something which is not the same but is somewhat comparable in Germany, a lot of help from central government. And those are the people with whom we compete. In a perfect world you would not require any help from government at all, but the fact is we haven't got a perfect world and it's not changing for the better all that fast.

Would it be true to say that the history of British governments has been much less firmly committed to keeping an aerospace industry going?

There's been a very high degree of inconsistency of policy. When you recognise that the life of a government is, say, four or five years and you recognise that it takes about eight years to develop an aircraft and get it actually flying, and then you expect it to have a twenty-five-year life, there's a total inconsistency of time here. And in this country we do have governments which swing from one extreme to the other. You don't see that same degree of swing in any of the other countries. So I'm afraid the political inconsistency is a major problem for manufacturing industry in the aerospace industry. But it's also true in a lot of other industries. The real problem is the Treasury. The Treasury happens to operate on a one-year basis, and our twenty-five-year programme is something that is very difficult to bridge. You'll find this with many industrialists, that the problem area is with the system the Treasury operates, a system which is inconsistent with industry.

There have been notable private ventures, like your own BAe 146 local feeder airliner. Do you see any more such projects?

I think there will be a very limited number of them, very limited indeed. In fact the 146 is not just the Brits, because we have got into risk-sharing involvements with the Americans and also the Swedes. But we take the majority of the bill there, and there is a limitation to that. Of course, the other problem that we face is a recognition that we have got to move up-market, because if you're in the high-volume lower quality market, other countries like Taiwan and Korea are ready to come in and take it over. We have to move up-market just as Jaguar has done with its cars, and that is expensive. But the number of projects in which we can do it on our own is very, very small.

Will you be tackling the main-line markets head-on or will you focus more finely, as you have done with the 146?

Some projects will be specifically aimed. The 146, the one we're doing ourselves, is basically aimed at a slot in the market and there aren't too many other people wanting to get into it. Some of the new Airbus proposals will be in competition with the Boeing 747. And that's going to be a tough one, no question about that, because Boeing has a monopoly and they're making some money on that aircraft now. There was a long time when they didn't, but they kept their courage and they kept going. We won't exactly be tackling Boeing head-on, but we won't be far off.

Looking at British Aerospace, what do you see as your unique strengths?

The unique strength we have is the very high skill level of our people. We have some absolutely first-class people who know exactly how to put an aircraft together, who know exactly how to design and do all those things, so I suppose it must be the technical resources which we have in people – it's the brain power – and my worry is that they will not be replaced, because we're not producing enough people with the technical skills out of our schools and universities; that's the worry for the future. Or alternatively, if a major project were to be cancelled, what's going to happen to those fellows? Are they going to succumb to what happened in the Sixties, the brain drain, and go across and work for Boeing and people like that? Our real strength is our brain power, and we had better make sure we keep replacing it and that we also keep it in this country.

Everything you say seems to suggest that projects in the future are most likely to see British Aerospace in partnership, whether it's on government-funded military aircraft or tackling the civil market?

For big projects, yes. I don't think there's any question in my mind that the market-driven requirement, the finance requirement for big projects, will force companies into partnerships. When we come to the smaller aspects of our company – if you like, some of the missile areas and things like that, where you are not talking anywhere near as much investment money, and where the product is relatively cheap and so you can sell it much more easily – then, no, I think some of them can be done individually. But the very big ones, yes, I think it's got to be partnerships.

SIR FRANCIS TOMBS, CHAIRMAN, ROLLS-ROYCE

Sir Francis Tombs was appointed chairman of Rolls-Royce in 1985 at a crucial time for the national aero-engine manufacturer. His task was to oversee the preparations for its relaunch into the private sector, while consolidating the company's long climb back to profitability, shaking off for ever the memory of the celebrated bankruptcy of 1971. Vital to both parts of Tombs' job is the need to convince potential investors that Rolls-Royce can continue to hold its own in world markets.

Tombs, 62, is no stranger to challenges. Knighted in 1978, he made a great name for himself as a turnaround specialist. In the past six years, he has twice been called upon to rescue former big blue-chips in mature industries. From 1981–3, as chairman, he masterminded the comeback of Weir, the Scottish engineering group. From 1982, he has been chairman of another engineering business, Turner & Newall – which also brought him the chair of AE, T&N's first major acquisition since its own highly effective turnaround.

Born in Staffordshire, Tombs began his working life in 1939 as a fifteen-year-old apprentice at the General Electric Company at Witton, where he stayed until the end of the war. Although his honours degree is a BSc in economics from London University, his career has been founded on technology, which has brought him several honorary degrees. He has been largely involved with electricity supply and manufacturing (returning to

GEC in 1958 to run its Erith heavy electrical plant for nine years). He became chairman of the Electricity Council for England and Wales from 1977–80, after previously rising to the chair of the South of Scotland Electricity Board. He is also a director of merchant bankers N.M. Rothschild & Sons (since 1981) and of Shell UK (since 1983).

Tombs' experience, especially at the Weir Group and Turner & Newall, was eminently suitable for Rolls-Royce. When he became chairman (after being a director for three years) it had already been much changed since the disastrous events of 1971. The painful process of turnaround has seen employee numbers halved in fifteen years, R & D refocused, sales techniques strengthened, and collaborations begun with major foreign competitors, including the US rivals GE and Pratt & Whitney. Joint ventures have become the only way forward in an industry where the development of a new product costs upwards of £1 billion. In 1985 Rolls-Royce invested some £234 billion in R & D (of which £134 million came from the government), a huge sum which, all the same, falls well short of allowing Rolls-Royce to go it alone in the major new developments.

Privatised or not, an independent UK engine-maker could not have succeeded without the government's help. But the company's efforts have paid off sufficiently to make privatisation perfectly feasible. Pre-tax profits reached £24 million in 1984, £81 million in 1985 and £120 million in 1986, on turnover of £1.8 billion. The order-book is now looking better than ever, but the future is dominated by the importance of continuing innovation in a broad range of products in the search for new markets. The current goal, which would give that all-important competitive edge, is to obtain vastly improved fuel consumption (as much as 25 per cent) from the coming generation of engines.

What direction has Rolls-Royce been taking in the Eighties?

It's been moving quite positively towards profitability, principally by rationalisation in the workforce and by capital investment in both manufacturing machine tools and in computer-aided design and computer control of those tools. It has also put a lot of effort into what we call modular development, that is, taking existing engines and adding together the bits, building-blocks if you like, rather than developing brand-new engines.

Your company's old independence, doing everything itself and on its own, appears to be a thing of the past, doesn't it?

Rolls-Royce is now a strong outfit in its own right, in profitability and in technical terms. We've had for many years quite a wide network of collaborations throughout the world. We collaborate with manufacturers in America, Germany, France, Spain, Italy, Japan and other countries, and we do that for a variety of reasons. One is to share technical risk, another very important one is to gain access to markets. It's becoming obvious to all of the three main engine-makers (the three companies with total engine capability are Pratt & Whitney of America, General Electric of America and Rolls-Royce) that a brand-new engine from the drawing board is unlikely to be launched by any single maker, because of the sheer cost. Therefore the importance of collaboration in relation to new engines will grow.

But it mustn't be thought that this leads to an easy or cosy life, because collaborations tend to be clearly defined in scope and application. They are entered into for the reasons I've mentioned – sharing technical risk and market access – and in areas where the collaborations don't apply we compete with each other with great ferocity.

How do you see demand for civil aircraft in the next ten to fifteen years?

We've been through a period of pretty unprofitable airlines continuing to run aircraft irrespective of things like fuel economy or sometimes even convenience. Therefore we have an ageing fleet throughout the world which will require replacement. Added to that, there is a modest growth in air travel, and we see the market for new aircraft as quite strong between now and the end of the century.

It's surprising to learn that even a large, big-thinking American corporation cannot afford to develop a major engine. Is this really so?

Yes. The big example of that is International Aero Engines, which has developed the V-2500 engine for the Airbus 320, which is selling very well. That's being built by a five-nation group; Pratt & Whitney owns 30 per cent of IAE, Rolls-Royce owns 30 per cent and the remaining 40 per cent is divided between Germany, Italy and Japan. That is a good example of a brand-new engine for a particular purpose, where the development cost was too great for Rolls-Royce alone and too great for Pratt & Whitney alone. The other three countries don't have the capability to develop such an engine on their own, anyway; they joined in to make parts and to provide important market access.

How much independence can you still have side-by-side with the collaboration? The BA project, for instance, seems to contradict that intent to go into collaboration.

First we have complete independence; we can design and develop a complete engine and we continue to do that, in what I described earlier as a 'modular' way – taking bits of existing engines, perhaps improving parts and adding them to other bits of existing engines. This is a fairly economical way of developing engines for new applications, and we will continue to do that. And so we shall remain totally independent, with a full engine capability in that sense.

In the case of the British Airways order, in which you mean the General Electric collaboration, we took a share in their large engine, the 6F6-8C, and they took a share in our medium-sized engine, the 535, which powers the Boeing 757. That was because neither of us had an engine in that range. There was always an overlap between our 524 and the 6-80C, and the agreement envisaged that we would continue to develop our engine as far as we could. Indeed in February we signed an agreement with General Electric that we would offer the developed 524 engine for the British Airways order, for which General Electric were also offering their 6-80C, but at the *lower* end of its range. So competition at the overlap point was always envisaged, and it need not preclude collaboration in the *higher* thrust-range of the 6-80C, where we don't have a competing engine.

Rolls-Royce is relatively small compared to its past and compared with Pratt & Whitney and General Electric. What special strengths do you rely on to stay in the race, to stop people saying it's time to squeeze Rolls-Royce right out of business?

First, it's not all that much smaller in output; it's considerably smaller now in manpower and it shares that situation with a lot of British industry. A lot of British industry was heavily overmanned in productivity terms, and so we slimmed in the same way as much other industry has. We're a very much more powerful company than in the Sixties because we have a wider stable of engines, a much wider market and a much more solid technology base.

Those are three very great strengths that make me quite confident about the future of Rolls. We are smaller than our two competitors but we're not that much smaller in terms of the engines we can offer and the recent successes we've had. We have sold a lot of engines, for example, to the 747s recently, far more than our size would suggest. The real difference between us and them is that they are parts of much larger corporations, and we're a stand-alone engine-maker. Now, that has advantages and disadvantages. The advantage is that it focuses our mind, we have to be very good at our job, we've got nobody else to pick up our tab. The general belief is that the diversity of Pratt & Whitney inside United Technologies and General Electric inside the large US General Electric gives them strength against adverse cycles. I think that can be exaggerated. Both those large conglomerates expect each part of their outfits to be profitable and don't tolerate poor performance, so that in a real sense their engine divisions compete as separate entities with Rolls-Royce, and are not all that different in size from us. I would add that when we make what comparisons we can on profitability and productivity, we're not too dissatisfied.

At one time Rolls-Royce was a rather expensive company to buy an engine from, rather production and technology-led and perhaps not so good at marketing. Is that something you've looked at?

Aircraft engines are expensive pieces of equipment, of course – a great consolation to those who travel in aeroplanes, because we wouldn't like them cheap and unreliable. It is a very demanding application; an aircraft has to stay up, has to defy gravity and has to fly for long periods. Reliability is a very important part of the deal. We are competitive with both General Electric and Pratt & Whitney, and we compete with them throughout the world.

About three-quarters of our output goes abroad, so we're not in any way cushioned by our home base, either military or civil. We have to live in a competitive world and we find it not too difficult to do so. I would say that in productivity terms we compare well with our competitors. That's not to say I'm satisfied; we have to improve and become much better than our competitors and secure a bigger market share.

Do you get beaten on price very much?

Occasionally, because sometimes pride is involved and people give engines away, or so it seems to us, and if the price becomes ridiculous we don't pursue it. There is a price which sometimes suppliers will quote to retain a valued customer, or for the sake of the spares business.

Are you satisfied with the amount of money you have available to spend, wherever it comes from, for research and development?

Yes. We spend about £250 million a year on total development, military and civil, and we find about half of that from our own resources and the other half comes from defence agencies – for example the European Fighter is European-funded; the Ministry of Defence funds their particular aircraft, the Department of Industry provides launch-aid for new engines and investment in particular projects. We would expect that to continue. We think that the overall investment in R & D is comparable with that of our competitors – it has to be. But we think that we are, for a variety of reasons, particularly efficient at the way in which we use it. We spend a lot of time looking at the way in which we control R & D expenditure and the way in which we can simplify – for example, by using computer modelling instead of running actual engines, because that's a lot cheaper and faster, and we've been quite successful in those areas.

What particular problems have you got to crack in the next five years?

The big problem is to broaden our market base further, to sell more effectively in the United States, where we have had a number of quite remarkable successes recently in the civil and military area. It's a country of considerable promise where we intend to expand.

Could the other two makers grow at your expense?

We've been increasing our market share in a number of areas and that can only be at the expense of the other two suppliers. I wouldn't wish to pretend this has been particularly dramatic, but certainly we've not suffered from competition. I think that they have both come to live with us, they both recognise that we have areas of the world, and areas of expertise that make us a solid and continuous competitor. I don't think that there have been any signs of either of them trying to drive us out of the market, and indeed the anti-trust legislation in the United States would make that very difficult. But more important is the fact that our sheer capability, and our customer base, would make it impossible.

From your experience of quite a range of industries, in the engineering sector particularly, what changes have you detected in the way business has been run?

I think a very much more professional approach to management, a recognition that working capital is important and that international productivity comparisons and wage rates are also important. We've unhappily had a tradition in this country, post-war, of paying relatively low wages and employing too many man-hours to make a product, and we've also been careless with the resources used within the company, principally working capital. I think all those things have changed, but I think also the labour and government climates have changed, and there's now a much greater recognition on the part of trade unions and government that we have to compete in the outside world. We don't live in a protected cocoon, which I think was the belief for some decades.

Why did it take so long for some of these things to sink in?

I think successive governments of all colours, post-war, have tried to pretend that we can live in isolation from the world and have been slow to realise that this is not the case. I think successive trade-union leaders have shared that belief that they can take a larger slice of the cake from somewhere, and somebody else will pay for it. And I think managements have not been sufficiently aware of the need to compete in the world at large, protected by our home market, protected by a belief that somehow things will come right. In a typical British way we've had to wait for things to get pretty bad before starting to adjust. That's regrettable. I think all three political parties share the blame, and the result is the very large unemployment we see today. If we had recognised the obvious facts twenty years ago, we could have avoided today's traumas.

Do you see any prospect of the slide in our share of the world market being arrested?

It won't be easy, and we have to face the fact that the newly industrialised countries are extremely aggressive, and have the principal advantages of people who work very long hours in a very conscientious and very determined way, for low wages and with a very cheap social infrastructure. The cards are stacked against us, so we have to use ingenuity at the technical forefront, and the same qualities that the newly industrialised countries use – determination, conscientiousness, commitment to quality – in order to compete with them. It's going to be very hard to grow our market share, but we need to do so in order to employ our population.

If you look in cold economic terms, we are a country with a very high standard of living, a very high standard of overhead expenditure in terms of government and social expenditure, and not that clever a productivity record. And we are trying to compete increasingly with countries who are much better off in all those respects than we are. We are gradually improving, but we need to do it much more rapidly.

What do you see as the main difficulties that still exist in running an industry?

The principal difficulty which the country has experienced post-war, and which may lie in the future, is the governmental system we enjoy, which has great advantages but is also adversarial. The two principal parties tend to contradict whatever has happened in the previous administration, to go back, almost as a matter of principle, on any changes made. That imposes tremendous uncertainty on industry. It makes it very difficult to plan, very difficult to have confidence. The most crying need is for a common agreement between the parties on the need for wealth creation before wealth spending.

Can you in Rolls-Royce, or indeed in any of the companies you've been associated with, get the people you want?

In general, the principal shortage is of graduate engineers and craftsmen, and a lot of companies are suffering from that. Rolls-Royce has a name which makes people want to work for them. It has quality and challenge. It looks very good on an application form to have worked for Rolls-Royce, and so on the whole we are privileged, we can get the people we want. Much of British industry, however, can't. The skill shortages, both at the craft level and the graduate level, are extremely serious. That's another huge problem Britain faces.

We are not producing from the schools the number of children taught numerate skills, by which I mean mathematics and physics particularly, who go on to universities and polytechnics. We're not producing the number of children who want to work in industry because of our cultural hang-up since the Victorian era. These are problems that successive governments have failed to address and the present government is only beginning to address.

You are also chairman of Turner & Newall, best known for motor components. The UK motor industry has shrunk to about half its former output – has that been a bad blow?

It's obviously been a short-term blow, because if you get used to depending on a home customer, adjustment is difficult. But the resulting need to go overseas, to make products that command the respect of Germans, Italians, French and Americans, is a very good discipline. We're going to have to compete increasingly, as a country, in the world marketplace, and the decline in the UK automotive industry has made companies like Turner & Newall, with its Ferodo brake-pads and Cooper's filters, go abroad and expand their markets beyond a purely UK base. That's probably the way in which British industry has to go. It has to forget the comfortable home base, sometimes with over-engineered standards, and compete on an open market with the world's industries. And we can do it.

Do you find there's a very big 'not-made-here' barrier in Europe or in the United States?

Yes, as there is in this country. You just have to work at that, and one way of doing it is to have a presence in the country, have a plant in the country as well as exporting to it. We do it in Turner & Newall in America, in France, in Germany and Italy. We have plants there and we also export to those countries; and it's probably the way we expect foreigners to behave when they're selling here. You can't just have an open door, to supply everything from outside. Every country is interested in employment. What you can do is establish sufficient presence to be regarded as a respectable member of the local community, and then export to them as well.

This seems to be one of the differences in attitude – ten years ago people didn't seem willing to make the investment to establish a presence. Would that be true?

Ten years ago, perhaps a little more, we were very self-satisfied, very committed to the cushy home market. We tended to design things for the home market at all levels of industry that the rest of the world didn't want – sometimes too expensive, sometimes just different. I think that has changed. We've become very much more international, very much more ready to manufacture elsewhere, as well as at home. This is sometimes represented as 'exporting jobs'. It's not. It's providing an opportunity for exporting on an acceptable basis to other countries.

THE ELECTRONIC SUNRISE

SIR JOHN CLARK, CHAIRMAN, PLESSEY
SIR GRAHAM WILKINS, CHAIRMAN, THORN-EMI
ROGER FOSTER, CHIEF EXECUTIVE, APRICOT COMPUTERS
PETER BONFIELD, CHAIRMAN, ICL

SIR JOHN CLARK, CHAIRMAN, PLESSEY

Alone among the seventeen top executives interviewed, Sir John Clark has a family link with his company. Plessey was the creation of a forceful entrepreneur named Allen Clark (who, like his son, was knighted). On his father's death in 1962, John Clark and his brother Michael took over the direction of the company. Their appointment was opposed by some members of the board, partly on the grounds of their youth – John Clark was 36 at the time. But subsequent developments have confirmed that he is a forceful manager in his father's mould, but with a marked willingness to develop and change the company and its strategy as needed.

In consequence, Plessey bears very little relationship to the firm Clark joined in 1949, as assistant to the general manager of Plessey International. After Cambridge, Clark had served with the Navy Volunteer Reserve in the war. His first industrial experience was with Metropolitan-Vickers (then a famous school for future engineers) and Ford Motor (which became equally famous for producing managers). Promoted to the Plessey board in 1953, Clark was general manager of the components group before his appointment as managing director in 1962.

Plessey had made its reputation, and Sir Allen's fortune, by supplying components, principally to the radio and aircraft industries. Today, largely as a result of his son's strategy, Plessey is a diversified electronics group whose main strength is in telecommunications – which accounted for around half of the company's £1.46 billion turnover and £162.5 million operating profit in 1985–6. Electronic systems and equipment are the next largest, accounting for another £618 million of sales (35.5 per cent), but much less (a quarter) of the profit.

In aerospace and engineering, the position is reversed: only 8.3 per cent of sales at £120.7 million, but 15.6 per cent of profit. The company also has a large business in micro-electronics and components (£161.3 million), while its fifth major activity is computer peripherals. This concentration on well-developed areas of corporate strength has been a relatively recent development. Plessey has been notable for continual evolution as the technology and markets have developed – not just in Britain, but in the world.

The group already derives 29 per cent of its turnover from outside the UK, but Clark has been placing great emphasis on the necessity to build up its international presence – above all, in the US and in telecommunications. The purchase of Stromberg–Carlson, the last available US independent manufacturer of public telephone exchanges, is thus crucial to Plessey's ambitions overseas; just as the System X exchange developed for British Telecom, for which Plessey is the lead supplier, is vital for the future of the company's largest business.

System X, and its slow start in export markets, have been a subject of controversy – and controversy has never been far away from Plessey. But Clark has time and again shown himself to be a robust and resilient manager with a strong sense of priorities and the ability to earn a consistently high return on capital – over the last seven years, never less than 22.6 per cent before tax and interest and as high as 34 per cent. In that period, turnover has doubled, while pre-tax profits have come close to trebling. Given the difficulties in many sectors of electronics, Plessey's longer-term performance, despite the three-year profits plateau to 1985–6, reflects the continuous investment in technology and in management quality on which Clark has based his ambitions.

How has Plessey changed during the Eighties?

Changes have taken place, not just in the Eighties, but over the last twenty years. We had a very, very wide range of products, and it became apparent that, in the main, most of those products either were, or would become, international in character. The competition is international, and in some cases the companies in the specialist product fields were considerably larger than ourselves. We therefore decided that we needed to concentrate on a number of core businesses. This we did by the selection of public telephone switching, private telephone switching and associated office automation, defence electronics in the broadest sense of the word, and the supporting technologies of semi-conductors – the silicon chip. Now, that meant that over time we had to divest ourselves, in the main by sale of companies, of those things that did not fit into that essential core selection.

What's the aim of this policy of concentrating on fewer and more-specialised product lines?

The objective is to get to a position on what we call the 'experience curve' that enables us to invest in people, in product and in plant, on a scale comparable to that of the competition. But again this is specialist investment – vertical investment in a product or product family, rather than horizontal investment.

Have there been any other aspects of managing the business where you've had to sort out problems? People talk a lot about productivity, about investment, about developing markets and so on.

In this company, we like to divide the job of management between what the Americans call 'mowing' and 'growing'. That means you've got to have a staff that is essentially directing its time and energy in two directions. First, to make sure that the day-to-day operations of the company are being adequately performed – like getting orders in, making sure that development programmes are kept up to date, and getting production out of the door on time to meet customers' needs. In the second place, you need to have an organisation *in situ* that is going to secure the future of the company. In that respect we have spent a great deal of time on forward planning, both product and market.

We now have a well-developed planning system that is an amalgam of, initially, the Boston Consulting Group approach; then the Texas Instruments OST system, which stands for the setting of objectives, strategies and tactics; and finally the approach of General Electric of America, which is essentially based on establishing your 'strategic business units'; to simplify it, you establish what are the businesses that you really think you are in, by doing an effective competitive analysis.

You are now very strong in specialised defence and electronics, in switching and telecommunications, in radar. How do you see the world markets ahead of you?

In the mainstream defence electronic industries, we believe that we've got a strong enough base to maintain ourselves in a technical lead against competition. Likewise, we are in a good position in semi-conductors and also in private switching. We freely admit that we would wish to be larger in public switching, that's what we call telephone main exchanges. And of course this is one of the main reasons why we bought our company in America which is involved in this field.

There seem to be three possible problems in that area. One presumably is that System X, as it is now, is a UK product; two, the office automation area, where you could use switching technology, is a very tough one to get into; the American company you have acquired isn't exactly a market leader in the US telecommunications sector.

Firstly, I can't accept your implied observation that System X is purely for the UK market. The contrary is the case. It is, in our belief, one of the most modern telephone switching systems in the world today. It is quite capable of being tailored to meet the needs of any international telephone network, and now that we've got a well-established installed base in the United Kingdom our expectations for the development of exports for System X appear to be more and more promising with the passage of time.

Your second question relates to office information systems. It's an extra-ordinary thing that the companies in computers have not been wildly successful in getting into private telephone exchanges; and likewise, com-panies in private telephone exchanges have not, to date, been particularly successful in computers. However, if you take the private telephone exchange, we are now offering extremely complex systems that enable the customer to handle voice data and video signals. We're far from sure that there is a need for a private telephone switching company to be in the computer business at all. We think that has yet to be shown.

Turning to your third point, our American company, Stromberg-Carlson, has been an established supplier to the independent telephone companies in the United States for some forty years or more, maybe. The AT&T company has now been broken up, from that were spun off seven major Bell Telephone operating companies. Each one of these is very nearly as large as British Telecom in its own right. The fact is that, on the basis of the existing products in this relatively small company, we are able to address something like 70 per cent of the total market requirement for all telephone companies in North America. Now, one has to go through an elaborate process of testing; I think it's fair and truthful to say that Stromberg-Carlson has got further to date in passing Phase 1 of the Bell Telephone companies' test procedures, and is a very long way down the road in passing the tests for Phase 2. That puts us effectively in pole posi-tion. So we take the view that our American company is facing a most exciting future.

So this opens to you a market potential many times greater than the one you have here?

Absolutely. The battle that's on really is the battle to become a third supplier, or possibly even a fourth supplier, for these telephone companies. And there is, of course, no guarantee that their existing suppliers will necessarily be able to maintain the position that they've enjoyed to date. We would hope to erode the market shares of established and existing suppliers.

How will you carve up the work, and the development programmes, between the Plessey home companies and Stromberg-Carlson?

The first major point to understand here is that, once you've established a customer base in public telephone switching, that customer does not wish to see the basic system or systems he's adopted changed. He wants, and is looking for, continuity of supply over a long time-period, and we understand this completely and accept it. Integration is a desirable thing, because integration naturally should save money and make your development spending and other investments cost-effective. And, of course, there is quite a degree of commonality in components and in sub-systems, as between the switching systems required for the North American market and for the rest of the world. It is in these areas that we are assessing the extent to which we can benefit by getting our engineers to work more closely together.

How important do you think acquisition now is for a company like yourselves tackling international markets. Is it a vital factor?

You have to realise that, as far as Europe is concerned, the public sector – which includes telecommunications, electricity, gas, coal and of course defence – has in no way been liberalised so far to any appreciable degree. The member states of the Community have continued to protect these basic industries, and it's only now that we're beginning to see some of these barriers being broken down. First, of course, the administrations must develop common network standards so that the various manufacturing companies can address those networks. Beyond that, how far you will be required to manufacture locally, or will be able to deal in direct export business, is presently a matter of conjecture because that depends on various government policies.

So this means that it's likely the European market can only be tackled on a co-operative or acquisition basis?

I believe so, as things stand at the present moment. But Europe has to be regarded as a large and attractive market, for the very reason that the European Economic Community was set up in the first place. The barriers will have to be broken down because, in the long term, Europe must compete. If Europe maintains a separation of national interests then it will never be in a position to capitalise on its buying power or purchasing power. Of course, one of the most significant and important commodities that any government has, in order to make its industries effective, is its own public purchasing power; and its own public purchasing policies are therefore quite vital to the development of its indigenous industries.

Does your relative smallness as a company, in international terms, make you vulnerable in terms of product and market development?

I don't think so, because, as I said earlier, we decided to specialise around what I've called our core business. I am relatively satisfied that our position in three of those core businesses is secure; but naturally we are looking to the fourth – the field of public switching – to become larger.

Are there any aspects of your business in which you are big in world terms?

Believe it or not, in our own chosen field of silicon componentry, where we are in what they call the 'custom-design' business, we are probably within the first half-dozen in the world, and are looking to a very, very considerable expansion in this field over the next five years. In private switching, likewise, we are now a very considerable force. On defence, if you take individual product areas, I would think that in military radio sets, in radar, in naval warfare, we have as good a position as any of our competitors.

Do you see any particular issues confronting the British electronics industry as a whole in the next five or ten years – things it must sort out strategically?

You can't really generalise about the electronics industry. You've got to look at consumer electronics and divide that from professional electronics, and then, of course, you've got computers, you've got telcommunications and so on. And each of these sectors has its own problems. But, without any doubt, the generalisation that *is* applicable to them all – and particularly today to consumer electronics – is that in international terms we have a very, very long way to go as against, say, the Japanese.

We've seen in the United Kingdom what the Boston Consulting Group called the demise of the British motorcycle industry, many years ago now. We've seen the demise of the radio industry. We've seen the demise of the audio industry. We've seen a massive penetration by the Japanese of the television industry. At one time we had up to a dozen, if not more, manufacturers of televisions in the UK. Today we're down to a bare handful, and unless not only the electronics industry, but British industry at large, wakes up to the character of international competition, the nature of it and the size of it, then there's no future for British manufacturing industry.

I think that governments have an enormous responsibility here, to the extent that they have the power through their public procurement policies to make sure that the indigenous British industry isn't damaged through policies like the pursuit of inward investment. You can have a situation where your indigenous industry is investing a great deal of its own resource into a given product area, and yet your inward investor is simply an assembler of goods, and he's not therefore competing on equal terms in any shape or form with the British manufacturing company. The inward investor, in almost every case, is no more or less than a satellite factory of a foreign country, but the consequence of bringing more competition into the UK – where probably a lot of competition exists already – doesn't make the cake any larger, it just spreads it more widely and more thinly. In the event, it's almost bound to damage your indigenous British manufacturing company.

What do you see as the main obstacles to progress, the main difficulties in running a company in Britain?

I don't think there are any external forces that are working to the detriment of British industry, as far as I'm concerned. I would regard the problems with this company – aside from these areas of government policy that I've just touched on – as problems that need to be dealt with by its management, and I would make the same point for the rest of British industry. Napoleon had a great adage; he said there's no such thing as a bad soldier, only a bad officer, and I think that comment applies as well today as it did then – and certainly to British industry.

Why do you think it took so long for British industry to respond to problems that had become so evident?

There was, and probably still is, a great lack of professionalism of management in British industry. I agree with you entirely that the signs have been on the wall for years. This issue of competitive analysis, based on an identification of what is called the 'strategic business unit', is something that's been taught in business schools for the better part of twenty years, in one form or another. Some companies saw the need to go into strategic planning and adjust their policies and their investment accordingly. Others didn't, and are suffering very badly today. Whether they can survive the course is a matter of conjecture.

How do you define the strategic business unit?

A strategic business unit is essentially based on the nature and character of competition. If you have competitors that are much larger than you, you have a problem because that competitor will probably have much better management, both in depth and in personality. He will almost certainly have a greater ability to invest, because he will be generating more money than you. And at that point you will have to take a decision as to whether you can get somewhere on what is called the experience curve, by matching his management competence and his investment characteristics – or whether you are going to get out of the business. If you decide that you can stay in, you can either do this by indigenous growth and investment, if you can find it, or by acquisition. But it is a strategic decision that has to be taken in one form or another.

Would you say that it's a very simple formula, but one which a lot of people have failed to apply?

That is absolutely correct.

SIR GRAHAM WILKINS, CHAIRMAN, THORN-EMI

Sir Graham Wilkins is one of the rare British industrialists who has moved from the summit of one great company to another. At Beecham, where he was chairman and chief executive until mid-1984 (retiring at 60), Sir Graham won a famous reputation for his work in building up the ethical pharmaceuticals business. Founded on a family of synthetic penicillins, this side of Beechams had become the main engine driving the group forward.

Wilkins had, however, also served in the consumer products sections of the company in a career that began in 1945. He became executive vice-chairman in 1974 and took over the chair the next year, as the second man in succession to the legendary H.G. Lazell, the creator of the post-war company. Since leaving Beechams, Wilkins has taken on a number of positions. Currently, he is chairman of the Review Body of Doctors' and Dentists' Remuneration, president of the Advertising Association, and a non-executive director of Hill Samuel amongst others.

He was also non-executive at Thorn-EMI (as deputy chairman) before becoming chairman and chief executive at a crucial moment in the company's history. Knighted in 1980, Wilkins is a West Countryman whose BSc comes from Exeter. Like H.G. Lazell, who was known as Leslie, Graham John Wilkins is not known by either of his given names: he is called Bob. The problems he found at Thorn-EMI were very different from those at Beecham. Although both companies had grown phenomenally post-war under dominant leaders, Lazell was a professional manager, while Sir Jules Thorn was an inspirational entrepreneur. Where Beechams had grown mostly by organic means, Thorn-EMI (as the hyphenated name implies) is the product of several large mergers – some under Sir Jules (especially in the TV rentals business, where the group is the largest force), some under his successors.

The latter-day acquisitions, in particular, created as many problems as they solved. The company wasn't helped in tackling these problems by the inadequate managerial inheritance from the days of the founder's autocratic rule. The result was a crisis of confidence and a total reversal of growth in profits: in the year to end-March 1986 the company earned £44 million after tax on £3.3 billion of sales. That was only half the profit earned in 1979–80, when sales were 50 per cent lower.

Plainly, drastic action was required. The company has been restructured into four main business sectors after disposals which brought in more than £200 million and helped to reduce a heavy burden of debt (including the sale of the cinema interests brought in with EMI). The divisions are the £885 million Rental and Retail, which includes High Street names such as Rumbelows, DER, Radio Rentals and the HMV shops; Technology (£852 million), including defence electronics sensors and security systems and the Inmos semi-conductor company; the £718 million Music division, which takes in Capitol Records among other labels – including the huge EMI classical output; and Consumer and Commercial, whose brand-names in appliances and lighting, with £684 million of sales, have included Tricity, Bendix, Moffat, Kenwood and Lightstream, and which also takes in Ferguson (£370 million). The latter has emerged from the restructuring drive as a vastly more efficient producer of televisions and videos.

The fruits of the group's reorganisation have begun to come through strongly: in the half-year to September 1986, on slightly reduced sales, pre-tax profits rose by £30 million to £41.5 million, while earnings per share multiplied sevenfold.

Thorn-EMI, like many other companies, had reached a certain point of decline at the turn of the decade. What was going wrong?

As with many British companies, they had just not kept up to standard with what was happening in the rest of the world. Thorn-EMI was about as good as most of British industry, but that just wasn't good enough in inter-national terms. There may have been some overmanning; there's no doubt that British industry in general was overmanned in terms of its competitors internationally. It's fair to say that in common with much of British industry, we probably didn't invest as much in new up-to-date equipment as we ought to have done.

What's been the response to that situation during the past five years?

You can really divide the last five or six years in Thorn-EMI into two periods. The first period was just after the merger. I don't think the two companies were ever merged or integrated together as closely as they might have been. Even as recently as a few years ago, you had people who looked upon themselves as Thorn people and others who looked upon themselves as EMI people. Now that's obvious nonsense in a company that has been put together with the object of reaping the benefits of the merger. We have addressed ourselves to that. I think we can safely say that all of our senior management do now recognise that Thorn-EMI is a merged company, and look upon it as one corporate entity.

Has there been any re-orienting of the product market strategy?

Very much so. Thorn goes right back to the days of Sir Jules, when it started off manufacturing light sources. To a very large extent under his leadership it was a production-oriented company. What we're doing, and have done, is to improve our production techniques and our production cost, and to graft on top a marketing philosophy and a marketing attitude to our future.

We've changed our organisational structure, and we've got rid of quite a few things that didn't fit; we were heavily involved in traditional engineering, and we no longer are. We have reorganised the company into four major profit centres for management purposes so that we have good management teams operating in each of those sectors, and we've pushed the profit responsibility down to the individuals running those sectors. They are not only responsible for their profits, but judged on their performance.

What do you see as your growth markets?

The first thing one has to define is, what is growth? Do you set yourself a target that you must grow by so much? The basic problem this company has is that it's inadequately profitable in any of the sectors in which it operates. That doesn't mean we're not profitable; but if you take an international standard of profitability, our profit on sales was only about 3 per cent; whereas the very minimum we ought to be achieving is something like 7½ per cent. That would only be the first target; we ought to be up in the 10 per cent area. So that's our first ambition, to make all of our existing businesses more profitable than they are, so that we can achieve what I call a more internationally competitive standard of profitability.

Some areas of our business will obviously grow faster than others – this is inevitable in a business with the sort of spread that we have. We are continuing to improve our profitability on our rental business – both in the United Kingdom and overseas – and although there is still growth in the United Kingdom there is, of course, much more growth outside. Of course, other areas in the business are growth-orientated. Music is a very clear example. Our music business is reasonably profitable outside North America. If we could only get the North American market up to the same level of profitability as the rest of the world we would have a significantly profitable business on our hands. That's obviously why we're focusing a good deal of attention at the moment on North America.

Does that imply that appliances, lighting and electronics, technology and consumer electronics are more difficult areas in which to make a profit?

The technology business, taking it in general, is one of our most profitable areas, but we do not compete head-on with the major international companies such as Texas Instruments in the defence or various other areas. We concentrate our efforts in more limited areas where we can be internationally competitive. Our technology business is very satisfactorily profitable – although we could still improve it. In technology we are really very strong in radar, we're very strong in thermal imaging and we're very strong in sensors and in security systems, and those are the areas in which we'll continue to concentrate.

How do you rate in appliances and lighting?

We're about number four or five in the world in terms of lighting. It is one area where we have significant research activities of our own and we're quite well ahead. But we do need to focus our attention and, in some of our more traditional areas, invest in more up-to-date manufacturing equipment, which will make us more efficient. In appliances the United Kingdom market is by any standards fairly small. We have quite large brand shares, but probably too many brands. The question that we're obviously facing up to is, have we invested enough? Do we need to invest more in terms of more up-to-date equipment? We're certainly already investing a lot more in terms of design and development in this area. Should we be looking more at a European market for appliances? That is about the maximum size of the market you can look at, because so many of these things are quite heavy and you can't really look beyond Europe. We do have quite significant businesses in a few areas – for instance Kenwood, our small appliance business, is quite a large business in France. But we had to sit down and decide how we wanted to develop that appliance business in Europe – whether we wished to go into every market in Europe or whether we wished to limit it; or whether we wished to stay in all appliances – that is, in cookers, refrigerators, laundry equipment and small appliances.

We convinced ourselves that in cookers there *was* a market that we could be in, and we built a new factory in Spennymoor to produce electric cookers, which is the most up-to-date cooker manufacturing unit in Europe. Our refrigeration factories had not been modernised, and we were obviously looking to see whether we thought it was worthwhile spending the money to modernise in relation to the potential returns. In the end, we decided it was more sensible to sell our major appliance business to Electrolux.

What sort of strategy have you adopted for your Inmos semi-conductor operation?

Inmos is a totally different company, and its products are totally different to that which we bought less than two years ago. We obviously bought Inmos at the wrong time, but then none of the experts predicted that the bottom would fall out of the market as it did. When we bought Inmos, it was just making a profit, but it has lost money since because of the way in which prices have fallen in the commodity areas. We've now stopped producing all commodity products. We are limiting the Inmos activity to more highly specialised ones, and in particular the transputer – the computer on a chip. We certainly have eliminated or drastically reduced the losses; we've reduced the size of the business. The transputer is a major British invention, obviously ahead of its time, and we feel that we must give that team and the transputer a period of time in which we can determine whether we can make it into a viable and profitable commercial operation. It will still take us probably another year before we know that.

Inmos is simply a component supplier for computers. We do not manufacture computers, nor do we have any intention of doing so. The transputer will only be successful if major computer manufacturers decide to develop and redesign new equipment round that particularly big advance in technology. We are obviously trying to persuade all of them that they ought to do so. But if they developed new products round Inmos's transputer, they'd be making their other products obsolete, and most companies wish to choose when to make their own products obsolete, if they can.

What do you think are your main competitive strengths for building on in the next five years?

We shall only remain in any business sector where we believe we have adequate management of a high enough calibre so they can compete with anyone in the rest of the world, and where we do feel we have an advantage either in product innovation or in marketing skills or preferably both. That will be the limiting factor as to which areas we decide to invest in – do we have the correct people, do we have the adequate marketing skills, do we have a big enough presence around the world, and can we make good enough products cheaply enough?

What aspects of the competition do you find the most challenging?

In the British market, the thing that many of us find slightly disturbing is the way that so many British customers appear to think that if it's foreign it's better than made in Britain. That's certainly not true of the things that we make. If you take our Ferguson television sets, they are manufactured as cheaply and as efficiently as any sets anywhere in the world; their reliability is just as good; and in fact we are currently producing television sets for Japanese companies who will put their own labels on and will sell them into Europe. That's a clear measure of the quality and reliability of the sets that we're making. This is symptomatic of what we're trying to do in Thorn – to be absolutely sure that we have the right product and we can make it at the right price.

Do you see a future in co-operative ventures?

There are two problems about co-operative ventures. The first is, are you going into a co-operative venture to obtain technology from the other side? The second is, are you going into a venture whereby you will act as a manufacturing or marketing base? In the television case we are simply manufacturing sets for JVC. That's not a joint operation in any way at all.

Undoubtedly we shall continue to have good relationships with many of the major Japanese companies, because that is quite clearly where so many of the new inventions in electronic technology are coming from at the present time. And they're sufficiently large and sufficiently profitable that they can afford to spend vast sums of money on the research and development for the new products. Our own British scientists are just as good, just as inventive as other scientists around the world at the moment, but you do need to spend quite a lot of money on research and development. And at the moment we are not adequately profitable to do that.

Is the low profitability you mentioned earlier a criticism of your own efficiency?

Profitability is a combination of factors. You really need to have a significant share of the market in any one area. If you do, then you ought to be the leaders in terms of setting the price, rather than being the followers. Although we do have large market shares in certain sectors, it is not always the case that you can set the price that you would wish, because of import penetration. Take microwave ovens. We have a factory producing them very efficiently, very satisfactorily. And what do we find? The United States, which had been importing a lot of microwave ovens from Korea, suddenly put on a very high tariff which in effect stopped all Korean microwave ovens going into the United States.

The Koreans still continued producing, and all those ovens that were going to the United States are now coming into Europe. Now, you may argue that the consumer in Europe has benefited because that has meant a considerable reduction in price. But they're less sophisticated ovens than the ovens we're making. We were about to launch a new, quite updated, very well-designed model, and we just couldn't afford to because the price was too low – nothing to do with our manufacturing costs. The fact is that Korea is still treated as a developing country, and actually gets almost preferential treatment and it is not possible to mount an anti-dumping action against them; whereas they ought to have to compete on equal terms.

What lies at the bottom of a successful revival?

The one factor which is the most important in any business is to get the right people in the right positions and with the right sense of responsibility. If Britain cannot get management which is at least as good as that in any other country, then we shall not succeed in beating or meeting those other countries on equal terms. I'm now confident that we've got not only the right organisational structure, but we've got some very good people in the right places within the business.

The big question comes back to the selection of people in the first place. Do they have the right attitude of mind? Experience is not the be-all and the end-all of everything – it's important, but it's the attitude to business, the intelligence and the right degree of delegation, too. There are always good people in every organisation. We've been able to promote quite a few people from within Thorn to more senior positions and they're doing very well indeed.

What has happened to British management over the past twenty years?

There has been a significant improvement in the standards of British management over this period. Perhaps one factor, although it can only affect a small number of people, is that a lot of the really good management people have been overseas to work and to live and to operate: that does show you that there are different standards, things that can be achieved if you really get down to it. Apart from that, I think that management education in the United Kingdom has improved tremendously over the years. There is no doubt that in recent years British management in certain sectors has become as good as any management anywhere in the world. The introduction of business school courses has been helpful. Companies are recognising that you need to have general businessmen as well as special experts, and sending the right people on management courses is bound to have been beneficial. But perhaps most important of all there is a recognition that the world does not owe us a living and that, if we want to sell our products overseas and make a profit, they have to be competitive in price, they have to have style, they have to have an overall aura which satisfies the consumer.

ROGER FOSTER, CHIEF EXECUTIVE, APRICOT COMPUTERS

The careers of Roger Foster and his company, Apricot Computers, are completely intertwined. Unlike the other companies covered in the broadcasts, Apricot is an entrepreneurial creation with a very short history – its beginnings date back only to 1965. It characteristics are typical of high-tech companies; but so is the profile of its financial history, thirteen years of dynamic growth, followed by a startling plunge into loss.

What is untypical at Apricot is Foster himself. Aged 45, he is an accountant, not a technologist, and his financial and management skills were widely credited for much of Apricot's success in a British small computer industry which has seen all too many under-managed disappointments and failures. Foster qualified as a chartered accountant in 1962 and began his career in the chief accountant's department at GKN, the engineering giant. He stayed there only to 1965, leaving to found Applied Computer Techniques – a computer bureau of the traditional type, supplying businesses with their data processing needs via a mainframe computer.

In its first decade of life, ACT developed vigorously from this beginning, both in size (it became one of Britain's largest bureaux) and in the scope of

the services provided. ACT was quick to see the promise of mini- and
micro-computers. Foster's idea of a 'total computing company' gave him a
wider view of the unfolding DP market: and the distribution of Sirius, an
American 16-bit micro-computer for business use, gave ACT a clear lead
in the British market (IBM then had no product, and was thus not a factor,
while Apple, the US leader, made remarkably little headway in the UK).

The company went public in 1979 and achieved a spectacular Stock
Exchange success to match its soaring profits – up from £373,000 before
tax in 1978–9 to £11.7 million only six years later, a rise of 3127 per cent.
From a low of 13.7p in 1980, the shares reached a peak of 295p in 1984, a
gain of 2053 per cent. But the business was changing fundamentally. The
company making the Sirius micro failed in the States. The future of ACT
came to hang entirely on its own product, the Apricot – but this had to
compete for its sales in a market dominated by the new presence of IBM.

When the PC market ran into a growth recession, ACT (which had tried
and failed to get a foothold on IBM's home ground) suffered severely. In
1985–6, the £11.7 million profit of the year before turned into a £1.47 million pre-tax loss: the shares fell as low as 43p. Against the background of a
market that has become even more competitive, Foster, in this new high-
tech business, has been forced to adopt a programme strikingly similar to
those of his old-line contemporaries: reducing headcount (from 1200 to
700), dropping unprofitable and unsuccessful lines, and striving to move
decisively up-market into areas where Apricot (the company's new name)
can achieve a clear product advantage.

In addition to its manufacturing activity (based in Glenrothes in Scotland), Apricot has important businesses in computer distribution and
services. In the first six months of the 1986–7 financial year, the new
strategy was rewarded with a marked turnround in profits on much reduced
sales – £2.5 million pre-tax on a turnover of £32.8 million. The year before,
£48.1 million of sales had generated a £4.6 million half-year loss.

*In 1985 you had the most difficult year in the group's history. What was the
problem?*

It was really a series of problems that compounded the situation. Two principal ones: first the rate of growth that we had achieved. In three years, we
had, from organic growth, gone from a turnover of about £8 million to
nearly £100 million. And though at the time that seemed pretty easy, and
we were very pleased with ourselves, I think we had outgrown the management or the depth of management in the company without growing some of
our own internal control systems. Probably for the twelve months before
the disaster, we were running pretty well out of control, though we didn't
realise it. So over-extended growth was a principal reason, for which we
paid a heavy price.

The second reason was the well-publicised disasters throughout the computer and electronics industry which had probably shared a similar pattern, that is, a huge boom between 1980 and 1985 and, following that huge boom, a great slump. So those two things together really caused an extraordinarily difficult year for us. We made sizeable losses following a period of some twelve years of continual growth in both sales and profits. However, we believe we are out of that now. Hopefully, we are poised to return to a growth path, albeit at a greater level of stability than previously.

You also had a foray into the United States market from which you withdrew fairly quickly. What happened?

We did have an opportunity to enter the United States market. A particular group of people in America wanted to handle our product. It was at a time of great success for the company, and we took a chance; we financed it separately from our main company because we knew the risks involved, and it clearly was a high-risk venture. We committed close on $20 million of funds to the venture. But in terms of the US market, that really is a small sum.

With the benefit of hindsight, we would have needed a great deal more money than that to have succeeded in the strategy. We would also have needed a year of boom for the industry over there, whereas in fact 1985 was a year of slump in America as well as in Europe. So we really didn't do well. We sold quite a few machines but, in terms of overall penetration, not sufficient to make it a viable long-term venture.

In the end, we decided that it would not be right to commit any money from Apricot plc here to the venture. It was too high-risk, and so we actually pulled out of America. We sold off the company we had there for a nominal sum, to the management, and we converted the shareholders' shares in that company to shares in plc over here – we did honour our commitments.

What is your new product and marketing policy?

There are two real differences between the new product range and old. We've now got a range that is 100 per cent IBM-compatible, as it's called in the industry. Prior to that we had a range of machines that were special to Apricot, and though we had a lot of software on them, we were not standard with what has now emerged as the clear industry standard, IBM. We decided that we had to become fully IBM-compatible, in order to reap the benefits of that approach. People estimate that some 100,000 programmers are working for this IBM-compatible world every day. Being able to hook into that is a priceless asset.

We believed we could use our own technology to do two things: to be IBM-compatible, and yet to keep the special features of our computers that had really been the hallmark of Apricot's success – their style, their extra performance, and the more advanced technological features.

The second major change: it was clear to us that, at the bottom end of the personal computer market, there was tremendous pressure on prices, and indeed, in the bad year of 1985, selling prices of computers at the bottom end of the market fell by, on average, 40 per cent in a year – a year in which costs had fallen by perhaps 8–10 per cent.

No company can remain viable with that amount of change. We looked to the future and we thought, we can see that happening again. The bottom end of the market is almost like consumer electronics, and will follow a similar pattern: people like Amstrad coming into the market, just moving a box, and you've got all the other Taiwanese and Koreans making things with virtually no overheads, with cheap labour. We really felt that wasn't the area of the market in which we could see any chance of sensible long-term profit. We made good profits in the past out of it, so we'd had our run, but now was the time to get out.

What was the alternative strategy?

The area of the market for the future, which we were already involved in and which will be the basis for the company in the future, is the higher end of the market. It's the area where you add value, so you are actually adding expertise, know-how, training, software. It really isn't easy for someone in Taiwan to be able to copy that sort of know-how and service. So we had to move into the more added-value areas. The timing in that respect was right, because new, more powerful processors are emerging in the personal computers which will actually enable them to challenge the much more highly priced mini- and main-frame computers, which at the moment are a huge chunk of the overall computer marketplace. So, just as one market was getting torn to shreds, another market is beginning to open up, a market which probably holds even greater potential riches for the next five years than the personal computers market did in the past five. We're now concentrating all our development and all our energies on multi-user systems, priced typically around £10,000 or £20,000 – offering all the advantages of the personal computer, but with the power of the much, much larger, more expensive computers. There is a fabulous market there, and that's a market in which we must compete, of course, with people like IBM and DEC and Hewlett-Packard.

Aside from the multi-user systems, are you also tending to focus more finely on particular users?

You have put your finger there on one of the great changes in the industry. Everybody did tend to follow a sort of horizontal attack, making broadly based products for broadly based markets. When the slump came in 1985, people began to decide where their markets lay and which parts to specialise in. We were no different. We really decided to focus on certain areas, one of which is the multi-user area, using personal computer technology. But you've also, to some extent, got to focus on particular industries. We were fortunate, because one of the most profitable parts of the Apricot Group, which showed large profit growth even in our bad year of last year, was a 'focus' company which concentrates on the City of London – ACT Financial Systems. We have developed, in-house, a range of some 2000 packages under the name of Quasar, and we sell these into very large City banks, merchant banks and stockbrokers. We actually sell computer hardware as well as software. But the essential sell is that we are offering a solution to a particular problem.

What we want to do is to apply that experience in certain other chosen specialist areas. That is one of our success stories and one that we intend to expand greatly over the next few years. There are other areas where we are adding value. We've put a big investment over the past few years into the maintenance of computers after you've sold them, and this is now a very sizeable business; we're probably in the top three or four maintenance companies in the country, with some 160 engineers. It's very, very profitable to us and, of course, very stable. At one time we talked only of growth; now we talk of stability, steady growth, sustainable growth – these are the watchwords for the future.

Looking at the company now, with this new range of equipment, what do you think your main assets are?

We've filled what was the gap in our range – we needed software compatibility with IBM. That's the main change. What we've done is to keep the classic features of Apricot: our technology is generally more advanced; our machines generally are smaller and take up less space on the desks, and they are more user-friendly – that is, easy to use. So we concentrate on those features, advanced technology to make life easier for everybody.

One of the other great keys that we've added with our new range, which no one else in the world provides, is the facility to upgrade from our cheapest machine to our most expensive machine. We are virtually unique in offering that facility, though it would be considered quite normal in the mini- and main-frame world costing hundreds of thousands of pounds. When your machine runs out of power you can replace it with a more expensive one by exchanging various parts of it. The manufacturer does that for you. We have brought that facility down to our range of personal computer style products.

What are the most critical factors in today's competition?

IBM probably has some 40 per cent of the market worldwide for personal computers. So they always tend to be the company that you judge against and obviously they have a fine reputation for quality and again for customer service. But equally they are a high overhead company and they are very large. We can do very well against them because our overheads are much smaller than theirs, which enables us to offer much more attractive prices.

Secondly, because we are smaller, we are quicker to the market with new technology. Now in a marketplace where there isn't any great new technology that wouldn't be important. But in an area like computers where there is a great deal of new technology, being able to produce a design and bring it to market in twelve months – which is typically what we can do compared with the industry standard of two years or more – does mean that we are always that much more ahead technically. So we can win in terms of advanced technology, and we can win in terms of price performance because of our lower overhead structure. So that gives us a significant advantage against the industry leader, and that generally would be true of the others in the market.

The other interesting thing is that, generally speaking, in the computer business IBM is the market leader, and then you have a strong local manufacturer in every country. In America, for instance, that would be Apple, who are clearly the number two in the personal computer market to IBM. In Italy it is Olivetti. In the UK it is Apricot.

How do you keep up with tomorrow's technology? The next super-chip or the flat screen, for example – do you simply buy into that when it arrives?

We do buy in that sort of technology. It's generally true that everybody in the world does, so that doesn't give us any disadvantage over anybody else. The technology of a computer these days is so complex that you get great specialists. A company like Intel in America is undoubtedly the worldwide leader in terms of processor design. So we buy our processors off them, but then so does IBM; we are all buying from the same source. Your example of flat screen technology is largely the prerogative of the Japanese, and again we all buy from the same sort of sources. These great steps in basic technology of processor and screen are created by specialised component companies. Actually, being small compared with one's rivals sometimes has an advantage, because when technology is new and they're just first commencing volume manufacturing, they'd rather have a company like Apricot that buys in thousands than a company that's going to buy in millions. So we can often get that technology maybe a year ahead of a huge buyer, and that gives us that time lead which is very important to our philosophy.

It's often commented that Britain and Europe in general have missed the boat in computers. Would you accept that?

In the whole area of information technology this is considered to be true, and regrettably there is quite a large degree of truth in it. However, there are what I would call substantial pockets of resistance, of which we would hope that we at Apricot are one, where we feel we compete genuinely with the best in the world in our particular area. But overall it is fair criticism that the great advances have probably been made by the Americans and the Japanese.

Are there particular kinds of development and research that you think we could have done, where we've abdicated?

We do not do anything like as much applied development in this country as we should. We do quite a bit of pure research in terms of universities, but when it comes to applying that technology, that is probably where, traditionally, this country has fallen behind. The funds to apply technology to real practical situations have to be supplied by industry, and industry, by and large, has probably not put sufficient of its investment into research and development.

How would you explain that?

It's almost a cultural thing in many ways. America and Japan, which are the two great centres, actually have totally different cultures. You can maybe see that this country falls between the two stools. In America it's all winners and losers. So if you've got an idea or piece of technology you can raise money, speculative money, and really have a go at the market. Either you'll become a huge success, courted by everybody in America, or you'll be one of the many companies that just goes bust in a big way. It's very risk-reward orientated, but so many people have a go that there's a fair few winners that create this technology and create the companies of the future, and that's the American way. Japan, on the other hand, works a totally different system. They have huge companies, very little of the development is done by 'start-ups', as we would call them here or in America. Most development is carried out by the huge electronics companies. They are massive companies, so they develop a large number of projects and just work on what we would call the numbers game; some win, some lose. They just work on a percentage of the ideas they have and, because of their huge size, they just write off the losses on the losers and then come back with the second wave and the third wave.

Both the American way and the Japanese way are successful, though I suspect the Japanese way is, long-term, more successful than the American. Here in this country you haven't really got either the Japanese philosophy or the get-rich-quick and have-a-go philosophy of the Americans. We therefore tend to be fragmented in our approach. The banks, I believe, are not sure whether they're backing high-tech or not backing high-tech. And you've got, traditionally, a political system in which you see wild swings in the attitudes toward industry, depending upon whether you have Conservative or Labour government. So, at the cultural level, we don't really have the support that the Americans and the Japanese have.

That makes it a tough environment to succeed in the UK, and generally I would say my comments are pretty true of certain European countries. But nevertheless, against that trend we have got a tremendous independence in the UK, an independence of research and independence of feel, that I believe does lead us in certain areas to succeed very well. But it is 'pockets of resistance', regrettably, rather than being a major player on the world scene in terms of information technology.

Against that different cultural background, when one looked at industry in the Seventies, things had got quite depressing. What do you think has happened in British industry as a whole over the past ten years?

The famous British malaise has been recorded *ad nauseam*. The problems of unions and attitudes of management did cause a serious decline, and I do think that in the last few years we've seen a big shake-up in industry and I think in this country very much for the better. I live and work in the Midlands, where there's been a decimation of industry over the past five or seven years. But I've got to admit that the industry now left in the Midlands is a lot more efficient, a lot sharper than it was a few years ago.

So the medicine has worked: industry I would say is in better shape than it was. But at what cost? At the cost of wiping out maybe as much as 25 per cent of businesses here in the Midlands, and the cost, of course, of millions of jobs. But yes, industry is now more efficient than it was, though I think it's going to take generations before we really get back into the mainstream, competing against the Far East and America.

Why is that?

We have improved because the malaise was so deep that it wasn't too difficult. With the big cut-backs people would get much more efficient, and that is what has happened. But from now on, if we want to gain efficiency, it will require huge long-term investment – and I'm not convinced that the whole industrial structure here lends itself to huge long-term investment. And that is what it needs.

Do you think that, as things get better – or feel better – people will slip back into old ways and take the pressure off themselves?

I'd like to think not. A lot of people have had a very tough time over the last few years and therefore it will take maybe a generation before everybody forgets how tough those times have been. So I'm optimistic that people won't slip back, that industry overall is sharper than it was and that we can continue the improvements that have commenced in the last few years.

PETER BONFIELD, CHAIRMAN, ICL

Few companies have had a more involved or unhappy history than ICL. Its difficulties were inherent in its formation as a merger of two independent companies that had operated profitably in data processing before the advent of the computer. That origin gave ICL the strength of a large customer base, from which flowed a uniquely large market share in an IBM-dominated industry. But every successive merger, as ICL absorbed all its British main-frame rivals, only added to the problems of achieving a coherent, combined organisation able to compete with IBM in the long term.

Doing so on equal terms was impossible, given IBM's far greater resources and market strength outside Britain. The government therefore repeatedly became involved in various ways and at various times, notably by preferential treatment for its own computer orders, as the ICL shareholdings changed and the marketing demands intensified. So long as the main-frame business prevailed, ICL's UK base saw it through – thanks to the brilliant improvisation by which a machine designed in Canada, and bought in with Ferranti's computer business, had been developed into the successful 1900 range.

But the evolution of the mini- and micro-computers provided severe new tests for an organisation that still showed unhelpful signs of unconsummated mergers. After the 1978–9 financial year, when ICL made £45.7 million profit on £624 million of sales, the company slid down into the recession of 1981 – losing nearly £50 million on £711 million of sales. Peter Bonfield joined the company in that year as group executive director, worldwide operations. He came from Texas Instruments, like the then managing director of ICL, Robb Wilmot. An engineering graduate from Loughborough, Bonfield had worked for TI in Europe, the US and the Far East.

Internationally minded and experienced, thoroughly versed in semiconductors and computers, Bonfield, now 42, is a model of the new high-tech executive. As a director of ICL, he had a ringside seat as the vicissitudes of the company continued. In its last phase as an independent private company, Sir Michael Edwardes briefly held the chair – but an unexpected takeover bid by Standard Telephones & Cables ushered in a new era. The initial reaction was that a weak ICL would be a burden on a strong STC – but the reverse proved to be the case.

As STC's profits plunged, taking chief executive Sir Kenneth Corfield down with them, ICL emerged as the jewel in the crown. Revenues passed the billion mark, and pre-tax profits reached a record £54 million. This reflected a remarkable improvement in sales per employee, which doubled between 1981 and 1985. The gains were not the result of short-term measures, but the pay-off from some years of reorientation. ICL had decisively abandoned the old strategy of competing with IBM across the board, opting instead for market-led specialisation, together with international collaboration to strengthen its product line.

The company is divided into four big businesses: office systems, main frames, network systems, and applications – of which those in the retail trade have been a particular source of strength, exemplifying the new strategy from which ICL plans to increase its market penetration both at home and abroad, where it now obtains two-fifths of its turnover.

When did ICL's crisis occur?

Our crunch point was about five years ago. The company had grown very quickly during the Seventies, probably grown at more than 25 per cent a year. And then the growth rate dropped off dramatically and the cash flow situation was very poor. Basically the company ran out of cash and therefore needed to be totally reconstructed on to a different basis to get moving again. What we had to do was re-size the company; the overhead was too big for the size of the company that we had.

So we spent probably a year re-sizing it, which meant reduction of workforce, reduction of plant, reconstructing the way that we did business, reorganising, retraining, and specialising in specific areas. Also, we set up a whole series of collaborative arrangements so that we could get access to other people's ideas and technology, to force the company to look outwards. I think it had got relatively introspective, looking primarily at the UK market, instead of the world marketplace. And computers is definitely a world marketplace.

How did you change your attitude to the market?

We basically said, it's no use looking at just the UK marketplace, we are in an international business, so we set our sights higher and looked internationally. We were obviously relatively large in UK terms, but not in international terms, and we had to come to terms with that. We said, if we're not big in international terms, then we'll specialise. Rather than try and compete with the big US multi-nationals across the board, we would only compete with them in very specific areas.

That was one major change. The other change was to try and get the company to think smaller, act as though it was a smaller company. We were organised in the traditional manner of British industry – with a big sales organisation, a big manufacturing organisation, a big product development organisation. All the decisions came up to the top of the company, and therefore it didn't move very quickly.

So we broke the company down into much smaller units – what we call business centres – where the marketing people and the development people get together, mostly under one roof. They attack a particular part of the marketplace. They're typically of the order of 100 to 200 people, whereas previously our product development operation was of the order of 4000 people.

The marketing is now focusing on narrower sectors. Does this mean that the product itself is more narrowly specialised or that the selling operation is more concentrated on particular bands of industry?

We decided that we would need an integrated product range covering a wide range of computer and network systems. It was obvious that we couldn't develop all those products ourselves, because we just didn't have the resources. In the UK, for instance, we've specialised in retail. I would think that now we are the largest supplier of retail systems to the UK retail marketplace. But they are total systems: we sell computers, networks, consultancy, software, even as far down as the training booklets, all into that industry. It's very much a specialisation.

What do you find are the most critical factors in the competition, what wins the orders?

Basically, knowing what the customer wants. It sounds very trite, but you have your people close enough to the customer, so they really know what the customer needs. We work primarily with two or three opinion-leading customers, find out from them what they need and then we go off and systems-integrate it. It's a method that the Japanese have used: they sit and talk and watch and look for what the marketplace needs, then deliver it.

Have you seen the effects of this policy in your sales?

We think so. The sales stagnated in the early Eighties; in fact, we had just about zero sales growth for a year or two. But since probably 1983 we've averaged just over 13 per cent, which is about the same growth rate as the largest company in the industry. So we're pretty pleased; it certainly has translated into sales, but most important, it's translated into the bottom line, where we've had quite encouraging growth in profit. We're now generating cash, whereas a few years ago we were consuming it at a large rate of knots.

You've also run a big co-operative venture on the main-frame Series 39, with Fujitsu of Japan. What were the reasons for that, what are the advantages?

The reasons initially were to share development costs. We're not big in the overall main-frame market, and in fact Fujitsu themselves are not that big compared with the largest in the business. Therefore we thought that we'd pool some of our resources. We did a deal with Fujitsu; it only covered the semi-conductor part of large main frames, not the total product line. We said we'd design our computer products using their parts, so that we get the benefit of reduced development cost and a reduced repeat cost; and the parts are then sent back to the UK and we make computers out of them.

With all collaborations we feel there must be a win-win situation; you can't have somebody winning and somebody losing. Fujitsu gained by ICL becoming a major customer of theirs in Europe, which we weren't previously. We used to buy most of our semi-conductors from the US, so we transferred to the Japanese. And that collaboration has been going now for just about five years and I think has been an excellent example of give and take on both sides. We've now extended our collaborations to cover all sorts of products and services. And we are one of the few companies in the UK with a main board director whose sole role in life is to encourage and monitor collaborative programmes.

Do you think this kind of collaboration is going to be a permanent way forward on some lines?

I personally think so. Where the industry is global, nobody has the resources to do everything. Even the largest competitors in our industry actually work with other people to gain knowledge, to share development costs, and that sort of thing. Across Europe we've had some success. ICL has had a collaborative research programme going with Siemens of West Germany, and Bull of France, for about three years. We've got a joint development operation based in Munich; and of course the Alvey programme in the UK, the Esprit programme, the Eureka programme, are all designed to try and get European companies to work closer together, to share and exchange technology. But I think it's going to go downstream, to be much more prevalent in joint marketing as well. It's the people that manage collaboration best that will probably win, long-term.

There might be those who will say there's a great danger here, that if you get in with a large company you may eventually end up as a satellite to that company – in effect, its out-of-town manufacturing and marketing organisation. How are you going to make sure that doesn't happen?

There are risks. If anybody starts dancing with a bear they have got to decide how to control the risk. We went into this very much with our eyes open. We set up arrangements where we are not totally locked in, so that we do have some flexibility and, where possible, we've kept the intellectual property rights or the technology ourselves. You've got to understand what you give up, but you've also got to understand what the other partner, which may be a competitor, also gives up. As long as you have that understanding at the start, the collaboration can work.

There can be some very substantial long-term benefits, not least of which is getting the people exposed to a different part of the world marketplace and the world culture. Our engineers in Manchester now are very familiar with what's going on in both the US and Japan – and the other way around. It's been very well done. In fact a lot of the Japanese engineers now speak English with a Manchester accent; we think that's real success!

How important is size to a company like this? ICL isn't quite in the top twenty, which is still dominated by the American companies. Is the scale of your operation big enough?

To get into the commercial marketplace, you've got to be able to satisfy the customer that you are going to be big enough to stay around; not just big enough to produce one or two machines but big enough to support the machines, big enough to support the next generation product, and big enough to understand his business.

The second critical aspect is whether you are big enough to generate enough profit to produce enough R & D to produce the next products. ICL's turnover last year was just over £1 billion and we put over £100 million a year into R & D; obviously you need to be a certain size to be able to afford that. So size is critical. We can overcome some of the size problems by means of the collaborations, so that we don't have to develop everything ourselves. Actually, with our web of alliances around the world, we feel bigger than number twenty in the world; I think our impact is bigger than that anyway.

You've also reorganised the business into smaller units, though. What's the thinking behind that?

If you're too big then it's hard to actually be responsive to the marketplace. We actually want the company to be perceived as in some aspects acting like a small entrepreneurial start-up company. That was one of the most significant things we did in restructuring the business. We had to find new managers who wanted to be entrepreneurial. By and large ICL had not trained multi-discipline managers; they'd been functionally trained. So we mounted a very large programme in conjunction with the London Business School, and US universities as well, to train our managers to think laterally, to think outside of their own disciplines, to train them. And then we took a lot of risks with some very young people. I guess the company had an aversion to anybody under forty, thinking that they obviously didn't have enough experience to be able to manage anything. So we picked some bright people, gave them as much education as we could, drew a line around their business and said, that's yours! – and then cast them adrift. It's worked very well. It certainly puts a different complexion on how the customers perceive it because they see a much more cutting, thrusting, market-led company than previously.

What effect did this all have on people inside the company? Did it raise morale once they knew what you were striving for?

Initially the morale was very poor. Obviously, when we restructured the overhead, we had to lay off a lot of people, and there was a lot of concern about whether the company would survive. So we went on a major programme internally, just on communications, to get everybody involved with what we were doing. But that took about two years, probably more, to percolate through the company and get everybody to say, well that is a good idea, we understand where the company is going.

Now, we communicate directly to each employee, we run videos, we run booklets, I go around and talk to the people. In fact, after the merger with STC, we set up a programme and within two months I'd talked to just about every individual person in ICL – that's 21,000 people – in groups of about 2000, just taking questions and telling them what was going on.

We've spent a lot more time in breaking down the operation into smaller teams, so we can do team briefings. The people on the shop floor should know what they're doing. We have demonstration areas to show where their bit fits in the overall operation to make people feel that they're part of a team that knows where it is going. I think that now it's starting to work through the morale. It's better, but it certainly took some time.

What do you think your greatest assets are now?

We've got a group of highly talented people within the company. They are very responsive to change, they are very responsive to new ideas, to working with other people, and we've got a good culture being developed where putting the customer first is a way of life, putting quality first is a way of life. And, of course, we've got an enormous technical base within ICL. About 40 per cent of our people have been with the company for more than twenty years.

We've got an enormous reservoir of talent. What we now want to do is not treat it as a reservoir, but as a fountain, so that we're putting people in at the bottom who can grow with the company. The key thing in the long term is a lot of talent but highly responsive talent. We've now got the ability to move quickly, and I think that's going to be downstream. It will separate the winners from the losers.

In your view, looking back on the Seventies, what were the most fundamental things going wrong?

There was total resistance to change, not only in the UK market but total ignorance of what was happening in the world. The world markets were changing dramatically and a lot of European companies, not just the UK companies, reacted much too slowly to what was going on, with the competitive advantages in some areas shifting out to lesser-developed countries. So the workforce was less flexible, management was less flexible, the approach to business was less flexible, while the outside world was changing very, very rapidly indeed. I encourage all my managers to look outward all the time. I encourage them not to sit in their offices but go out and talk to customers. I talk to at least five or six customers every week around the world and ask them what is going on, so that I can sense and feed back into the company what needs to change. And then, every time I'm asked in the company what the fundamentals are, I say: no change equals no business. It's a risk, it makes people unhappy, it's hard to deal with, but you have to do it. During the Seventies there was a total reluctance to do it; reluctance from the unions, reluctance of the people – and I think reluctance from the management to force the issue of change. And a lot of that advantage has gone to the people who are much more willing to change – the Japanese certainly, the Koreans, Taiwanese, and now the other Europeans.

Looking at managers across British industry, in what ways do you think they have forced changes and improvements?

Look at the structures of companies now. They're much more dynamic in the way that the boards have changed. Certainly the age level, the experience level, has changed. There is much more receptiveness to putting new ideas, new people in. I've worked in the US for ten or eleven years, and I came back to the UK in 1981. The contrast I saw shortly after that, from when I worked in the UK in the mid-Seventies, was as different as chalk and cheese. The managers are more worldly, most of them have travelled – all my managers have operated and worked overseas as one of the requirements. They are much more flexible, they look at a world industry very pragmatically.

A lot of it seems to boil down to taking more notice of the customers?

There is no business that can survive without listening to the customers. It sounds like an old truism, which it is, but it's actually a lot harder than you think. If you've got some very dedicated technical people, they would much rather develop in the isolation of their labs rather than get involved in the rough, tough business of commercial exploitation. So you have to force the issue. This doesn't happen by remote control, you have to lead from the front and get in there and force it. We found that 'co-locating' – which is our great computer word for putting people down on adjacent desks, but putting the engineers opposite the marketing people and forcing them to work together – has produced magic results. They previously thought that marketing was something people did with flashy shiny suits; but I'm trying to encourage everybody in ICL to be a marketing man. All our engineers have been put through marketing awareness programmes, and that in itself has made for quite dramatic changes.

What do you think are the chief obstacles that industry faces as a whole?

Within the UK, one obstacle is just the size of the domestic market. There is no doubt that, with a large domestic market, you can accelerate products into that marketplace quickly. You can just see what happens with the US domestic market and the Japanese domestic market, where they establish their domestic base first and then push off into the export base. What we've got to do is to regard the total European market as our home base. The Commission has now set 1992 as the date when there will be a fully fledged European market. Companies have really got to get in there and try and exploit that effectively; and with assistance from governments, because we do need some help to break down obstacles in standards and this sort of thing. If we can do that, we will have a bigger home base.

Has your investment in education and training been part of a deliberate policy?

Absolutely deliberate. When the company was in bad straits five years ago, we insisted on two things: one was that we would not reduce our investment level in research and development, which we didn't; and secondly, we would increase our level of training, management training, marketing training and general training. That has really started to pay off. We started initially with a very large marketing training programme, we then expanded that into management training, and we've put over 2000 people through that training programme. I would think it's one of the largest of its kind in the UK, and the results have paid off handsomely.

Finally, is there still a serious gap in British industry's performance?

Gaps in productivity in certain areas, yes, but certainly in a lot of areas the companies have caught up, the whole country has caught up. What I always like to do is not bench-mark against where we've come from, but bench-mark against where the competition is. So just because ICL had a 20 per cent improvement in productivity, which is good, I rely on everybody to say, don't measure against that – what did the competition do, did they do 20, did they do 25, did they do 15, are we closing the gap? Within ICL we think we have closed the gap dramatically, and on most of our measures we are now up with the best in the world. I would see that in a lot of other UK companies. But there is no cause for complacency, and just measuring against yourself is no measure. Always measure against the best of the competition, whether it's in Japan, Korea, the US or Europe.

HALF-WAY POINT IN CARS

SIR JOHN EGAN, CHAIRMAN, JAGUAR CARS
GRAHAM DAY, CHAIRMAN, ROVER GROUP
JOHN BAGSHAW, CHAIRMAN, VAUXHALL MOTORS
DR JOHN PARNABY, GROUP DIRECTOR, LUCAS INDUSTRIES

SIR JOHN EGAN, CHAIRMAN, JAGUAR CARS

When Sir John Egan took on the chairmanship of Jaguar Cars in 1980, the famous cars had become infamous – above all for unreliability. Once a symbol of excellence in British design and engineering, the luxury car specialist was sinking fast: sales had halved to 14,000 in just two years, and the business was losing over £4 million a month.

According to Sir William Lyons, Jaguar's founder and president until he retired in 1974, Egan was the very man he would himself have chosen to run the company. Trained as a petroleum engineer (he gained his BSc from Imperial College, London, in 1961), the Lancashire-born Egan first worked for Shell, from 1962–6. From there, he progressed via the London Business School, where he added an MSc in business studies to his qualifications, to General Motors, where he was general manager of the AC Delco Replacement Parts Operation.

That experience took him on to BL in 1971, where, as managing director of Unipart, he was responsible for the successful build-up of the subsidiary's business in the years to 1976. After an interlude as corporate parts director at Massey-Ferguson, he moved to Jaguar in 1980, at a time when it was by no means clear that Jaguar had any hope of survival at all, let alone any hope of privatisation (which came in August 1984) or a return to profitability. But Egan knew what had to be done. He identified the myriad failures in parts and the dealer network that were destroying Jaguar's image and then set to work to eradicate them.

Egan imported the much-publicised quality circles from Japan, as well as robot technology, and at the same time started to develop Jaguar's own engineering to new heights. By 1985, annual expenditure on R & D had risen to £22.9 million, and the long-awaited launch of the XJ40 in October 1986 was one of the most successful introductions in Jaguar's history. It confirmed Jaguar's new status as the leading supplier of specialist luxury cars, with a following on both sides of the Atlantic, not only for its models but also for its shares: offered at 165p in 1983, they have been trading at over £6 as the markets have gradually come round to Egan's view that the company is a money machine.

Egan's determination to get things right has in fact brought extreme improvements to both productivity and sales. There were redundancies in 1980–1; and by 1986, 3.9 cars were being produced per employee (three times the 1980 figure), with total production up 200 per cent from 13,791 to 41, 437. In the same period, retail sales were up 28 per cent in the UK (to 7579), 22 per cent in Europe, and a massive 709 per cent (to 24,464) in the US, Jaguar's key market. Compared to a loss of £52.2 million in 1980, pre-tax profits five years later were £121.3 million on turnover up 348 per cent from £166.4 million to £746.5 million.

The architect of this remarkable revival was knighted in June 1986. Egan has emerged as a highly articulate spokesman for the new wave of managers in British industry and for the necessity of achieving quality by design and maintaining it by effective management at all levels – including that of the supplier firms.

Around 1979–80 Jaguar was in a bad way. Output was below 14,000 cars a year. What had gone wrong?

Probably everything. The company had been run for some years on functional lines as part of a much larger organisation, BL. People had concentrated on all kinds of corporate objectives and not on manufacturing a good product as the principal objective. So quality was one very big problem; the whole production process was very ill-organised and disjointed; there was very bad timing, very large inventories, very low productivity. The cars weren't selling; the dealers weren't very interested in the product; nor were they doing much of a job to satisfy the customers with the products they had. So most things had gone wrong across a pretty broad spectrum.

You could claim to have had a quite remarkable recovery in the last five years. What are the main things you've done?

Of course, we had some very good cards. The original Series 3 car that was the basis of the company's business was fundamentally very good, and an extremely beautiful car. Indeed, the readers of one American magazine voted it the most beautiful four-door sedan of all time. That was a very good card. Also, the people who worked for the company did have a lot of affection for it. They were willing to allow a lot of change to take place to enable the company to survive. This affection carried on right through to the dealers and the distributors. There were some dealers throughout the world who really did want to do the job well: certainly, as soon as we gave them the room to manoeuvre and the challenge, they answered it.

One of the other key aspects was production efficiency. What did you have to do?

In terms of our manufacturing processes, the first thing we did was to concentrate on quality and getting it right first time. There is, incidentally, a productivity multiplier on quality: if you start getting things right first time the whole production process flows through much easier. We also put right the inventory control aspects of the job and actually got a lot better planning into our production processes. This was a good solid platform for going for productivity improvements. It really meant organising work better, giving better leadership, and people working harder. To help that we brought in a production bonus; people on the shopfloor earn something like 27 per cent of their wages through the production bonus. All of these things came together to allow a management-led increase in overall productivity. I don't think we were asking people to run around like greyhounds; but we were indeed organising the job so much better that people could work at a much steadier pace throughout the day.

But you also looked very hard at the engineering aspects of the car, didn't you?

In terms of the quality control aspects we did an awful lot of research with our customers to find out the kind of things that were going wrong with the car. We had to re-engineer quite a lot of it. In fact, I hardly know of a part number that we didn't have to re-engineer on the old Series 3. Of course, all of that was bringing in good disciplines when it came to designing new products. We were able to utilise all of the lessons we'd learnt in terms of the development process on the old product and put those into place as disciplines for the design of new products.

When you say re-engineer, what were you actually doing?

If customers had complained of something going wrong, we'd take a look at that particular component and find out what things could possibly lead it to go wrong. For example, in one particular component – the automatic gearbox – there were something like sixty or seventy components which we had to help our supplier redesign. Indeed, at one stage something like 25 per cent of our engineering effort was being spent on helping suppliers redesign their own components.

How far have you strengthened the engineering side of Jaguar?

In the six years since 1980, we've raised the staff and hourly paid employees in engineering from something like 250 in 1980 to over 1000 today. We're just half-way through a capital expenditure programme of over £50 million for a new engineering centre which will be fully open by the end of the year; at which time the total headcount in our project engineering department will rise to about 1300 people. The budget of our project engineering department will have gone from something like £5 million to £35 million. So the whole engineering effort is on a completely different scale.

Looking at the relationship with suppliers – because they are surely vital people – one gets the impression that it had become a rather careless and over-trusting one. Has it changed?

We're like every other car-maker, we make about half the car and we buy about half from outside suppliers. There were bad information flows through to the suppliers. They often didn't know how badly their products were faring in the field. We put those communication processes right. We manage, in most cases now, to agree with our suppliers that they pay for the full cost of failure, so they have a tremendous incentive to achieve the quality levels that we require. What we found in the United Kingdom is that where the board of directors really want to make a first-class product, they'll end up doing it. When they haven't made up their minds what they want to do, then you find that you don't get a good product. It's really all to do with the attitude of mind of the senior management of a company as to whether they want to achieve excellence or not. Wherever there's a good management team, you'll find there's a good product as well.

What else have you done to get better performance from suppliers?

We've had to spend a great deal more on the whole communication process with suppliers. We've had to define our specifications much more carefully. Indeed, there's a whole portfolio of specifications for each component, covering not only what we expect the component to do, but also the process controls in its manufacture. We also insist on a very high degree of communication within the supplier firm, so that everybody involved in the manufacture of the piece for us does understand what's expected of them. These procedures have improved the communication processes enormously and create the framework into which good quality can be put. For example, we now insist that most of our critical products are controlled by statistical process controls. We are very quickly putting these controls into all of our own manufacturing processes, and we expect all our suppliers to be capable of doing what we can do.

Does Jaguar have to be successful in the United States to succeed at all?

Yes. Something like 75 per cent of the people in the world who can afford to buy a Jaguar live in the United States. Often we don't really understand the enormous wealth of some parts of that country. For example, we have a dealer on Long Island who will sell over 1000 cars this year. That might be more than we'd sell in Belgium and Holland combined. That's from one dealer outlet. In the city of Los Angeles, we'll probably sell as many cars as in half of Europe. The immense wealth there means that, if you're in the luxury goods business, you have to create an effective marketing effort in the United States to be successful.

It's a fiercely competitive market, though; because all of the world's car-makers try to make a success of their business in the United States. The wealthy buyers can afford to buy anything, so if your product isn't an excellent one, you won't be able to sell at all. Quite a number of European car-makers have been driven out of the States because they haven't been able to compete.

What have you done to ensure that Jaguar cars can compete – not just in the US, but in all world markets?

What we did was to put together a small team of the service managers from Saudi Arabia, the hottest market, Canada, the coldest market, Germany, where they drive the cars the fastest, and Australia, where they are driven on a lot of rough roads – as a feedback to our board and to the engineering and manufacturing groups, to demonstrate just how well or how badly our cars were faring. After that very small beginning, we created testing stations in all the extreme marketplaces, so that we could not only test our existing products but, more importantly, the new products in these very testing environments. For example, our XJ40 sign-off included 75,000 miles on the roads round Timmins, Ontario, which is one of the coldest places in the world; also 75,000 miles in Phoenix, Arizona, which is very hot, and on the dust roads out in the deserts in Australia and the Oman. They also included 25,000 miles at full speed round a test track in southern Italy. The original drawings say that that is what the car is expected to do. We try to make a car which is extremely strong, extremely rugged and capable of putting up with all of the difficult circumstances that it will have to face.

One gets the impression that the label 'Made in Britain' had become something of a turn-off to a lot of overseas buyers. Do you get that feedback these days?

In the history of things, we've only been doing a bad job, as it were, for say twenty years. Just as Jaguar's own reputation was able to turn around fairly quickly, I think the reputation 'Made in Britain' can also be turned around fairly quickly. Britain still does have a reputation for doing things well at the top end. We're very good at the luxury end of the marketplace. Certainly 'Made in Britain' is, and has been, no turn-off for people making luxury cars like ourselves. If we manage to keep our industrial product improving, especially the quality and the reliability, I don't think 'Made in Britain' need be a turn-off. Strangely enough, I'll tell you the country that'll probably be most difficult to get back one's reputation in: this country itself!

Do you detect a kind of sackcloth and ashes feeling?

No. I think that, in a way, the British customer had to put up with more of the poorly made British products. There's always a feeling in people, especially British people, that they're doing a good job; it's everybody else who's doing a bad job. But if you've taken part in a company's programmes like those at Jaguar or some of the other companies that have made massive efforts to improve their products, you know what's gone into it and you can appreciate such efforts in other people's products. Certainly there are now a growing number of manufacturers – for example, in the domestic appliances industries – who are beginning to make products which are European leaders in quality and reliability. So I don't think for one minute Jaguar is the only company, I think lots of others are beginning to make very big strides in terms of their quality.

Where does Jaguar see itself going in the next four or five years? Is the recovery programme complete, or are there still more nuts and bolts to put in place?

I'd say that we're about half-way through. There's two areas where we have to concentrate. First of all, we have about £700 million to spend, at the rate of something like £125 million a year, to put in place all the modern equipment that we need to do the job properly, our engineering centre, our robotics programmes, our machining centre programmes and so on – vast capital expenditures. In a way, we've missed out a generation of capital expenditures. We're using, very often, equipment that's twenty years old. We've missed out on the investment programmes in the Seventies, and all these big investment programmes have to be put in place.

Secondly, I think we have an enormous training and motivation effort still. The car industry was pretty well near rock bottom in terms of leading and motivating large groups of people to work in harmony together to a common purpose. I think we've done a good job, we've made good improvements, but we're still again only half-way there.

What do you see as the outstanding national problems?

The problem we've got in this country is that, compared with our competitors in Germany and Japan, from top to bottom, the workforce is probably badly educated – only a third or a half the number of degrees, 'O' levels, 'A' levels and so on – and we, like any other company in the UK, have to put a tremendous impetus into training, and also into creating the motivation environment where the first line of supervision, for example, can do a very good leadership job. Often we've seen foremen in this country as a sort of oiler of the wheels, whereas really the most fundamental part of his job is to be a leader. And I think often we haven't understood in this country that business, especially big business, is an enormous leadership challenge.

Are you saying that there's been a shortfall in investment, both by society in general and by companies themselves, in training and education?

Yes, I think if we're to criticise British people for anything, we've been very poor managers of the resources we've had at our disposal. Clearly our educational processes have not been up to scratch compared with even our European competitors. We haven't managed our large industries very well. But one does get the impression now that a lot of people are beginning to concentrate on the absolute basics of putting these things right.

How much ought companies to invest in training?

We spend something like 1.25 per cent of net sales on training. This compares with something like 2 per cent for a similar German company, so we still have some way to go. But we spend something like eight times the national average on training; so many companies in the UK really have hardly started on this long road.

What makes life difficult in running an industry in Britain these days?

I don't think there's been any coming together of the lines of, say, trade unions and management. All parts of our way of life have to be adversarial. Why should we get so angry at each other? Why should unions want to destroy managements and *vice versa*? There seems to be an enormous gulf between unions and management. For example, I keep asking my trade unions are they interested in helping a fine company to grow and to become wealthy, from which they're going to get a good return? Or are they simply demanding more money for doing less work? If they're doing the former it's quite easy to get the two sides together down a common track of wealth creation. If they're just simply grabbing more for doing less, then of course the company will go out of business. That's one absolute gulf.

A second major problem is that standards throughout most of Britain are low in every way. It seems that we're willing to have poor service in hotels and restaurants, and dirty streets, and so on. When you're trying to pick up a whole company to run at international levels of competence, it's difficult when the whole environment around you is often willing to accept second and third-rate standards.

Those are two of the major problems in terms of making your company into a world-class performer.

You were also talking earlier about lack of investment in the Seventies. Do you think that has created a very big shortfall which is holding Britain back?

I really was talking about the particular gap at Jaguar Cars. We were owned by the State at the time, and it was spending something like £2 or £3 million per annum on capital investment within Jaguar. (So, by the way, the State didn't turn out to be a very benign owner of the company.) Whereas we're having to spend something like £100 million per annum now. That was our problem; however, for many years there seemed to be a notion in British industrialists' minds that they could spend a third of what their competitors were doing on research and development and on new capital investment and still compete. Obviously it's nonsense. If they're doing it, you've probably got to do it as well.

What do you think is going right now – in general – compared with, say, five to ten years ago?

We're seeing around us many companies, especially our suppliers, beginning to achieve world-class levels of quality standard. We have a Supplier of the Year award ceremony every year, where something like thirty-eight British suppliers will be getting these awards. We really mean these are world-class standards, these are excellent companies. It does your heart good to see the enthusiasm and excellence generated within these companies.

It's a painful process, because we're actually having to recreate the industrial fabric of the nation at a time when there has been almost a world recession. It's much easier to do it when the rest of the world is growing. But we see a lot of companies fighting and inching their way forward. There's a lot of courage and a lot of strength in a country with the heritage of the United Kingdom. If we keep on trying, and as long as we don't believe there's any magic wand that the government can throw in and suddenly make it all easy, then we might make it.

What has been the effect of varying exchange rates in the last five years?

Our general strategy is to be a world-class competitor in what is, generally speaking, a relatively weak economy. So in a way you win twice. Sometimes the exchange rate makes it particularly difficult, and we have to concentrate far more on productivity and cost-effectiveness; and sometimes the exchange rates become very easy, and you are concentrating more and more on putting together the cash which enables you to spend a lot more money on long-term investment and research and capital investment programmes. So, in spite of the fact that exchange rates have fluctuated, we have been able to change our approach, depending on which cycle of the ups and downs we're actually in. We also tend to stabilise our exchange rates by a policy of currency hedging, which has meant that our own internal exchange rate has fluctuated much less violently than the actual spot rate. What we've always tried to do is use these variations to push home the various programmes at any particular time.

But presumably the weak pound, in the long term, is not a good thing for the health of industry?

One had a feeling when the pound was very challenging in the early Eighties, when it was up at $2.20 or so to the pound, that you had to be very, very hard-working to have any chance whatsoever of survival. And I think a lot of progress was made faster. It's not a medicine I'd recommend again, but generally speaking it is vital not to live off a weak exchange rate. One had the feeling that in the Seventies people just simply made money which was basically eating their seedcorn – they were living off an easier and easier exchange rate.

GRAHAM DAY, CHAIRMAN, ROVER GROUP

Graham Day, 53, is the odd man out in Britain's car industry in several respects: the only Canadian running a major motor firm, the only lawyer, the only man with no previous experience of the industry whatsoever. His appointment to the job of chairman and chief executive at Rover Group is a consequence of that company's history – probably more chequered than that of any large business in the West. In particular, Day owes his post to the continued State ownership of the last British-owned car-maker in the mass market.

Day came to Britain only in 1971, again as a government appointee. The job was chief executive of Cammell Laird shipbuilders, half owned by the State through the Industrial Reorganisation Corporation. His career until then had been largely involved with the law. The son of an Englishman who emigrated to Canada in the early 1920s, Day graduated from Dalhousie University in his native Halifax, Nova Scotia, and practised law until he joined Canadian Pacific, the transportation conglomerate, in 1964. His work in the legal department brought him into contact with many aspects of CP's huge business – all forms of transport, hotels, telecommunications, property, labour negotiations.

Day's closest connection with shipbuilding was setting up CP's bulk shipping subsidiary and its ship procurement programme. Despite this limited background, Day in three years reduced Cammell Laird's accumulated losses of some £9.7 million to less than £4.4 million. He was promptly picked to prepare for the nationalisation of the industry and to become its chief executive. When the nationalisation was held up, he refused to renew his contract and returned to Canada. His stay at home, in academic work and with Dome Petroleum, lasted until 1983, when he at last took on the job for which he was originally intended.

As chairman and chief executive of British Shipbuilders, Day presided over the reconstruction and contraction of the deeply depressed industry. Three years after his return to Britain, in March 1986, the government offered Day the same post at BL. Its almost immediate change of name to

Rover Group symbolised the fate of a company that had once contained many of Britain's leading *marques*: Austin, Morris, Jaguar, Wolseley, MG, Triumph, Riley. The group has lately been developing its product line with new models which have been designed in collaboration with a leading competitor, Honda of Japan.

The company has lost money for a decade. After-tax losses of £1.4 billion in nine years led the government to attempt a sell-off of all its commercial vehicle interests to General Motors, with a possible sale of the car side to Ford. That was killed by political opposition, but Leyland Trucks has been merged into Daf: Day had made it clear that he would not shrink from any action necessary to achieve a viable solution for the group. Its £3.4 billion of sales and 77,000 employees still make it one of Britain's largest businesses – and one whose operating efficiencies have been greatly improved by the management, industrial relations and equipment reforms initiated under Sir Michael Edwardes earlier in the decade. That improvement has been crucial in obtaining further government investment, without which the company could not survive in the highly competitive conditions of an over-supplied European industry.

In the late Seventies, despite reorganisation and writing off losses, BL was at a very low ebb. What were the main reasons?

They included inadequate attention to the market; therefore the market was progressively being eroded as a result of the initiatives taken by competitors. Part of that lack of success in the market was a result of very erratic industrial relations in all the plants. If you added those together – and there are other examples – you'd say the company wasn't really focused. Sir Michael Edwardes – to whom I, like anybody who sits in my job, has to remain grateful – certainly addressed the industrial relations situation, and the climate in which I operate today is very different. The way in which we respond to the marketplace still has a way to go. Of course, you don't change attitudes all that quickly; one of the themes I am trying to develop everywhere in the business is to heighten the awareness of all our employees to the marketplace and the need to respond to the customer.

What's been going right, what's been turned around?

The second important legacy from Sir Michael Edwardes was the push towards productivity, and that is understandably linked to the change in the industrial relations climate. But with that change came the justification for significant investment in plant and technology. In terms of getting units down the line and out – expressed any way you like, say, cars per person per year – we are certainly as good as the best in Europe. So the combination of the industrial relations and the investment, which led to productivity increases, has given the company, not a full lease on life but a good leg-up into the Nineties.

Despite the investment in productive equipment the man in the street often imagines that you're still putting it together with spanners, doesn't he?

That's right, and not only the man in the street! We run endless tours of the plants, not only for employees and their families, but also, for example, members of Parliament. Most recently we had an industrialist who some of my colleagues took around, who couldn't believe the level of technology. He had – and he is not alone – an idea of men and women in grimy overalls working in a 'satanic mills' kind of environment; and when you see spotlessly clean floors, high intensity lighting, lasers, robots, people punching up line-side computers, it's not what you anticipate. But the business of manufacturing sophisticated products – and certainly today's automobile or any vehicle is very sophisticated – has necessitated a change, not simply in technology, not simply in the hardware, but also in the general working environment.

On productivity measurements, you suggested that the group now is right up in the European league. Is that enough?

Productivity is not the be-all and end-all. You have to build into that quality and reliability, and indeed the product itself has to be appealing to the consumer. Then you are looking at a future product plan, because it takes four to five years to produce a new product. We are trying to anticipate what consumer trends are likely to be four and five years away. That is a very sophisticated, time-consuming and, I suppose, risky exercise, because I don't actually think any designer of any consumer product ever gets it totally right.

The motor industry as a whole has been a by-word for bad industrial relations. One or two commentators have suggested that the problem at the moment is 'contained' – people are scared to death of unemployment. Is that a fair comment?

The advance is much more positive. I wouldn't deny that the thought of losing one's job at any level concentrates the mind, and I think that that has been a positive factor – particularly on an individual basis – whereby the individual employees realise that their future and the company's future are absolutely linked. But also in the process, management – albeit belatedly – has become much more alive to the need to communicate. We all do it imperfectly but I think we do it better.

Last year, we sustained the downstream consequences of strikes at one of our major suppliers, Lucas. As we were running 'sole-sourcing' for a lot of our components, we felt the downstream consequences in less than forty-eight hours. And we had to shut down a number of operations. So it isn't only industrial relations in one's own establishment, it's in the establishments of those upon whom one relies.

How do you see the future of your industrial relations evolving?

We have just concluded in a very mature negotiating environment a labour agreement in our cars business, which extends for two years and pays a base increase of 3 per cent which is in line with inflation. We did some consolidation of some of the long-standing bonuses. But importantly we've created, in the negotiation, opportunities for employees to enhance their take-home pay as a result of continued efforts on the productivity front; and now, very importantly, extra take-home pay on the basis of external measurement of quality.

What I don't want to do is put jobs at risk by increasing basic unit labour costs, but the very fact that take-home pay is increasingly linked to productivity and quality and reliability makes the employee's personal objectives for himself or herself, and the company's objectives, essentially the same. Some of those in the same industry have had settlements well in excess of 20 per cent – Jaguar being an example. Jag is a profitable company, and I suppose in the short term they can pay that, but I'm very interested to see what it does to their unit labour costs.

Looking at the success of the group in the car home market, I think its share is still only around 16 per cent of the market?

Our market share cooled off, starting in the third quarter of 1985. We finished slightly under 16 per cent for the whole year of 1986. That reflected a number of factors, including, at least in my perception, that we hadn't got a lot of our advertising as we would wish – getting people to understand our product and all about it. But we've changed our whole advertising strategy: that's been helpful – volume rose in the first quarter of 1987.

Even things such as the colour we paint certain products, to the way we present them, have impacted. Have we ensured that enough of our products for certain market sectors have sun-roofs, have we ensured that we've put the kind of radio-cassette player in the car which is going to appeal, for example, to people in their twenties or early thirties? There's a number of things we've had to look at in the marketplace, which I think have improved our market share. A critical factor, of course, has been the way in which the over-capacity in the market generally, in the world, particularly in Europe, has resulted in tremendous price pressure. One certainly can increase one's market share by pricing changes and that may give a temporary fillip to one's ego. But at the end of the day, the most important thing is the profitability; that's the only thing which underpins a business and sustains it.

Is the price warring over? And do you face any other problems in raising market share?

I hope and believe we've got through a bit of the silly period, and I've said publicly – which gives some of our dealers some distress, and I'll repeat it again – that market share in isolation is not the only god to worship. It is a fairly complex formula of market share, of product mix, of profitability, and so on. Also, for us, it's sustaining our total production. After a very modest performance for many years, with in some cases complete withdrawal from markets, we've now moved back very strongly in export. We've been selling well, for example, within the EEC, in Europe generally – sales in 1986 were up over 14 per cent over the previous year. We've gone into the United States with the new Rover 800 series and with the Range Rover. And I can see that perhaps on the car side alone a third of our production will find itself sold in overseas markets in 1987.

The other element which has not helped us in the domestic market is the continuing debate about the business generally. The very fact that the government holds the majority of the shares indicates there's never a close season on us; we're always open season!

If people go to buy an imported car, they know nothing about the company and the country of its origin, or very little except what the advertising says, and they look at the car on its merits. In France, where we're up about 26 per cent, someone looks at one of our products, they either believe that the dealer and his employees are paying attention to them or not, or they like the product or they don't, and they take a decision. The fact that we're majority-owned by the government, that there's a continuing debate in Britain about us, doesn't interest the Frenchman or the French lady at all. So we enjoy some of the benefits in the overseas markets which our competitors enjoy in Britain.

Does market research suggest that the home consumer's image of the company has an adverse effect on the decision to buy?

We had a problem in bringing perception in line with reality. I receive letters from a wide range of customers, ex-customers, potential customers, and of course, we have been commissioning a lot of research in the marketplace – and people do hold views of us which are not valid. They may have been valid at one time, they may be partially valid now, but they are distorted. One of our problems is to try and bring perception in line with reality and that is a very difficult thing to do.

You need a catalyst. For example, I don't know if Sir John Egan would agree, but he was working very hard in Jag in bringing about the changes which have conferred such benefit on them before he left the BL group; but the privatisation exercise, I believe, operated as a catalyst to enable John to have people focus on what he was doing which was positive, and he's built on that strength. I think we need a similar catalyst and I'm not sure what that catalyst is likely to be. One of the things I toy with is the idea of continuing to focus on our successes outside Britain with the hope that as we go from strength to strength increasingly people at home will say, maybe we'll look at their products again. But in the meantime we've changed the way in which we organise the domestic market, and I have a significant level of confidence that we will do better in 1987.

Are there crucial market tests outside the consumer market?

Well certainly the fleet user-chooser market; in other words your employer provides a car as part of your employment contract, and you can choose, depending on your rank, one from column A, column B, column C manufacturers and so on. It's a very important part of the market. But the important thing is that, while it's paid for by the employer, it's still the individual who is making that selection. So we have to get to that individual the same way that we get to the individual who is purchasing with his or her own money.

Another important sector of course is the leasing or car rental side. We've recently been able to crack, for the first time in five years, the Ford monopoly at Avis. We've now sold Avis 2500 cars against, say, their yearly purchase of about 9000 cars. Now, while 2500 cars is very important to us, of more importance is that Avis has actually taken a buy decision – not because we're splendid chaps and we've worked very hard on them, but because they had a wide range of cars on test for a protracted period and were satisfied not only by the cars and the economics of purchasing them, but also because the cost of repairs and all the other features that go into it are very positive.

I suppose the thing that ultimately clinched the deal was that the resale values of our cars are climbing. The obvious example is the Rover 200 which has a very high resale value, so that makes the economics for the car rental people much better. I take a lot of reassurance from the fact that we are making progress in areas which I can always take as test markets.

How do you propose to cope with the fact that your model development costs are the same as anybody else's, but your volume of sales is so much smaller than, say, VW or Fiat's?

We are carefully considering what our future product strategy has to be. It's absolutely correct that for us to produce a model costs the same as for someone who is selling a million off or two million off. That drives us down two paths. One is, we've got to make sure that our models and the positioning of those models in the market are absolutely right; our margin for errors is much less. Secondly, for some market sectors we go along the collaborative route. The Rover 800 is the first strategic collaborative venture for us, which was with Honda, with whom we've had a relationship since 1978. We were able to produce an executive market car which combined our individual skills in a way which, I believe, produced an optimum product for us both, and at a lower individual cost. We're currently involved again with Honda on another product for another market sector, which we code-named YY (incidentally the 800 was XX). So YY is now progressing and we hope to have that product, in its different guises, into the market in, say, 1989.

Will you be moving decisively up-market?

Like a lot of sophisticated businesses in developed countries, we will perforce be driven up-market. Again, people view 'up-market' as meaning we're going to restrict our product range, and only going to build cars in the executive or luxury class. Not true. We can take a small car and move that to the upper echelon of the small or basic car market – so we have moved up-market. The whole question of segmentation of markets is becoming very much more sophisticated. We have to segment the markets in a way which enables us to present a product to the marketplace which the consumer can differentiate.

What do you see as the main priorities over the next five years?

I see marketing in the broad sense of the word as the priority. Included in marketing is not only that we become increasingly more responsive to the customer, wherever that customer may live and whatever language he or she may speak, but marketing in the sense of ensuring that – not only on a product basis but on a corporate basis – the perception of us is in line with the reality, and, of course, ensuring that the reality is something we are proud of. Marketing also includes the realisation on the part of all our employees that the product has to be seen as something of value which people want. So I'm taking marketing not simply as a misnomer for selling, but really as conveying the broad messages for the business. This is the ultimate priority, and if we get that right I'm confident we can deal with the manufacturing and some of the other elements.

Does anything make business in Britain difficult to run?

I don't think it's necessarily difficult to run business in Britain. I manage here by choice and I upset some of my Canadian colleagues by saying I prefer to work in Britain, I find it more comfortable, I find it easier, I find the response time better than I used to find in Canada. And I think if you were to speak to Japanese businessmen, both those who've established plants here and those who may be seeking to establish plants here, they view the British industrial and commercial climate as the most attractive within the EEC.

I talked to you earlier about my belief that the whole climate for business is more positive – industrial relations and so on – than it used to be and I think we are seeing some of the fruits of that in some of the investors who come into the country. So for those of us who are already here and managing established businesses it doesn't mean that life is easier, but I think it is an encouraging environment in which to work.

If you wanted to invest more in professionalism where would you put your money?

I think I would worry about investing in people first and in hardware second. You can invest in hardware – up goes your depreciation charge and, if you borrowed money, your servicing charge. But unless you have the people right it's not going to be fully productive. If we go down the education track, you and I would be here all day; but I'm concerned about investment in people to produce professional managers, not managers by accident, and I think that starts very early in someone's career. We have continual dialogue with a number of universities in the country, some of which are most discouraging, others of which are very, very encouraging, and of course we work with the ones that we believe have focused on the future appropriately. I'm frequently, more frequently than I would like of course, referred to as someone who's had one of those North American applied educations. I guess it means I didn't do a PPE at Oxford or Cambridge, so I generally then pepper my conversation with Latin quotations just to prove I'm not entirely without the benefits of some education. But I'm not arguing that Britain should produce a North American education model, but rather to recognise that we have to create wealth in the country, that in order to create wealth we can't simply manipulate in the City, we have to have that generated from, say, manufacturing. If that is to happen we have to have better and better people in manufacturing, and those people have to be trained, whether their basic education is in engineering or in finance. But that's not what's critical. What's critical is what they do after that. Taking your point about the word 'professionalism', the need is to take those people on from their specifically applied training into training them to understand business and how it works. Market segmentation, product differentiation, all has to be understood in theory and in practice if one is to be involved in marketing. You don't get that in an engineering school, you don't get it in finance – you get it, I think, in a formalised business education, which can be done on block release, day release, sending people away to short courses, or perhaps sending them away for two years. But that's where I'd put my money.

JOHN BAGSHAW, CHAIRMAN, VAUXHALL MOTORS

John Bagshaw's career in General Motors, for which he has worked since 1948, has in its latter years fitted the now characteristic pattern of the multi-national executive. Now 61, he was born in Sydney, and served in the Royal Australian Navy in the war. He studied mechanical engineering after leaving the service, and then joined GM-Holden, which used to dominate the Australian car market. For thirty years, Bagshaw built up unrivalled experience in sales, rising through successive promotions to become Holden's director of sales.

His success in Australia led to transfer to Detroit in 1978. GM was beginning, after a period of benign but costly neglect, to pay far more attention to its international business. Bagshaw was director of the overseas marketing staff before moving briefly to the domestic sales side for Pontiac. That assignment was ended by Bagshaw's move to Britain, where he took over car marketing for the Vauxhall subsidiary – then a poor also-ran, not only to Ford, but also to BL.

Bagshaw was quick to see that Vauxhall's marketing problems were inseparable from its production inefficiencies. His success in improving delivery performance was instrumental in taking the company back into the crucial fleet market. Without that, the remarkable rise of the Cavalier, which doubled Vauxhall's share of the overall British market, would not have been possible, and the survival of Vauxhall would have been in grave doubt. After eleven months on the marketing side, Bagshaw became director of Vauxhall's car operations – but before long he was on the multi-national escalator again.

His new job was the control of sales, service and parts for GM's cars all over Europe. Following in the footsteps of Ford, the American giant had set about integrating its European operations into an effective, powerful force. Tens of millions have been invested, mostly in developing a superior range of cars in all the main categories – from the mini (Nova, made in Spain), via Astra, Cavalier and Carlton, to the Senator-Monza range at the top. The design and production lead, however, is unequivocally placed with the West German Opel.

In early 1986, when Bagshaw returned to Vauxhall as chairman and managing director, the emphasis in GM's European philosophy had shifted from winning market share (at which it had been spectacularly successful) to reducing the heavy losses that had resulted. Vauxhall's own financial record is appalling. Profits were only made in one of the ten years from 1976 to 1985. Although home sales in units had doubled over the period, losses rose from under £2 million on sales of £514 million to over £47 million on sales three times the value.

Even that is a far better performance than in 1980, when GM's 30,670 employees generated a loss of £83 million. Since then, numbers have been cut to 12,467, as Vauxhall has shifted towards an assembly rather than a manufacturing operation, with a high (but now reducing) proportion of its sales imported directly from the Continent. As chairman, Bagshaw has moved in forthright Australian style to improve productivity still further, to bring more of the manufacturing into Britain, to modernise the facilities and to return to profits. All British car firms have been adversely affected by a price war, operating mostly through dealer discounts, that has stemmed from European over-capacity and the desperate struggle for market share. Bagshaw, however, is one of the new realists who are hoping to restore stability – and profitability.

The motor industry in Britain in the Seventies was more or less the symbol, because of the publicity perhaps, of what was going wrong with all British industry. What was the underlying problem?

It's got to be management. We were having some horrendous industrial relations problems right through the industry. I arrived here at Vauxhall to do some research work back in 1979. We had an unfilled customer order-book that you couldn't jump over, and yet we couldn't get the cars out of the plants, and people were just walking away from our products and going and buying wherever they could because we just couldn't satisfy demand.

There was a lack of realisation – maybe at the shop floor level, certainly at the supervisory level – of the simple need to meet a customer's demands, and nobody was paying much attention to it. The frustration and the rage when you went round and talked to fleet customers was unbelievable, and if only we could have video-taped some of that and played it to the whole organisation we would have realised what we were doing to ourselves.

If that was really the basic problem, what about the product and the quality?

When you've got that sort of unrest within the plant, and you're not building the cars on time, and you've got industrial disputes that are stopping the line, you can't build quality. The only way you can build quality is to build it right first time. And that wasn't happening, so the quality was crap.

What has been the price of all that?

Lost market share to imports, loss of profit to the manufacturer, and loss of jobs.

How many jobs have been lost in your company?

We've got a rather complicated situation because we're branched between passenger cars and commercial vehicles. If you take a look at what Vauxhall Motors was back in the Seventies, you're looking at a very complicated passenger car and truck organisation. Now you're looking at a streamlined passenger car operation which is my responsibility. At the moment we're operating with around 12,500 people. That's much less than it was back in the Seventies.

Since the late Seventies what has been the response to that situation? What have you done about it?

There's been a much greater realisation of what we are giving our customers. We widely publicised the results of the findings in talking to our customers and their dealers. We set out on a programme to get Vauxhall well again, and I think it's history now that we moved from 8 per cent to around 16 per cent market share in the next five years. It was only done by satisfying customers, and by working very closely with all levels of management, and with our trade unions, and through them down to the shop floor. There's a great awareness now right through our operation that we must satisfy our customers' needs; they are just not going to wait any more. And I'm sure that was a key factor in us gaining those market share advantages.

What happened in terms of quality, design, productivity?

We are now within one or two rating points of the best General Motors products built in Europe, with the products that are coming off the line at both Ellesmere Port and Luton. That has been done again by an awareness that we've got to get quality right. We've been identifying where we did have quality problems, we've even – in some cases – sacrificed attainment of schedules in order to build quality, we've put a lot of investment into better equipment, and we've also considerably upgraded our paint plants. The bodies that are coming out of that new paint shop at Luton are absolutely outstanding. That's really been the sort of thing that's been going behind the quality drive.

Has the injection of technology also been important? Have you managed to get totally up to date with that?

The cars that are being built at our Ellesmere Port plant are going through robotic gates, which allows us to build the bodies very accurately and improve the fit and finish. We've got a lesser amount of automation at Luton, but it's a different type of body construction, so that allows us still to maintain very high quality standards. We've also upgraded the quality of our dealer network. We just haven't been satisfied with letting the cars go out the gate and expecting them to be delivered to customers without an upgraded professional attitude by the dealers.

We've got what we call a 'golden quality handover' system, where the dealer and the customers jointly sign off on the pre-delivery and handover of the car, and that's made a big difference. So we're trying to get a total professional attitude right from the time we build the car until we get it into the customer's hands.

Your other question was productivity, and that is an area where we have made considerable gains. We've got a two-year wage agreement which was negotiated in 1985. That has allowed a lot of stability in the negotiating process. We are now within a few minutes of building our cars to the same levels – the same number of hours to build a car – as our other plants in Europe. Now, that sounds pretty good, but unfortunately in other parts of the world our competitors are building cars in a lot less time than we are, and that's a problem we haven't got right yet; that's where we are going in the future.

What's the underlying cause of that lag? Is it to do with equipment, work organisation?

Not so much equipment, but work organisation mainly. If you take a look at a certain new plant that's gone up in the north of England – a green-field site hiring in labour to new work standards – that competitor is stating that, in the next round of expansion they'll be building about 100,000 vehicles with around 2500 people. Now, we're building 200,000 vehicles with 12,500 people. You can't compare apples and oranges because we do a lot more in-house manufacture with that 12,500 people than the new plant. But it really makes you wonder what are they going to do up there to get so efficient and so effective in terms of labour? This is an area that we, and I'm sure all our other local manufacturers, are looking at very hard, to see how much of it is work standards and how much of it is the difference between 'in-house' versus 'supplier' manufacture.

Are you beginning to get a closer relationship with your suppliers?

We have to tighten up on the way that we deliver the order to the supplier. We've got to get much more rigid tolerances on what we want, we've got to set quality standards, we've got to make sure that that supplier has set up a mechanism in his own organisation to ensure he can meet them, do self-inspection there. If we run into trouble, then we will go and help inspect in the supplier's plant, so we know that when the truck comes in and delivers a box to us that we can get, if not 100 per cent, 98 per cent parts that we can fit immediately.

Half the quality problems, if you went down and talked to some of our employees on the line, half the problems we've got is terrible frustration. A person has got a certain amount of time to complete an operation, and if the material is not there, or the part won't fit where it is supposed to fit, or the bolt won't go through the hole for some reason, you can't blame the worker for it, you've got to blame management – the management that allowed that part to come onto the line knowing, or not knowing, that it won't fit. So the poor employee's standing there being blamed for it all, but we haven't put the mechanism in place to let him do it right first time. And that is why I blame management at all levels for any problems before going out on a union-bashing exercise and saying, hey, you won't co-operate with us!

A lot of the problem in this country is that people have been tending to have a 'we and they' relationship for the workforce, instead of saying, together we've got to get it right: what can we do as management that will make it easier for you to do it right first time?

So at the moment you would find it difficult to be totally satisfied with the supplier relationship, the supplier performance?

No, I'm not satisfied – and *I'm* a supplier too, because we have in-house manufacture – in fact I'm totally dissatisfied with certain aspects of what we're doing. If we do a sheet-metal stamping, for instance, and then the worker has got to take a hammer to it to get it to fit on the line, that's not good enough. It goes right back into the engineering and design, in many cases, of those pieces; they've got to be producible and they have got to be fittable. I think we've got a lot of work to do in a lot of areas. That's us at Vauxhall and General Motors, and I'm sure it's the same for other manufacturers as well.

Where do you start on this? Is it a training exercise?

First of all you've got to identify your problem and then you've got to develop a responsible organisation that instead of saying, well that isn't happening over here, or, that's not my fault, would rather say, yes, we've got a problem, how can we jointly fix it? You've got to get that attitude, and changing attitudes is a long and painful process. But we really are getting at it. We've got some very high quality standards for General Motors in Europe, as a matter of fact even higher than the worldwide standards of General Motors. We are determined to get there, and we *are* getting there. But it's only being done by an awareness and a willingness to make sure that the customer is getting the best value product.

What would you say are the main obstacles to progress in the next five years?

The first problem I have is that, in my two assembly plants here, we're running at about 12½ per cent absenteeism. Now, that 12½ per cent absenteeism means that we have to bring more people in every day than we need to run the line, and that's cost. I talk to my competitors, and I talk to other industries, and I find that some of them are down as low as 2 or 3 per cent. So one of the first things we've got to do is find out what's the cause of our

12½ per cent. We know we've got a minority of our employees that are bending the rules on how they can get time off and beat the system.

If management allows those employees to get away with it, why shouldn't any other employee who wakes up this morning with a sick headache, why should he strive to get to work, when he knows that there's somebody else on his work team that's getting away with blatant cheating? So I'm taking the attitude that if somebody is sick, somebody has got a bereavement in the family, we'll give the utmost help to that person with their problems. But if there is somebody blatantly beating the system – not coming to work, forcing us to have somebody else standing in place in case he doesn't turn up – as far as I'm concerned that's stealing, and we are really going to get at it.

We've got to change management attitudes because out there we've supervisors that allow it to happen, really don't stand up to a confrontation with the schemers that are beating the system, so they're causing the rest of the people to say they don't care. And I'm taking it on as a personal challenge and I do feel very badly about it. If, just like a damn soccer team, two of your players don't turn up, how does the rest of the team feel? That is the attitude we've got to change around here.

Looking on the brighter side, what would you say are your main strengths, the assets that make you feel optimistic?

Our product programme is absolutely outstanding. We've got a range of products which is virtually second to none in the industry. We've built up a good relationship with our dealers. They are responding to our drive for professionalism, they've seen our market share come up, they are highly motivated. We've doubled the number of sales we're making each year, so we've got a growing number of Vauxhall owners out there who hopefully are loyal owners that will buy again. So we're building a very, very solid base for the future. But we are not doing it on a profitable basis at the moment. So we have really got to work to get profitability into this place in order to survive.

On the industrial relations side, do you detect more consensus here, more understanding?

Oh yes, I've had meetings with our trade-union conveners and I've invited them to join some of the task forces which we are setting up to address some of these key issues.

If there are work practices in our standard wage agreement that we need to change or negotiate, sure, we'll get into the normal union bargaining. But at least we should understand that, if we don't change the practices, we're not going to achieve the goal of coming first. How fast can we get to the goal together? That's what I'm asking them to do. It's quite a change; we don't normally do business this way. It's normally a confrontation. But they are as concerned about jobs as I am. I think they are as concerned about profit as I am, because they realise that if we are not profitable we can't survive. So I'm hopeful that as we move forward – and there are encouraging signs – at least we're all talking to each other rather than at each other. I'm hoping that we will see quite a turnaround. If we don't it will be a very sad day. I try and get out and around and talk to as many people as I can. And the big thing we have to do is get the awareness right through all levels that it's a team job that has to be done. It's not a management and a shop floor confrontation.

What about your other problem that, despite having a lot of up-to-date, successful models, you're still not making enough money?

We were talking earlier about the investment and where it went. We have an unhealthy amount of reliance on overseas suppliers for a lot of our material, and consequently we are far too susceptible to fluctuations in the pound. A year ago everything was looking pretty good at Vauxhall. The Deutschmark was around 3.90 to the pound. It made pretty good sense, all the material coming in from Germany. Today, the mark is down around 2.83, and for every pfennig we are in the red about £1 million. So the difference, from a year ago to today, is about £100 million, just on exchange.

   Now, we are scrambling as hard as we can go to re-source back into the United Kingdom. We're working very closely with the Department of Trade and Industry; they are identifying suppliers along with our purchasing people, and as far as humanly possible we are bringing components back into the UK, so we don't have the exchange penalty. But unfortunately, because of the placement of the major components such as engines and trans-axles – that's the big dollar items – we can't re-source as fast as we want in that area. So this is a real penalty. We are paying for the sins of the Seventies, if you like in that we are now so susceptible to the fluctuations in the currency.

Britain is now a net importer of motor cars, unlike France or Germany. Even looking at a company like General Motors in Europe, you say that Vauxhall has lost quite a lot of work out of Britain to other parts of GM. Are you going to be able to win more of it back?

We have got our Ellesmere Port plant now moving up very fast to 35 an hour, which is plant capacity. That has just about wiped out all the imports of the Astras and Belmonts that we saw two years ago. At Luton, we've got the new paint shop coming on stream, we're moving on to the plant capacity of 32 an hour. And there will be practically no Cavaliers now imported from the Continent. So, of the cars that we sell here, we will now be building nearly 70 per cent in this country, which is higher than it's been in years and years. Our reliance on imports is purely in the couple of cars that are relatively low-volume that we build in one plant, namely the Nova, which comes from Spain, and the new Carlton and Senator, which will be coming from Germany.

As head of Vauxhall in Britain, where do you have to go and fight these things out? Is it in Europe or is it back in the States?

We don't do any fighting. We've set up a new office in Zurich, which is a very, very good move, because it removes any parochial interest. If the office was in Germany, then it might be a different situation. We've now got a group of very talented people sitting in Zurich who can look at the situations and just move the pieces around without having any local self-interest. I go over flying my British flag, and I'm met in the hall by Dr Herke, my equivalent number at Opel, flying his German flag, and we march into Zurich on neutral territory, and the decisions are worked out very amicably for the good of General Motors Europe.

When one looks at some of the hindrances to conducting business in Britain, what do you think are the most important ones?

As we're digging more into the problems within our own company and talking to some of our suppliers and associated companies, it is evident that what is causing most problems is a serious lack of training in the preceding ten years or even further. We're finding that as we're moving towards more complicated equipment – more use of computers and things like that – people have never really been trained up to it. As I talk to people in a lot of other companies, we are all coming to an awareness that maybe we've done a short cut on training, and we're paying for it.

Do you see that it needs a really large increase in training investment?

I'm a fellow of the Institute of the Motor Industry and that Institute's prime function is to provide increased and better training. I'm stepping up our efforts in all areas to get this training. Another thing that came out of the discussion we had was, all right, you put a robot in and you expect a 58-year-old foreman electrician to service it. Now, when that man had his last lot of professional training, probably people didn't know how to spell 'robot' let alone build one! Yet we're asking him to supervise the electrical fitters.

That's not picking on anyone within our organisation but it's something that I'm starting to get an awareness of as I go and talk to more and more suppliers of the equipment. And a supplier will tell you that you just won't get the results unless you put the investment in helping the people; and it's not training an employee to make him more efficient, it's helping the guy to have a satisfying work experience. You get the pay-off in quality and a happy employee. It really is an investment.

DR JOHN PARNABY, GROUP DIRECTOR, LUCAS INDUSTRIES

Few companies have undergone so radical a change of culture as Lucas Industries. The characteristic insularity of much of British industry was especially marked in a company that for years had enjoyed the security of dominant UK positions in the motor components business (notably, electricals and brakes). But the strength of this position was inevitably eroded by the rise in car imports and the concurrent decline in British car production. The crunch year for the group was 1980–1, when it recorded the first loss in its history – £10 million after tax. The shock to its management was severe: but the response matched the severity of the shock.

Under chairman Sir Godfrey Messervy and group managing director Tony Gill, the company has attacked its core problems on every front. The brunt of change has been borne by the production apparatus. Where companies like Lucas used to pride themselves (wrongly) on the quality of their manufacturing, the purpose now is to make the performance match the pride. Dr John Parnaby, as group director of manufacturing technology, is at the centre of the extraordinary transformation under way at Lucas. An engineering graduate from Durham and Glasgow universities, he is charged with an overall programme of 'major change in manufacturing units' – a basic element in which is the introduction of the systems engineering principles that have been so successful in Japan.

That programme epitomises the effect to become world-class, without which the company couldn't face the future with any confidence. In addition to systems engineering, Parnaby is responsible for manufacturing development and business information systems. He brings a wide experience to those broad tasks, having worked in chemicals processing and general engineering companies as works director, general manager and managing director. He is also well known in academic circles. A former professor of manufacturing systems engineering, he is still a visiting professor in that discipline at Birmingham University. He is 49 years old.

Lucas's business is still heavily dependent on the automotive sector, which in 1985–6 accounted for £1.2 billion (72 per cent of sales) and £56 million (59 per cent) of profits. The latter figure was double the previous year's: strong evidence of the success of the switch to wholly new concepts of manufacturing, together with an equally far-reaching change in organisation – with responsibility devolved to unit managers and exceptionally heavy emphasis on training to provide the skills which the new concepts of management structure demand. The recovery in the automotive side (which lost money in 1982–3) was crucial to the rise in pre-tax profits to £89 million – the highest figure for ten years. Sales, however, have nearly doubled in that period, which is some measure of the progress that is still required. Lucas does not depend only on the automotive side for further advance; the aerospace business is already much more profitable (£285 million of sales, £31 million of profit) and the group is also in industrial products such as microwave equipment and ultrasonic cutters. The improvement in efficiency across the board has seen sales per employee rise by half since 1981–2. Equally crucial, the share of sales taken by the UK market has diminished over the period to 44 per cent, largely thanks to a major build-up in Continental Europe. That fits in with the group's self-declared 'vision' – which crucially includes the ambition to 'pursue and achieve full international competitiveness in all our chosen markets'.

What principles lay behind your re-orientation at Lucas?

We recognised that the skills of the emerging competition, that's to say the Japanese, resulted from the strategy they laid down for penetrating existing Western markets. This strategy led them to have three very important skills. One was to be able to manufacture high product varieties economically. Another was to achieve high product quality economically. And the third was that they were able to operate very flexible manufacturing systems with very flexible people systems. All of these skills resulted from having to concentrate limited resources on manufacturing development, and having to get into other people's markets by offering features which the competition couldn't – exploiting niches, and above all providing a cost and a quality advantage.

So really this meant highly reliable but cheaply made goods?

Yes, a general philosophy of being able to make high-variety products at the lowest possible cost but also of the highest quality. And those three things go together. Very *low* varieties can be made in mass-production systems at low cost; to make *high* varieties economically is difficult, and to achieve the quality standards is also difficult.

You looked at all this in the context of what was going wrong at Lucas, when in 1981 you made the first loss in your history. What did you find from your investigation?

The basic phenomenon that one sees is quite typical of British engineering and Western industry in general, in that much of the design of the manufacturing systems was based on 1930s principles and aligned to the manufacture of very high volumes of low varieties of product, through a period when we dominated world markets in many areas, and where our production engineering was quite excellent within that requirement.

However, as these sorts of manufacturing system are forced to compete with an aggressive new competitor who is offering high variety, there is a strong danger that people will modify them in a relatively piecemeal way, and will use panacea methods of buying pieces of equipment or computers to try and compete. If you're not careful you finish up with a very complex system, which still nevertheless has a backbone of a high-volume, low-variety business. And since these sorts of changes take place gradually, there's never quite the incentive to go right back to the beginning, use a new set of principles, and produce a new design of manufacturing system which is capable of high variety and low volume.

An example of a tendency towards higher variety, together with the requirement to increase the numbers of technologies used in the product manufacturing processes, would be one of our lighting factories which makes automotive headlamp systems. It used to make a relatively low variety of products, predominantly steel-formed headlamps, circular with a rim. Progressively, that very low variety has become very large, so the business now makes several hundred types of product.

Have more designs, more materials, more processes proved too complex for the traditional kind of mass-production unit?

Yes, indeed; the tradition of the mass-production unit and its design is based on a set of principles laid down by F.W. Taylor and Adam Smith. Basically, systems were highly specialised with highly specialised people in fairly narrow job slots, with not a great deal of change. Then all of a sudden you're faced with having to do exactly the opposite. So, if you don't take great care to produce systems which are as simple as possible to meet those requirements, they become unmanageable or uncontrollable. At the same time you have to recognise the need for the 'people' systems in the organisational structure to change, to get away from the highly specialised job function, to have flexible people, flexible jobs, flexible organisations – so they can cope with these new variety demands and the rate of change of these demands.

You set up special task forces to look at the manufacturing units. What was the idea behind that?

The basic idea was that, if you are to start a total re-design of business units, this is a multi-skill activity. It's not a job which can be done by an individual or by a group of specialists, it's a team job and it requires many inputs – inputs from young new graduates with manufacturing systems engineering skills and inputs from work-study engineers with a lot of experience. And you have to integrate all of that to solve the real problems.

The change isn't just technological, it does involve people, it does involve organisation. The team approach is a way of tackling that, but it also had to be supported by major efforts in education and training, because the principles which we used to design and run the dedicated specialised factories of the 1930s to the 1960s no longer applied. A new set of principles had to be learnt. We call this 'systems methodology'.

What has resulted from these working groups and from these studies?

The task forces have worked fairly widely across Lucas now, and in general have supported the strategy of decentralisation laid down by our chairman and managing director, which in itself was a recognition that old functional styles were not able to cope with the complexities and dynamics of this new game we are all playing. The principle is one of essentially dividing up into cellular units – small businesses if you like – whereby a company has a set of business units which are reasonably autonomous, which in turn are divided into product units. These in turn are divided into cells or modules, with each cell looking like a small business, designed and tailor-made for the job it has to do so that the people who operate it can understand it, and feel as if they are in control and part of a professional team.

Every business manager is now responsible for the totality of his business, embracing the market, the sales, as well as the product design and production?

Exactly. If you mix lots of dissimilar businesses together, it's very difficult to get the correct marketing into phase. If they're sharing a manufacturing resource, where each requires its own manufacturing strategy, you have a compromise. You have an average manufacturing strategy which is not 'best performance' for any one of them. And the Japanese, from the very beginning, decided to compete through manufacturing strategy.

By manufacturing strategy I mean the mix of machines and processes and people and systems and organisations, which that business requires to meet the demands of its market and achieve world-class performance – as measured in the normal business ratios like stock turnover, the ratio of staff to direct workers, the lead-times for manufacture, and the lead-times for development.

Would it be true to say that what you're trying to achieve is not a compromise worked out by head office, but an optimum performance which you get from people on the spot?

Quite right, and my job in Lucas as group director of manufacturing technology is really one of supporting and helping people with their own innovation problems. We operate a philosophy that whoever owns the problem, manages the solution – and pays for it himself. The individual business unit manager is in charge of innovation on his site, and any systems engineering resource which is applied is not solving his problems for him in isolation by taking them away; it's actually working for him. He's in charge of the solution, and the solution therefore matches what he perceives as his business need.

Do you charge your business managers for your time?

The business managers all have to pay if they pull in contract resources, particularly manufacturing systems engineers and business systems engineers, to help them with this task. It's another internal small business which sells factory systems engineering skills. But the principle is not one of taking the problem away and solving it and handing it back, it really is to support the man in the business to help him solve his own problems.

As director of manufacturing, what would have been the main functions of your job in 1966 and how does that compare with how you see your job in 1986?

The major difference would be the balance of time spent between operations roles and development roles. In 1966, which was at the tail-end of a lengthy period of something approaching steady state – that is to say high-volume, low-variety, consistent production – engineering technologies, the operations role, running things with increasing efficiency continuously, was very dominant. The last five or six years have been a period of quite major change and therefore a development role has had to become more significant, at least in a transient period.

We've built manufacturing development capabilities into every business unit, and we've got co-existing the development of the new alongside the operation of the existing businesses against their existing markets. And it's quite a difficult game to make these major changes, to carry out major changes in innovating manufacturing systems without upsetting the customer relationships; because the customer has every right to expect that, while that is going on, he will still get a good service, the best possible service under the existing system.

Can you explain the Japanese 'kanban' system which you operate at some sites?

It's a very simple system, and at the root of everything we are doing is the principle of make it simple – which is at the root of the Japanese success. It's primarily a methodology for providing a discipline for materials-flow control through a factory. It requires you to pick out in your products those which run through regularly, and to containerise the flow of those products, even though there is high variety, in such a way that when you sell a product of a particular type, the empty container returns to the provision point as an order for a replacement. The reason it is good is that, with a fixed number of containers in the system, and with everything containerised, it imposes a very simple discipline on materials-flow that can't get out of hand, and which the operating staff at the very lowest level can understand. It doesn't require works orders systems, it doesn't require computers. Therefore, instead of the data processing function running a factory, the people at your floor level are doing it themselves; they can understand that system.

This is part of our philosophy, we call it 'bottom up' development – simple systems owned by the people who have got to run them, understood by the people who have got to run them, which don't rely heavily on staff support to make them work. *Kanban* has many other benefits; it gives you short lead-times, it gives you savings – we've had as high as 99 per cent work-in-progress stock reductions in one factory by implementing that system, and it gives you much more reliability of supply. It's one of the steps towards becoming a 'just-in-time' manufacturer – one of many steps, but a very powerful and important step.

How do you now compare with the best competition in terms of manufacturing economics – because some of the comparisons you discovered between British and Japanese standards were actually quite embarrassing, weren't they?

It's patchy. We are a large company with a lot of business units. We have some business units which are world-class in all their competitiveness measures. We have others who have a long way to go. Our analysis of British engineering manufacture suggested that on the average, the Japanese measure will be between 10 per cent and 40 per cent better. But that was three years ago and in some cases we've closed the gap and gone the other way, where we are better in some measures. In other measures we've got a way to go. But of course it is a big job – methodology, technology, people systems, culture, organisational structures are all involved. You shouldn't underestimate the size of the job that British manufacturing is taking on in doing all this work.

You've clearly accepted the need to invest a lot of money in training.

That's true. We spent over £40 million last year, internally developing a wide range of training courses, a heavy proportion of which were in relation to manufacturing development. We have open learning courses on Japanese systems engineering, we've got courses on simulation that we've done ourselves. We've built up a modular structure of about forty modules of training and it's been done by our group training functions in collaboration with the business training units, but pulling in engineers to do the details, so the professional choice of methodologies was there; and also pulling in academic staff from universities and polytechnics who had particular skills. It has been inordinately difficult because when you looked around the British academic world, there actually wasn't a great deal of knowledge of these sorts of skills, so we've had to do a lot of studying of Japan and working through the world's literature to put all this together.

Has further and higher education failed industry?

Certainly higher education is well out of tune at the moment. If you look at the figures: Japan in 1985 produced 70,000 engineering graduates, Britain produced about 7000. Japan produced about 4000 pure science graduates, Britain produced 20,000. I think that goes a long way towards explaining why we seem to be good at inventing but not at applying, and the

Japanese are very good at applying and in competing through manufacturing strategy. What they've done is apply our technology of products, but they are *making* our products and that's really the main reason why we've got so many unemployed. It's nothing to do with automation or robotics, it's the applications culture at work.

In fairness, the DES recently has started to increase its efforts to improve the output of people in the area of manufacturing systems engineering. There have been a number of initiatives starting to go through the system – there's one at the moment going through the polytechnic system for increased courses in the area of manufacturing technology. We've really got to shorten the time-scales; it takes us far too long to change our established institutions, and we still have too many which are orientated towards the requirements of the 1930s. We are now in the 1980s, and we've really got to move a lot quicker.

You've instituted a great many changes. Have people reacted well – does it actually raise morale if they feel they're in a winning team, or do they not like the changes?

Everything I've described is a team approach. It's not an individual, it's not me, it's not a particular manager. We're all in amongst it, and when a team starts to see success, even if it's localised and it's small, morale starts to rise. If you go back four or five years, when we were all in the bottom of the trough and we were perceiving the size of the problem, morale was low; because it is only when you understand the structured approach for solving those problems that you start to have the confidence that you can solve them. In Britain there were all sorts of tall stories about Japanese success being a consequence of Japanese culture, when in fact it's Japanese professionalism, the use of knowledge, the excellent use of engineers. And once people get to understand that there is a structured way of solving these problems, morale starts to rise. So on the whole we are all feeling a lot happier than we were, now we know where we are going and we know how to solve the problems.

Looking at all the companies who've revolutionised themselves, one may wonder why it took so long? Why did it need such a big crunch to make it happen?

I suppose some companies responded earlier than others, which is a function of their culture. In general, the lag is a natural consequence of once being on top and having world prizes for production engineering. One also has to recognise that from the Japanese point of view they have the skills I've described because of where they started. They could only go up and that was the only way they could get into our markets. So it is quite complex and it takes people a while to get used to the idea that proven methods and proven principles don't actually work any more, because the next question then is – what are the principles and where do we get them from? And when you're dealing with these complex issues, finding the new principles and successful methodologies can be quite a taxing job.

If industry is to close this great gap that seems to be opening up in terms of trade, what are the things it most needs to look to in the next decade?

They have got to keep a very close monitor on their market and be sure they know what the customer wants, not what they *think* the customer wants. That's the difference between marketing and selling. Beneath that, they have to accept that every part of the business strategy has to be competitive so that the manufacturing strategy has got to be just as competitive as the product strategy. That in turn leads on to the idea that we have to have a much healthier regard for knowledge, and innovation through knowledge and through education, and therefore keep up to date, scouring the world for good ideas, not being embarrassed to admit that we don't know things.

Being willing to learn from other people is a critical part of that. This innovation process that we're going through is quite clearly education-led, and we have to recognise that we're now stuck with it forever. It's not a question of now moving back into line and then saying with a sigh of relief, that's it for another thirty years until the next crisis. It's got to be a conti-nuous improvement process, and if you look at the best-run Japanese busi-nesses who've already done all this innovation, the thing that strikes you about them is the structured management of continuous improvement.

Ten years ago most component manufacturers said that they were heavily dependent on a good home base in order to export abroad. Since then that home base has shrunk – car output in the UK is only 50 per cent of what it was. How international has Lucas become?

It varies across the different companies. Our Girling company is only 25 per cent dependent on the UK, and their factories generally are in Europe. Lucas CAV has factories across the world. Lucas Electrical is probably the least widespread of our companies in contrast to Girling, which is probably the most widespread. Girling have an enviable record in that most braking systems on Japanese cars are Girling designs, which is quite amazing.

Our aerospace companies are quite competitive in world markets and we are steadily increasing our overseas portfolio – and of course we are carry-ing through the same processes of manufacturing innovation in these com-panies as in our automotive companies. We are determined to be totally international and to compete through the excellence of our manufacturing systems.

MAKING IT

As this book was being prepared for publication, the political temperature in Britain began to rise in a familiar way. The campaign for the 1987 election had begun. Once again the Outs were castigating the Ins for the failure of their economic policy; and once again the Ins were castigating the Outs for the disastrous potential of their economic nostrums, and extolling the success of their own. The connection of either campaign with the business realities described in this book was not readily apparent.

The supreme reality is that economic events unfold remorselessly behind the political hubbub. Sometimes economics and politics are in tune – as over the aerospace industry's need for international collaboration. Sometimes the discord is distressingly audible – as over the development of the British electronics industry, for which no coherent strategy appears to exist. That, however, raises the question of whether government can or should form strategies, either for individual sectors or for industry as a whole. Isn't it wiser, as well as easier, to let the market look after its own?

The advocates of management by market can certainly point to the success stories in these interviews. Mostly, these managements found their own solutions in the marketplace, and all have framed their strategies around meeting the market. But it has been a messy process, and a painful one – especially painful for the hundreds of thousands who lost their jobs. Moreover, in the process British manufacturers were forced to abandon many of their former strongpoints. It isn't an experience that can safely be repeated.

In any event, government is itself part of the market, one of industry's largest customers. Nobody would argue that government has used its enormous purchasing power to any enormously, or even visibly, good effect. The opportunity to force high-quality standards on suppliers, Jaguar-style, has not been taken. Nor have the orders placed been matched to specifications that gave suppliers the chance to break into world markets. Across the whole field of government purchasing, policy and practice are un-co-ordinated and unhelpful.

A series on *The State of Government: Can Britain Be Better Managed?* would throw up many more examples. The equivalent interviewees would be senior civil servants and ministers. If they spoke the truth, the picture would be significantly less encouraging than that painted by the seventeen industrialists. Compared to industry, Whitehall is extremely inflexible, resistant to change and uninterested in results. While its senior executives are well aware of the defects, they don't advertise them until retirement – when it is others, not themselves, who will have to bear the brunt of change.

This Whitehall habit suggests an answer to the conundrum of relative economic decline; the fact that public opinion hasn't demanded and won decisive action. There has been no crisis in Whitehall, no threat to force reappraisal, agonising or otherwise. As most of the industrial interviews showed, the British often seem to need the spur of emergency to accept radical reform. In addition, the civil servants and their political masters, like most of the educated middle classes, are not personally and directly involved in relative economic decline.

That is the key. Revolutions, even peaceful ones, are invariably led by a discontented bourgeoisie – and Britain's professional classes, far from suffering relative decline, have prospered while manufacturing industry has struggled for survival. True, they have prospered less than their counterparts in other industrial countries. But these international comparisons have very little effect. Life at the top in Britain has been too comfortable for the endless words about industry's problems and their causes to result in calls for drastic change in a governmental system which has evidently proved powerless to arrest the process of decline.

The exceptions to the rule of complacency are the reforming managers, like the seventeen interviewees. Their position has been very different. They were not insulated from international competition, and felt its full force. In defending their businesses, they were defending their own futures. They were able – as most of industry's critics are not – to take the law into their own hands. But it's possible to detect a note of anxiety in the interviews as to whether society fully supports the kind of initiative that the best manufacturers have shown.

The danger exists that, in a less than congenial environment for great exertions, the firms that have been slowest to respond to challenge will relax and relapse into their old ways. Another two-nations divide exists alongside that between North and South: that between the sleepers and thrusters, or, more accurately, between the internationally oriented manufacturers and those who can still only see the English Channel with difficulty.

It should be said that not all of the thrusters are large, established groups with sales in the billions. Many are in the Apricot mould, niche players still in the hands of their founders – the type of company from which, of course, today's giants eventually grew. Much has been made of this new entrepreneurial crop, which is certainly a most welcome addition to the economic scene. But none of them carries the promise of creating a major manufacturing complex in this country; the orientation is heavily towards services; and the myth that services are an alternative to manufacturing is one of several firmly scotched in the preceding pages.

There is, however, a reality that can't be ignored. Building international success is a long-haul business. Building a national economic miracle takes still longer. In both cases, investment holds the key – putting off today's consumption to finance tomorrow's means of production. In the consumption-led economy of Britain, the priorities have been reversed. To the minds of several of the seventeen top executives, education and training are the acid tests; the tell-tale of society's readiness to invest in its future.

Without that investment in schools and universities, the state of industry cannot continue to improve at a rate fast enough to prevent further decline in relative performance. Much the same is true of spending on R & D. If Britain continues to accept second-best or worse in the development of its human resources, through lack of sufficient commitment of will and funds by the nation and by firms, second-best or worse performance will inevitably follow, as it has done for four post-war decades. If that happens, the last state of industry will be worse than its first – and that would be a miserable reward for the excellent endeavours of the Eighties.

INDEX